Educational Poli(

MW00778248

Educational policies aimed to reduce educational inequality and promote access and success for disenfranchised youth can backfire, do not always materialize, and often have the unintended result of widening opportunity gaps that lead to stark educational achievement gaps. Although policy reform is thought of as an effective way to improve schooling structures and to diminish the opportunity gap, many such attempts to reform the system do not adequately address the education "debt"— the legacy of unequal policies and the historic and pervasive inequalities that persist in and out-side of schools. In this interdisciplinary collection of case studies, contributors examine cases of policy backfire, when policies don't work, have unintended consequences, and when policies help. The volume includes domestic and international perspectives that illustrate each of the four policy scenarios. Through an exploration of the roots of school inequality and examining often ignored negative policy outcomes, contributors discuss what might explain the policy result and what we can learn to structure policies that enact stated intentions.

Gilberto Q. Conchas is Professor of Education Policy and Social Context, University of California, Irvine, USA.

Michael A. Gottfried is Associate Professor of Education Policy, University of California, Santa Barbara, USA.

Briana M. Hinga is Assistant Professor of Clinical Education, University of Southern California, USA.

Leticia Oseguera is Associate Professor of Higher Education at the Pennsylvania State University, USA.

Routledge Research in Educational Equality and Diversity

For a full list of titles in this series, please visit www.routledge.com

Books in the series include:

Educational Policy Goes to School

Case Studies on the Limitations and Possibilities of Educational Innovation

Edited by Gilberto Q. Conchas,
Michael A. Gottfried, Briana M. Hinga,
and Leticia Oseguera

Routledge
Taylor & Francis Group

LONDON AND NEW YORK

First published 2018
by Routledge

2 Park Square, Milton Park, Abingdon, Oxfordshire OX14 4RN
52 Vanderbilt Avenue, New York, NY 10017

Routledge is an imprint of the Taylor & Francis Group, an informa business

First issued in paperback 2019

Library of Congress Cataloguing-in-Publication Data
A catalog record for this book has been requested

ISBN: 978-1-138-67875-0 (hbk)
ISBN: 978-0-367-87845-0 (pbk)

Typeset in Sabon
by Apex CoVantage, LLC

Contents

1 Introduction

Conceptualizing the Intricacies that are Concomitant in Educational Policymaking that Determine Success, Backfire, and Everything in Between

Leticia Oseguera, Miguel N. Abad, Jacob Kirksey, Briana Hinga, Gilberto Q. Conchas, and Michael Gottfried

> Taken together, the historic, economic, sociopolitical, and moral debt that we have amassed toward Black, Brown, Yellow, and Red children seems insurmountable, and attempts of addressing it seem futile. Indeed, it appears like a task for Sisyphus. But as legal scholar Derrick Bell indicated, just because something is impossible does not mean it is not worth doing.
>
> (Ladson-Billings, American Educational Research Association (AERA) Presidential Address, 2006)

Policy reform is often considered an answer to promoting equity in schools. However, history tells another story. Numerous policy reforms have come and gone while deep-rooted inequity within the school system persists. Gloria Ladson-Billing's explanation of the "education debt" provides an elucidation of this problem (AERA Presidential Address, 2006).

Ladson-Billings reframes the focus away from the concept of an achievement gap (i.e., referring to disparities in standardized test scores between races and classes) to a focus on an achievement *debt*, explaining historical, economic, sociopolitical, and moral inequities rooted in the system. Historical debt refers to the legacy of inequitable policies and practices in schools. Economic debt includes funding disparities in education. The sociopolitical debt denotes the exclusion of people of color from the civic process. A moral debt points out the difference between what we state we believe to be right versus what we actually practice. The comprehensive intersections of these four debt categories paint a bleak picture for the hopes of education reform. Ladson-Billings—in her 2006 AERA Presidential Address—cites Derrick Bell as she explains that just because this debt seems hopeless to overcome, this does not mean it is not worth working toward.

In contrast to reforms addressing the achievement gap, addressing the education debt requires addressing systematic inequalities rooted in the system. This takes shifting the conversation from an achievement gap, which can exist without ownership, to the acknowledgement that the problem is owned in the form of education debt (Patel, 2015). A gap can be seen as something to fill, if a policy targets the right factor(s) to reform, without calling for a transformation in the conditions that created the gap. Attempts to reform the system by isolating and fixing factors within the system align with the understanding of reform as merely the reorganization of unethical practices that allows us to sleep at night (Wilderson, 2010).

This book attempts to understand ways we can work toward addressing the possibly insurmountable education debt, through policies. Rather than pose solutions to our education debt, the volume engages what it means for policies to address the education debt and how policies materialize within a system with deeply rooted inequities. We look at the intentions espoused by specific policies as well as the material unfolding of each policy. We include an analysis of the roll out of policies that met their stated intentions as policies, those that had unintended consequences, those that failed, and even those that backfired and made things worse. A look across studies opens a discussion about how stated intentions of policies materialize within a system that runs on debt.

What it Means for Policies to Address Achievement Debt

Scholars such as Gloria Ladson-Billings (2006) have critiqued the hegemony of the achievement gap paradigm, which has prioritized short-term solutions, and has promoted siloed investigations and interventions (Patel, 2015). What is often excluded from this discussion is how underlying systemic issues of racism, power, and politics shape both educational and social inequity. Moreover, researchers and policymakers often do not recognize the ways in which the achievement gap paradigm is rooted in historical processes that are intimately tied to anti-blackness, "culture of poverty" tropes and neoliberal restructuring (Baldridge, 2014; Dumas, 2014; Leonardo & Hunter, 2007; Sojoyner, 2016). This theoretical and policy perspective centers individuals and minoritized communities through a deficit lens. What has recently emerged from this perspective are shortsighted efforts such as personality-centered interventions to increase students' "grit" in hopes of stimulating academic achievement (Duckworth & Gross 2014; McGee, 2016). Aside from the moral and philosophical issues that belie such efforts, these types of interventions do little to address the systems, and structures that constrain the life opportunities of minoritized youth. Disparities in educational opportunities cannot be truly addressed until policy is dedicated to transforming the social and institutional conditions that hinder the healthy development of all young people—especially those from minoritized communities (Welner & Carter, 2013). This calls for a broader analysis and understanding of the fundamentally racialized, gendered, and class-based nature of inequality and its consequences for all aspects of human development. Within this broader perspective, systemic change must be centered on inequities that intersect with education, which includes lack of access to physical and mental health resources, inadequate housing, extreme economic inequality, food insecurity, immigration status, de facto segregation and lack of access to enriching activities.

Angela Y. Davis (1990) once defined the word radical as "grasping things at the root." The conceptual hegemony of the "achievement gap" is dependent upon an assumption that equity can be attained if: 1) the causal mechanisms that belie the systemic glitches are identified and that 2) these malfunctions can be ameliorated by liberal reforms or technocratic innovations. Scholars have noted the ways in which reform agendas fueled by colorblind ideologies and naïve meritocratic principles have often reduced and conflated equity with simplistic conceptions of "access" and "equal opportunity" (Pollock, 2001; Lewis, 2003; Philip, Jurow, Vossoughi, Bang, & Zavala, 2017), which do not address the structural and institutional nature of inequality. This framing obstructs the opportunity for a radical analysis of the historical and structural social formations that are at the root of oppression and inequality (Gutierrez & Jaramillo, 2006; Patel, 2015). Such polemical topics are often excluded from mainstream policy and research discourse. Some influential social scientists and policymakers perceive these concepts as value-laden, not objective, and ultimately unscientific, which has relegated researchers who ask such questions to the margins of academia (Hale, 2008). In the context of the current political climate, some education researchers—specifically those in the learning sciences—have called for education scholars to embrace these dimensions of research and establish a political theory of learning that advocates for the rights of minoritized communities (Philip et al., 2017). Research and policymaking are not value-free, ahistorical, or decontextualized endeavors. Politicians and activists all along the political spectrum tend to agree; laws and budgets are essentially "moral documents" (Ryan, 2014).

Policy Outcome Continuum

We engage the discussion of how policies materialize along categories of backfire, failure, unintended consequences, and success. While backfire is included under the umbrella of policies with unintended consequences, it has its own special category. Backfire occurs when a policy or intervention has the *exact opposite effect* of what it was intended to do (see Gottfried & Conchas, 2016). Policies that backfire are distinct from policies that fail or even policies that have unintended consequences. Therein lies the conceptual utility of "backfire" versus failure. Defining this distinction is an intention and contribution of this edited volume. The addition of failure, unintended consequences, and success will further add clarity to backfire. While unintended effects can be positive or negative, backfire is always negative. We argue that there is a need to specifically identify policies that backfire, as unintended effects often provoke a "we should have seen that coming" face-palm moment and require a reworking of the program, and failure requires an entirely new policy or program (or not, depending on how stubborn the "deciders" may be); backfire suggests a fundamental misstep in the program design that failed to account for some vitally important factor or structural consideration, whatever its basis. This design flaw led to the program not just failing, not just having unintended effects, but having an iatrogenic effect, or creating greater harm as a result of the treatment. All social and educational policies are intended to do good, so the understanding of how and why they go wrong is essential to understanding how stated intentions play out in a system that runs on deep education debt.

Intentions of the Book

This book was written to learn from attempts to move toward equity in the education system. The strengths of this approach toward educational equity include its coverage of a continuum of policy adoption, from success to backfire, as described above. It is academic and action focused in that chapter authors include conceptual frameworks describing policy implications with practical examples for those tasked with implementing or adopting policy. Also, we offer an understanding of the policy outcome through an asset-based perspective and challenge chapter authors to push the conceptual boundaries of the achievement gap and shift the discussion toward a more complete understanding of inequity that accounts for racism, power, oppression, and the historical structural antecedents of educational inequality. That is, rather than blame the student or actor for less than promising outcomes, we explain how multiple actors often work together, through historically structured cultures, to shape conditions for how the policy materializes. Through lessons of each study, we offer ideas for future academics, practitioners, and policymakers to consider as they oversee/implement policy improvement. A final strength of this book is its inclusion of international perspectives. We extend the contextual features of this book by including domestic and international perspectives that illustrate each of our policy scenarios. This is a first, unique opportunity to present a multifaceted, multidisciplinary examination of when educational policy and practice do and do not converge—and what lessons we can learn.

   This collection of chapters represents a multitude of disciplines and methodological approaches, located across the United States and internationally, and studies of different geographic regions and distinct youth and young adult populations—from early childhood education through adulthood. While the geographic scope and methodological approach varies, each chapter directly addresses three key questions:

1) What was the educational policy, and what educational intentions were espoused by the policy?

2) How did the policy materially unfold and how does this materialization fit within the categories of success, unintended consequences, failure, or backfire?
3) What might explain the outcome? And, what can we learn to structure policies that enact stated intentions?

The first question is central to any analysis of policy. It provides the landscape by which we can examine how a policy set out to reduce schooling gaps for a particular minoritized group. Once we understand the landscape (e.g., intention and goals) of the policy, it is feasible to move to addressing question two. Here, each chapter will evaluate the divergence between intention and material reality. Question two provides an analysis of the implementation of the policy and provides evidence of outcomes across the continuum. Finally, of great importance to this book is question three. This final question addresses reasons for the outcome—i.e., providing the readers with specific explanations and useful conclusions that may be used to address the achievement debt.

Organization of Book

Part I of the book focuses on the contributions of educational policies that backfire and make things worse for the populations the policies were intended to help.

In Chapter 2, "How Urban Education Choice Campaigns in Detroit Masqueraded as Equity and Social Justice and Worsened the Status Quo," Brownell discusses the schooling context in Detroit, and how school enrollment restrictions prevented disenfranchised populations from accessing education. While the notion, "I'm in" was propagated among the Midtown population, the policy backfired: quality schooling excluded specific populations through admissions criteria, which perpetuated the existing opportunity gaps for the city's youth and parents in the most underprivileged sectors.

In Chapter 3, "When Policies that Impact Students with Significant Disabilities in Michigan Backfire," Deschaine discusses the role of PA 198 in Michigan, a policy that established segregated schools for students with significant disabilities in 1971. While at the time the policy was considered "best practice" among educators, Deschaine argues that the segregation of schools for these students was met with the rise of pressure for the mainstreaming and normalization of access to general education classrooms. This chapter discusses several policies that attempt to provide support for students with significant disabilities, but emphasizes their backfire on individuals and school districts.

In Chapter 4, "When Zero-Tolerance Discipline Policies in the United States Backfire," Potter and Boggs situate the discussion of policy backfire using zero-tolerance discipline policies in schools. Through a sociological framework, the authors contend that zero-tolerance discipline policies undermine student educational attainment. Moreover, these policies, though originally intended to make schools safer, have reinforced and increased the school-to-prison pipeline, a clear perpetuation of the problem that these policies were trying to solve.

In Chapter 5, "When Free Schools in England and Charter Schools in the United States Backfire," Downes and Simon describe the Academies Act of the UK, a policy intended to create additional choice and competition for schooling for greater social mobility for students. Similar to the invention of charter schools in the U.S., the Academies intended to reduce inequity in schools by eliminating barriers seen to be blocking student success. However, research suggests that these Academies backfired and heightened stratification and debilitated social mobility in UK schools, amplifying opportunity gaps for students.

Part II examines the contributions of policies that failed. They may have been crafted with good intentions but clearly failed to reach their aims via a collapse in sustainable infrastructure to attain policy goals.

In Chapter 6, "When High-Stakes Accountability Measures Impact Promising Practices in an Indigenous-Serving Charter School," Anthony-Stevens juxtaposes the aims of a culturally responsive, local charter school with the realities of harsh accountability policy embedded within Adequate Yearly Progress (AYP) benchmarks. Using ethnographic research to portray an Indigenous-serving charter middle school in Arizona, the author illustrates the clear satisfaction of students, parents, and teachers with the school's learning environment for its students. Yet, with the school's failure to meet AYP thresholds, the school was forced to close its doors to its students. Anthony-Stevens suggests that while the goal of culturally responsive schooling was clearly desirable, this goal failed in the context of accountability measurement for this school, and more work is needed to understand potential for sustainable, equitable educational change.

In Chapter 7, "How Public-Private Partnerships Contribute to Educational Policy Failure," Fernandez, Loya, and Oseguera highlight the policy failure of a federally sponsored college access program. An analysis of the program reveals that overall implementation was hindered due to consistent communication breakdowns between schools and private, non-profit organizations. While the partnership between public and private entities is popular among reform efforts, the authors argue that these partnerships are not enough to reduce opportunity gaps for students. Further, they conclude that evaluation of programs is a key component to understanding policy success or failure, as these evaluation efforts lead to better coordination between stakeholders and improve the ability for program staff to collect informative data.

In Chapter 8, "The Failure of Accountability in the Milwaukee Parental Choice Program," Ford and Vélez discuss the results and overall failure of the Milwaukee Parental Choice Program (MPCP). Due to the fact that

MPCP was not held accountable among voters in the community, the program was never richly embedded within the city's education infrastructure. The authors argue that without a democratic mechanism to keep the program accountable, MPCP inevitably failed. They suggest possible solutions that address Milwaukee's policy failure.

In Chapter 9, "How Centralized Implementation Policies Failed the Austrian New Middle School Process," Geppert questions whether the policy implementation from a centralized administration is inherently fated to fail. That is, does top-down policy diffusion work, or what resistance does it face from schooling communities? Using a multiple-methods, multilevel design, Geppert demonstrates the challenges faced by the New Middle School in Austria, a new type of schooling that was introduced for secondary students. Ultimately, the goals of the school failed given the factors of parental power and school refusal to commit to an alternative education option for students.

Part III presents examples that illustrate the contributions of policies that produce unintended consequences through a disconnect between intentions and material implications. These cases offer new perspectives in policymaking by broadening the scope to consider who is affected by various policies and how these policies are mediated within systems, which determine the real impacts.

In Chapter 10, "The Unintended Consequences of School Vouchers: Rise, Rout, and Rebirth," Saiger discusses the impact of reform efforts that instituted school vouchers in the state of Ohio from the late 1990s. While Ohio successfully litigated the constitutionality of school vouchers for private schools—including religious schools—few voucher programs emerged in the early 2000s, which many educational stakeholders viewed as a policy failure for the voucher movement. However, Saiger argues that the movement produced an unintended consequence: voucher programs provided the groundwork for the future emergence of charter schools in the U.S., and their judicial efforts will likely enhance the ability for religious schools to successfully compete with public schools.

In Chapter 11, "Challenges and Unintended Consequences of Student-Centered Learning," Hubbard and Datnow present findings from a two-year qualitative case study of a public elementary school that uses a student-centered approach to contrast with the more traditionally conceived teacher-centered classroom. The authors argue that while this pedagogical reform had good intentions, the policy endured unique unintentional challenges, as the educators faced the contrast of this new approach with the traditional culture and structure engrained in school. Highlighting the importance of understanding the influence of current policy and cultural context, this chapter offers suggestions for future progressive policies aimed at introducing student-centered educational reforms.

In Chapter 12, "School Discipline Policies that Result in Unintended Consequences for Latino Male Students' College Aspirations," Huerta,

Calderone, and McDonough draw attention to the unintended consequence of aggressive school disciplinary policies on academic outcomes for Latino males through misidentification and the loss of class time for students. Framing this policy issue through Bourdieu's concept of cultural field and policy implementation theory, the authors provide insight into how well-intended policies may misalign goals and outcomes, stressing the importance of all students' contexts and life experiences when crafting policies that have the potential to hinder aspirations.

In Chapter 13, "When Special Education Policy in Ontario Creates Unintended Consequences," Jervis and Winton address the unintended consequences of Ontario's policy requirement that all students be formally assessed before qualifying to receive special education services. The authors draw on analysis from a study that examined the efforts of the People for Education to bring awareness to the underlying inequities of this policy initiative. They conclude that shortfalls in funding, the increased layer of privatization of schools, and neoliberal conceptions of parenting prevented much-needed changes to the province's policy. The authors make recommendations for which changes might curtail the inequities inherent in the current policy.

Part IV presents a series of studies that introduce policy initiatives from community to national levels, highlighting material implications that align with intentions written into the policy.

In Chapter 14, "Latina/o Farmworker Parent Leadership Retreats as Sites of Agency, Community Cultural Wealth, and Success," Nava and Lara examine how the Education Leadership Foundation—a leadership development community-based organization—in partnership with the Migrant Education Program use parent retreats for building leadership, and skill development of migrant farmworking families. Utilizing cooperative and community responsive practices, these retreats build on the Community Cultural Wealth (Yosso, 2005) in migrant communities as parents develop cohesive networks and community leaders to engage in school advocacy in the service of their children. They argue for the need to rethink the role of *testimonios* as a pedagogical tool in parent engagement and capacity building for leadership and agency in such communities. This chapter highlights successful policy development that comes from communities themselves rather than from top-down approaches.

In Chapter 15, "Bilingual and Biliterate Skills as Cross-Cultural Competence Success," González-Carriedo and Babino highlight the success stories of three recent high school graduates in a dual language program and the Seal of Biliteracy initiative—two programs that promote bilingualism and biliteracy. The policy goal of bilingualism and biliteracy seeks to enhance student academic knowledge and understanding in a cross-cultural context. The authors discuss how these goals were achieved for these students and how their pride and motivations for linguistic success were enhanced with these cooperative policies.

In Chapter 16, "Diversity-Driven Charters and Construction of Urban School Success," Wohlstetter, Wang, and Gonzales discuss the national reform goals of the charter school movement and how more recent charter school initiatives return the original aims of their invention. Particularly, the authors bring to light how many of the intended goals of charter schools have faced major challenges through the implementation process. However, new policies that have redefined charters have returned the reform effort to its origins, and successful decision-making within schools has facilitated the innovative education of students from diverse backgrounds and experiences.

In Chapter 17, "Reflecting on the Institutional Processes for College Success among Chicanos in the Context of Crisis," Rodríguez, Mosqueda, Nava, and Conchas pen that the education crisis facing the Latino community in the U.S. has received considerable attention. In recognition of the various factors that shape the disparity in Latino male outcomes, this essay focuses on the experiences of four low-income Chicanos within the U.S. context. Their counternarratives demonstrate that beyond "ganas"—motivation—key institutional processes, practices, and policies integrally shaped their experiences. This chapter provides a complex analysis of Latino student mobility from kindergarten to college and career.

In the last chapter, Chapter 18, "Refra'ming the Problematic Achievement Gap Narrative to Structure Educational Success," Ream, Ryan, and Yang summarize the nature, sources, and consequences of stubbornly persistent disparities in educational opportunity and performance, despite countless and varied policy initiatives intended to promote equity in schools. Drawing on the combined perspectives of ecological systems theory and the economics of human development, the authors recognize the nature and causes of social inequities, both within and beyond schools, as layered and overlapping and they question the unrealistic expectation that schools alone should be capable of remedying a long history of systematic and discriminatory gaps in educational inputs. The authors shift our attention toward how policy might better address the longstanding "educational debt" by acknowledging the social and institutional conditions that intersect with education. Specifically, they highlight new research that upends two problematic assumptions about how educational processes function beyond the formal K-12 setting. The first assumption contends that the beneficial effects of early childhood interventions inevitably fade, while the latter asserts that few educational benefits derive from affordable housing reforms designed to improve the neighborhoods of marginalized families. Both assumptions rely on a selective reading of research and have long limited the imaginable policy moves that might be used to reduce the achievement debt and advance educational and social equality. Ultimately, new research offers the potential to reframe the problematic achievement gap narrative, and, importantly, the policy agenda at a time when the population of U.S. voters and workers has become increasingly diverse and divided by widening social class inequality.

Utility of this Book and Contributions to Reducing Schooling Gaps

At its core, the schooling system in the United States is touted as the key way in which disenfranchised, underrepresented, and non-dominant populations can move up the ladder—socially and economically. Therefore it comes as no surprise that much of the educational policymaking time and resources are devoted to supporting student populations who are not given an equal opportunity to succeed. Over the past decades, we have seen an influx of state and educational policies designed in a way to reduce opportunity gaps and promote access and success for these groups by improving schooling structures and practices. While these policies have been diverse in approach, they are often united in asking how we can better improve schools to serve the needs of diverse student populations. While many of these educational policies have worked to partially alleviate temporary gaps, the deeply rooted inequities in the system persist. Within this context, many policies have failed, or, even worse, many backfired; that is, policies that were explicitly intended to address educational inequality for disenfranchised groups through changes in schooling structures and practices have caused the reverse effect—a widening of the gaps that they had set out to close. Generally, we present chapters that examine theoretical and empirically grounded work that elucidates the possibilities and limitations of educational policy in school and out of school contexts.

Other scholars and activists have laid the groundwork for the discussion for a systemic and historical understanding of educational inequity through their conceptual and philosophical contributions (Solorzano & Yosso, 2002; Gutierrez & Jaramillo, 2006; Ladson-Billings, 2006; Duncan-Andrade, 2009). At the same time, the achievement gap paradigm has continued to permeate throughout all aspects of American education research and policymaking. In this age of hyper-accountability and evaluation, it is ironic that the achievement gap's paradigmatic hegemony endures despite its disappointing track record of fulfilling its intended goal. This book aims to extend and renew this conversation by presenting empirical work from a wide array of research traditions that collectively illustrate how (mis)understandings of the roots of inequality contribute to policy backfire, failure, unintended consequences, and success. We ultimately hope that the findings of the studies in this volume compel researchers and policymakers to "steer the ship" (Lipsitz, 2008) beyond the achievement gap paradigm.

As we transition to a new conservative education era, it is imperative to consider the roots of inequality. We should be aware of catch phrases that sound promising, such as "allowing every child an opportunity to succeed," or, "families should be given more choice to send their children to good schools" without investigating the full spectrum of negative outcomes that are likely to ensue. If we learned anything from history, it's that sweeping reforms to "fix" problems are all too often short sighted and exacerbate inequities, as we never truly addressed these gaps systematically. This volume is now timelier than ever. We urge the public, researchers, and policymakers to respond responsibly to ensure that the root causes of inequality are considered and addressed so as to not exacerbate the very inequities we set out to combat.

References

Baldridge, B. J. (2014). Relocating the deficit: Reimagining Black youth in neoliberal times. *American Educational Research Journal, 51*(3), 440–472.

Davis, A. Y. (1990). *Women, culture & politics*. New York: Vintage.

Duckworth, A., & Gross, J. J. (2014). Self-control and grit: Related but separable determinants of success. *Current Directions in Psychological Science, 23*(5), 319–325.

Dumas, M. J. (2014). 'Losing an arm': schooling as a site of black suffering. *Race Ethnicity and Education, 17*(1), 1–29.

Duncan-Andrade, J. (2009). Note to educators: Hope required when growing roses in concrete. *Harvard Educational Review, 79*(2), 181–194.

Gottfried, M. A., & Conchas, G. Q. (2016). *When school policies backfire: How well-intended measures can harm our most vulnerable students*. Cambridge, MA: Harvard Education Press.

Gutiérrez, K. D., & Jaramillo, N. E. (2006). Looking for educational equity: The consequences of relying on Brown. *Yearbook of the National Society for the Study of Education, 105*(2), 173–189.

Hale, C. R. (2008). *Engaging contradictions: Theory, politics, and methods of activist scholarship*. University of California Press.

Ladson-Billings, G. (2006). From the achievement gap to the education debt: Understanding achievement in US schools. *Educational Researcher, 35*(7), 3–12.

Leonardo, Z., & Hunter, M. (2007). Imagining the urban: The politics of race, class, and schooling. In *International handbook of urban education* (pp. 779–801). The Netherlands: Springer.

Lewis, A. (2003). *Race in the schoolyard: Negotiating the color line in classrooms and communities*. New Brunswick, NJ: Rutgers University Press.

Lipsitz, G. (2008). Breaking the chains and steering the ship: How activism can help change teaching and scholarship. *Engaging contradictions: Theory, politics, and methods of activist scholarship*. University of California Press, 88–111.

McGee, E. O. (2016). Devalued Black and Latino Racial Identities: A By-Product of STEM College Culture?. *American Educational Research Journal, 53*(6), 1626–1662.

Patel, L. (2015). *Decolonizing educational research: From ownership to answerability*. London: Routledge.

Philip, T. M., Jurow, A. S., Vossoughi, S., Bang, M., & Zavala, M. (2017). The learning sciences in a new era of U.S. nationalism. *Cognition & Instruction*. Advance online publication. Retrieved from http://cognitionandinstruction.com/engagements-the-learning-sciences-in-a-new-era-of-u-s-nationalism/

Pollock, M. (2001). How the question we ask most about race in education is the very question we most suppress. *Educational Researcher, 30*(9), 2–11.

Ryan, T. J. (2014). Reconsidering moral issues in politics. *The Journal of Politics, 76*(2), 380–397.

Sojoyner, D. (2016). *First Strike: Educational Enclosures in Black Los Angeles*. Minneapolis, MN: The University of Minnesota Press

Solórzano, D. G., & Yosso, T. J. (2002). Critical race methodology: Counter-storytelling as an analytical framework for education research. *Qualitative Inquiry, 8*(1), 23–44.

Welner, K. G., & Carter, P. L. (2013). Achievement gaps arise from opportunity gaps. *Closing the Opportunity Gap: What America Must Do to Give Every Child an Even Chance*. New York, NY: Oxford University Press, 1–10.

Wilderson, F. B. (2010). *Red, white & black: Cinema and the structure of U.S. antagonisms*. Durham, NC: Duke University Press.

Yosso, T. J. (2005). Whose culture has capital? A critical race theory discussion of community cultural wealth. *Race ethnicity and education, 8*(1), 69–91.

2 How Urban Education Choice Campaigns in Detroit Masqueraded as Equity and Social Justice and Worsened the Status Quo

Cassie J. Brownell

On a visit to Detroit in fall of 2013, I first saw public schools advertised in the same manner as the numerous charter schools of my previous home of New Orleans. There, brandished along a major highway into the city, stood a billboard encouraging local parents to declare, "I'm in" and commit to Detroit Public Schools (DPS) while simultaneously promoting Detroit's Midtown "Community of Schools." Fresh from the streets of corporate school reform in New Orleans, I was initially taken aback by the presence of the Detroit Public Schools' billboard itself. Curious about the state of public education in the city and the inception of the "I'm in" campaign, this chapter charts the enrollment campaign and the paradoxical possibilities of "shopping" for schools supported by then emergency financial manager Robert Bobb. The chapter specifically provides a deep and critical conceptual understanding of the limitations and possibilities of educational policies with respect to issues of equity and social justice.

While serving as an educator in post-Katrina New Orleans, a city now overtaken by the charter school movement, I became accustomed to seeing streetcars, bus stops, and bumper stickers advertising the many choices parents had in educating their children. After Hurricane Katrina ravaged the city, the Orleans Parish School Board and the Recovery School District, the local operator of the public school system, slowly relinquished control of the city's public schools to charter school operators. When I left the city in 2013, New Orleans was home to only five schools managed by the Recovery School District (Recovery School District, 2013). An additional 60 charter schools were managed by various private entities and charter organizations.

Many Americans view urban, metropolitan centers as especially in need of an improved school system. Few Americans, however, fully take into account the many obstacles large cities and public school districts face in establishing sustainable school reforms. They instead overlook particular constraints inhibiting successful steps toward equitable education. Therefore, Americans must now consider the intersection of current school reforms and the political economy in an effort to move urban education to a more equitable and socially just framework.

What was Detroit's "I'm in" Campaign Policy?

This research employed a method of qualitative critical content analysis (Holsti, 1969; Krippendorff, 2013). In addition to the DPS billboard (see figure 2.1), district and school websites, and individual school brochures alongside internal and external school reports were included in this study. Publicly available primary source materials (e.g., external communications, policy data) gathered across the course of the 2013–2014 school year also served as data sources.

Additionally, multimedia resources, such as public media, open-access blogs, and DPS archived social media, served as rich data sources. Utilizing content analysis, with a specific focus on Krippendorff's (2013) six guiding questions (e.g., *What is the context relative to which data are analyzed? What is the target of the inferences?*), I analyzed the relationship between these data sources while making inferences across such sources to take into account the culture and time in which each appeared. Moreover, I explored how this policy was intended to support families and promised new possibilities, through the framing of school choice, but how this goal ultimately backfired.

Figure 2.1

The photograph on the 2013 billboard displayed a young African-American girl, brightly dressed while working on a computer. Smiling, the young girl appeared relaxed as she easily completed an individual task using technology. In the distance, along pale blue walls reaching to a high ceiling, a suited African-American male—presumably the teacher—mingled among a handful of African-American students diligently engaged in their studies at their desks. The students sat distanced from one another in the seemingly large space rather than an overcrowded classroom. The image portrayed joy and limitless possibilities for learning.

Visually, the narrative of the 2013 billboard presented a hopeful illustration of learning and engagement within the reformed DPS. Local news stories from the same year, however, still rendered a majority of students serviced by DPS as "at-risk." Many students within DPS were noted as coming from the lowest socioeconomic class with parents who themselves had limited education. These findings demonstrated how education within DPS was not yet equitable, fair, or just when compared with neighboring townships or nearby charter schools (Guerra, 2013). Additional findings illuminated how the "I'm in" campaign backfired and failed to fully account for the sociocultural context of Detroit public education while sustaining socially unjust practices and perpetuating the commodification of schooling in Detroit.

Refracted through Labaree's (1997) purposes of schooling and seen through a neoliberal lens, this chapter investigates the following research questions: *How does the "I'm in" campaign take into account the sociocultural context of Detroit public education? Does the "I'm in" campaign promote socially just or unjust practices of/for schooling? In what ways do the DPS billboard and larger "I'm in" campaign account for the commodification of education within the city?* Divided into three sections, this chapter first explores the sociopolitical context of education in the city of Detroit and asks, "Who's out" in DPS's "I'm in" campaign? Next, I analyze the paradoxical relationship of the purpose of schooling embedded within the "I'm in" campaign through critical content analysis. Finally, I contend in my findings that public education is actualized as a private commodity rather than a public good through critical analysis of the DPS billboard, the "I'm in" campaign, and other promotional materials. I end with a discussion of the limitations and possibilities of structuring urban school success.

Detroit's Ground Zero in Urban Education: Contextualizing the Campaign

The challenges of school reform are well documented within urban policy literature (Judd & Swanstrom, 2010; Dreier, Mollenkopf, & Swanstrom, 2004; Massey, 1993; Stone, 1998) and urban education literature (Bulkley, Henig, & Levin, 2010; Cucchiara, 2013; Orr & Rogers, 2010). Variants like competing interests and political ideologies are often challenges that are considered as well as specific structures and school reforms. These often result in racial or class cleavages (Henig, Hula, Orr, & Pedescleaux, 2001) and persistent marginalization of and within particular communities. Without taking into account the storied histories of urban areas like Detroit, scholars and policymakers misunderstand the sociocultural context in which policy is enacted. In turn, they sometimes create more limitations than possibilities for teaching and learning in urban education.

In recent years, the city of Detroit has taken center stage across various media platforms as a primary example of the urban crisis. This has been particularly true following the city's financial fallout and debt explosion. But what led to the city's fall from grace? Many Americans approach this answer with a deficit viewpoint. Thus, blame comes in many forms—from editor Nolan Finley's declaration that Detroit's present situation is a "self-inflicted, rolling disaster" (Aviv, 2011, p. 6), to the commonly held belief the race riot of 1967 is the primary reason for White flight to the suburbs, to the "What if?" questions surrounding each mayor's decision-making (Bomey & Gallagher, 2013). Detroit schools have been plagued by economic and racial inequality. This is in part due to deindustrialization, but, like many other major U.S. cities, also persistent, racialized poverty (Bulkley, Henig, & Levin, 2010; Cucchiara, 2013; Orr & Rogers, 2010).

The 1930s and 1940s were a formative era, both in the social and economic history of the city (Sugrue, 2004). During this period, Detroit was bursting with employment opportunities, dominated by auto industry giants Ford, Chrysler, and Chevrolet. While people of all races came to Detroit seeking new employment opportunities, large numbers of African-Americans were flooding the city. Commonly referred to as the "Great Migration," huge numbers of African-Americans fled to Detroit seeking employment and hoping to escape the poverty and racial caste system of the South. However, many African-Americans found their new home in the North to be quite similar to the world they had hoped to leave behind, with "hostility, racism, and discrimination nearly as bad as in the South" (Judd & Swanstrom, 2010, p. 133). As more and more African-Americans began to move toward Detroit and other Midwest cities, middle class White families with access to automobiles began making their way to the suburbs in what would quickly become known as "White flight." Improvements in transportation infrastructure contributed to Whites' initial exodus from the city (Mollenkopf, Dreier, & Swanstron, 2001).

The 1950s were a prosperous time for many in the city of Detroit, but changes in the urban economy and labor market also had negative results. More specifically, housing separation and "ghettoization" along racial and class lines became more prevalent (Massey & Denton, 2003). Many neighborhoods that were home to White, working-class citizens formed organized efforts to "protect themselves" against the invasion of African-Americans that would, as one Detroit citizen stated, "just destroy everything in the whole neighborhood" (Judd & Swanstrom, 2010, p. 134). Through restrictive covenants, White citizens were able to keep African-Americans from buying property in White neighborhoods, resulting in continued racial seg-regation. An additional tactic Whites used in their attempts to keep Afri-can-American families from "violating the sanctity of racial boundaries" (Sugrue, 2004, p. 24) was intimidation. Such efforts, in conjunction with the doubling of Detroit's African-American population and the limited pool of housing, led to a metropolitan area densely populated by African-Americans during the postwar era (Sugrue, 2004). This trend was similar across several U.S. cities (Henig, Hula, Orr, & Pedescleaux, 2001).

Detroit was once the fourth largest city in the country. In the early 1960s, the city was home to nearly two million people, with 400,000 children enrolled in the city's schools. After decades of change, framed by racial mis-trust and the race riot in 1967, many more Detroit citizens began to flee the city for the developing suburbs, causing property values to plummet (Bomey & Gallagher, 2013). The exodus of industry contributed to the fall of the Detroit urban area with the dawning of new technologies and auto-mation. Thus, joblessness plagued African-Americans in Detroit from the 1970s through the 1990s.

Debt and (Re)Development Characterizes the Detroit of Today

The city of Detroit has faced a financial crisis since before the recession of 2008. As outlined above, in the decades leading up to the new millennium, the city saw a dwindling tax-base and an increasing need for public assis-tance. From 1962 to 2012, the city's revenue fell 40% despite the imple-mentation of the 1962 income tax, the 1970 utility tax, and the 1999 casino revenue tax, among many others (Bomey & Gallagher, 2013). One possible explanation for this enormous decrease in revenue is that higher taxes con-tinue to push people out of the city.

Detroit, like many other major cities, is working to recreate itself in order to attract people, particularly wealthy populations, back to the city. This is evident in the renaming of various neighborhoods (e.g., Cass Corridor to Midtown) that is done even against residents' wishes (Fahle, 2013). Renam-ing is a means of bringing about reinvestment in particular neighborhoods (Peterson, 2012). By renaming specific areas of Detroit, the city's govern-ment is attempting to entice businesses to relocate to the area and contribute to redevelopment of the city.

Detroit's Choice Reforms as a Divisive Decision

The segregation of Detroit's children, particularly along racial and class lines, is not an accident (Mollenkopf, Dreier, & Swanstrom, 2001). With marginalized populations left behind, Detroit's property values and city rev-enue decreased dramatically (Judd & Swanstrom, 2010). This was especially during the final decades of the last millennium. Simultaneously, the question of what to do with the city's failing schools quickly became headline news

(Dzwonkowski, 1999). Yet, the segregated nature of Detroit is not only the result of institutionalized oppression, but more directly, legislative policy (Massey & Denton, 2003).

Like other predominantly African-American U.S. cities, the city of Detroit has implemented a number of different school reforms across time (Henig, Hula, Orr, & Pedescleaux, 2001). While officials in Detroit were serious in their attempts at implementing a range of school reforms, few reforms had staying power. The trend to implement new reform in Detroit is therefore not new, but tracking the number of reforms introduced since the new millennium is a daunting task. Additionally, the landscape of Detroit schools appears to be ever changing with new names—of management officials, of schools, and of policies—frequently littering local news media. With many different educational reforms happening all at once and with many of these reforms overlapping, placing a single current reform within the urban literature is difficult. Many reforms from recent years are already outdated, including the "I'm in" campaign. Yet, underlying tensions due to race and class remain prevalent across time.

The country's 2009 economic downturn contributed to Detroit's continued change in demographics. After President Barack Obama named Arne Duncan the United States Secretary of Education in 2009, Duncan declared Detroit Public Schools to be "ground zero" and an "educational disgrace" (Aviv, 2011). The education scene remained besieged by the economic downfall of the city itself. Decaying and decrepit school buildings were surrounded by neighborhoods of foreclosure and blight. Unemployment and poverty were on the rise while the actual number of children in the city continued to decline (Data Driven Detroit, 2012). With fewer children in the city, many areas schools were closed.

Due to the declining enrollment of students and the bleak predictions for the 2009–2010 school year, the state of Michigan swept in and took over the Detroit Public Schools, naming Robert Bobb as the emergency financial manager. Charged with turning the schools around and with making them financially viable, Bobb partnered with the advertising agency Leo Burnett to develop the "I'm in" campaign. Aimed at recruiting and retaining students, organizers created a counternarrative to reverse the negative perceptions of the city's public school system and introduce new possibilities for teaching and learning. In an effort to renew confidence in a system plagued by corruption, the greater Detroit community would need to be emotionally engaged in the restoration of the Detroit Public Schools.

Paradoxical Possibilities and the 2013 "I'm in" Billboard

For my own investigation, I situated my inquiry within Labaree's (1997) three competing purposes of schooling—democratic equality, social efficiency, and social mobility. For Labaree (1997), "citizenship training," "equal treatment," and "equal access" originated with the same goal of preventing educational stratification and, thus, social stratification (p. 44). However, Labaree (1997) argued that the stratified state of contemporary American education resulted from an undermining of democratic ideals thanks to prevailing models of social efficiency and social mobility.

This line of logic is closely aligned to literature surrounding neoliberal ideology in education. It stresses privatization and competition while being rooted within a framework of free-market capitalism and globalization (Olssen, Codd, & O'Neill, 2004). As noted by Giroux (2004), the promotion of market-based practices often resulted from a desire for a more anti-bureaucratic system. Many proponents of neoliberalism remain suspicious of services deemed public. According to neoliberalism, communities are well served—both socially and economically—through restricted government intervention in their lives and the flourishing of free markets within which they can act according to their own rational self-identity (Harvey, 2005). In terms of education, parents then are "shopping" for schools whose own mission and goals align with preparing their students for continued education and future success. Neoliberal ideals, however, often lead to less transparency within/of the system as parents and students are left confounded by the choices available to them and—further still—how to access these options in schooling (Dunn, 2013).

Advocates of neoliberalism often promote market-based practices under the guise of democratic ideals. Neoliberal ideals are used to foster individual freedoms like self-selection of schooling for one's own children (Apple, 2001; Giroux, 2004). Yet, it is here that the question becomes whether such "freedoms" are extended to all people equitably or whether, as Labaree (1997) would suggest, these "freedoms" reproduce unequitable power relations. In other words, many limitations are inherent in the "possibilities" outlined by proponents of neoliberal ideologies. In the section that follows, I build on existing literature about the purposes of schooling and neoliberal education reform by bringing to light particular instances of neoliberal principles masquerading as democratic ideals.

Neoliberal ideology purports that "public schools are charged with providing individual students the knowledge and skills that they will need to pursue personal gain in college and the workplace" (Mirra & Morrell, 2011, p. 410). As evidenced in DPS mediated communications, students appeared adept to meeting market needs while actively engaging in and learning through 21st Century skills. For example, the "new" Detroit Public Schools emerged as attractive in both their appearance and the offerings available to students and families. By featuring a clean, open space in conjunction with the promotion of 21st Century skills, DPS attempted to push the counternarrative developed in the "I'm in." campaign through the photographic portrayal highlighted on the billboard.

The young student working at the computer embodies numerous buzzwords associated with 21st Century skills. Not only was she portrayed to have the ability to "Apply Technology Effectively" in the billboard photograph, but she appeared able to "Work Independently" and as a "Self-Directed Learner," 21st Century skills that will enhance her own productivity while promoting economic growth ("21st Century," n.d.). The serene learning space in the background reveals students that "know when it is appropriate to listen and when to speak" and are conscious of how to "conduct oneself in a respectable, professional manner," proficiencies demonstrating the 21st Century competency of how to "Interact Effectively with Others" ("21st Century," n.d.). The images of student adaptation to market needs and of student engagement in learning further suggested social efficiency as a purpose of schooling within the Detroit Public Schools.

A Case of Commodifying "Community" Schools

On the surface level, the photograph on the billboard promoted education as a public good. Yet, the four schools listed alongside the billboard's image are promoted as individual products. The billboard is an advertisement and ultimately presented the commodity of education as a *private* good. Parents and students, as consumers in the market, appeared to be presented with choice. Naming four specific schools in the Midtown area—Burton International, Golightly Education Center, Spain Elementary/Middle School, and Detroit School of Arts—fostered interest and built confidence in letting parents know what choices were available to them within the market of Detroit Public Schools. Suggestions such as these stimulate parental choice in "shopping" for a school that provides a myriad of learning possibilities and will produce a well-rounded student.

Several principals of the "Community of Schools" listed on the DPS billboard advanced the neoliberal ideal of the commodification of schooling during a WDET radio interview in 2013. During these interviews, the principals positioned parents as consumers and schools as products. One principal, for example, told audiences, "we have our wonderful, excellent, top-notch staff members [. . .] trained with customer service" (Fahle, 2013). A second principal similarly discussed the role of the Midtown Detroit Public Schools as part of a newly transformed school system, and commented that the schools act as "hubs of our neighborhoods," but with "better customer service" (Fahle, 2013). In agreement, a male school leader discussed his school's many "customers" while his colleague claimed, "we have a product you want" and encouraged parents to "check us out" (Fahle, 2013). The show's host agreed with the principals' comments, citing Midtown as "fertile ground to recruit students," but also noted the challenge they faced in "convincing people to stick around" (Fahle, 2013).

Interesting to note is that it was not only the principals' words that were used to "recruit" families to claim "I'm in" and join the Midtown "Community of Schools." For example, Golightly Education Center referred to itself as a "Midtown, Detroit Public School with a *suburban, private school presence*" [emphasis added] in its 2013 brochure (Golightly Education Center, 2013, p. 2). Rebranding not only to the public school system as a whole—but also individual schools—was a strategy used to sway families to choose public schools in the city's Midtown area. Three of the four schools, for instance, were recognized as Detroit Public Schools' Centers for Excellence and have undergone a name change in the last two decades. Additionally, in 2013, each of the schools required an application to be completed for acceptance (Detroit Public Schools, 2013c). The Detroit School of Arts, one of four magnet schools in the city, required an audition (Detroit Public Schools, 2013b), while Spain Elementary/Middle School placed all students on academic probation during the first semester of enrollment as a student (Detroit Public Schools, 2013d). As a Skillman school and boasting partnership with over 25 organizations, the Burton International Academy's application process in 2013 included a family interview and grade level assessment while demanding a 2.5 GPA and recognition of good citizenship for all applicants (Detroit Public Schools, 2013a). Expectations and standards for enrollment, as outlined above, influenced the decision of families and individuals to apply, perhaps intimidating specific disenfranchised populations. One clear limitation—some families faced ineligibility due to previous school grievances. They may have been prevented from completing the application process at all. Put another way, neoliberal ideologies touted possibilities yet perpetuated social and educational inequities.

Lessons Learned for Structuring School Success

Through this micro-read of the "I'm in" campaign, and the 2013 Midtown billboard in particular, one can see how the Detroit Public Schools system upheld a framework of social mobility as the primary purpose of schooling. Influenced by neoliberalism, public schools within the city, and advertisements in areas like Midtown, promoted schools as products for consumption. Nevertheless, minimum expectations for admission were put into place. Such acceptance procedures give rise to questions about whether this is done to keep particular populations out (e.g., "at-risk" students, students with special needs, students with previous disciplinary records). Strict application criteria allow schools the ability to declare students academically and civically unprepared for enrollment. Where then do children named as deficient turn for schooling? What options remain for children not eligible for attendance? A foray into answering such questions would benefit from extended research and study.

Billboards, like the one utilized in this content analysis project, remind parents of the many options and possibilities available for their own child's education. Some view the evolution of advertising as a positive development in school reform. Such advocates for school reform state schools must explain why their school is the best place for a child, but this practice also prompts school leaders to take an active role in meeting privatization and market demands (Spalding, 2013). Paired with government policies "facilitating takeovers of 'failing' public schools" and grounded in the principle of individual merit, educational stratification comes by default (Lipman, 2006, p. 101). In turn, the status quo is maintained.

One point of consideration for future research is the relationship between Detroit's longstanding educational history and the city's contemporary landscape of school reform. In order to more closely gauge student enrollment in the Detroit Metro area, the city's current economic state in conjunction with the process of (re)gentrification must be explored more deeply. Researchers and policymakers must continually ask questions about whether and how a mirage of school choice is created for historically marginalized communities. How are families encouraged to opt in to a class-based system while they remain disenfranchised by larger institutions and structures? How are access and choice being monetized? In what ways are policies and systems framing equity as something that can be purchased? While one can predict education will continue to shift due to changes in educational policy and through school reform at the state and local level, one must also wonder if the Detroit Public Schools will undergo such drastic changes that the city will more closely resemble the educational structuring of New Orleans, a city whose own history created a graveyard of public schools.

References

21st Century skills definitions. (n.d.). *Museums, libraries, and 21st century skills.* Retrieved from www.imls.gov/about/21st_Century_skills_list.aspx

Apple, M. W. (2006). *Educating the "right" way: Markets, standards, God, and inequality.* Abingdon, Oxford, UK: Taylor & Francis.

Aviv, S. (Producer). (2011, May 10). *Dan Rather reports: A national disgrace.* [Television broadcast]. New York, NY: Central Broadcasting Service.

Bomey, N., & Gallagher, J. (2013). *How Detroit went broke: The answers may surprise you—and don't blame Coleman Young.* Retrieved from www.freep. com/interactive/article/20130915/NEWS01/130801004/Detroit-Bankruptcy-history-1950-debt-pension-revenue

Bulkley, K. E., Henig, J. R., & Levin, H. M. (2010). *Between public and private: Politics, governance, and the new portfolio models for urban school reform.* Cambridge, MA: Harvard Education Press.

Cucchiara, M. B. (2013). *Marketing schools, marketing cities: Who wins and who loses when schools become urban amenities.* Chicago: University of Chicago Press.

Data Driven Detroit (D3). (2012). *The 2012 State of the Detroit child report.* Retrieved from http://datadrivendetroit.org/wp-content/uploads/2013/02/D3_2012_SDCReport.pdf

Detroit Public Schools. (2013a). *Burton International Academy*. Retrieved from http://detroitk12.org/schools/burton/

Detroit Public Schools. (2013b). *Detroit Schools of the Arts*. Retrieved from http://detroitk12.org/content/school_profiles/files/2012/02/dsa-app.pdf

Detroit Public Schools. (2013c). *Golightly Education Center*. Retrieved from http://detroitk12.org/schools/golightlyeducationcenter/

Detroit Public Schools. (2013d). *Spain Elementary-Middle School*. Retrieved from http://detroitk12.org/schools/spain/

Dreier, P., Mollenkopf, J. H., & Swanstrom, T. (2004). *Place matters: Metropolitics for the twenty-first century*. Lawrence, KS: University Press of Kansas.

Dunn, A. H. (2013). *Teachers without borders? The hidden consequences of International teachers in US schools*. New York, NY: Teachers College Press.

Dzwonkowski, R. (1999, January 3). We aim for a new century, and some things we better not miss. *The Detroit Free Press*. p. H.2.

Fahle, C. (2013, August 28). Detroit public schools marketing to midtown parents. *The Craig Fahle Show*. Podcast retrieved from http://wdet.org/shows/craig-fahle-show/episode/detroit-public-schools-marketing-to-midtown-parent/

Giroux, H. A. (2004). *The terror of neoliberalism: Authoritarianism and the eclipse of democracy*. Herndon, VA: Paradigm Publishers.

Golightly Education Center. (2013). *Brochure*. Retrieved from http://detroitk12.org/content/school_profiles/files/2012/02/Golightly-Marketing-Brochure_2013-2014_PDF_V4.pdf

Guerra, J. (2013, October 24). The education gap. *Michigan Public Radio: State of Opportunity*. Podcast and transcript retrieved from http://stateofopportunity.michiganradio.org/post/education-gap-transcript-and-audio#.Umm_YUc8J8k.facebook

Harvey, D. (2005). *A brief history of neoliberalism*. New York, NY: Oxford University Press.

Henig, J. R., Hula, R. C., Orr, M., & Pedescleaux, D. S. (2001). *The color of school reform: Race, politics, and the challenge of urban education*. Princeton, NJ: Princeton University Press.

Holsti, O. R. (1969). *Content analysis for the social sciences and humanities*. Reading, MA: Addison-Wesley Pub. Co.

Judd, D. R., & Swanstrom, T. (2010). *City politics: The political economy of urban America* (7th ed.). New York: Longman.

Krippendorff, K. H. (2013). *Content analysis—3rd edition: An introduction to its methodology*. Thousand Oaks, CA: Sage Publications, Inc.

Labaree, D. F. (1997). Public goods, private goods: The American struggle over educational goals. *American Educational Research Journal*, 34(1), 39–81.

Lipman, P. (2006). This is America. In Ladson-Billings, G., & Tate, W. F. (Eds.), *Education research in the public interest: Social justice, action, and policy* (pp. 98–115). New York, NY: Teachers College Press.

Massey, D. S. (1993). *American apartheid: Segregation and the making of the underclass*. Cambridge, MA: Harvard University Press.

Massey, D. S., & Denton, N. A. (2003). *American apartheid: Segregation and the making of the underclass*. Cambridge, MA: Harvard University Press.

Mirra, N., & Morrell, E. (2011). Teachers as civic agents: Toward a critical democratic theory of urban teacher development. *Journal of Teacher Education*, 62(4), 408–420. doi: 10.1177/0022487111409417

Mollenkopf, J. H., Dreier, P., & Swanstron, T. (2001). *Place matters: Metropolitics for the twenty-first century.* Lawrence, KS: University Press of Kansas.

Olssen, M., Codd, J., & O'Neill, A. M. (2004). *Education policy: Globalization, citizenship and democracy.* Thousand Oaks, CA: Sage.

Orr, M., & Rogers, J. (Eds.). (2010). *Public engagement for public education: Joining forces to revitalize democracy and equalize schools.* Stanford, CA: Stanford University Press.

Peterson, P. (2012). The interests of the limited city. In Kantor, P., & Judd, D. (Eds.), *American urban politics in a global age* (pp. 14–26). New York: Pearson.

Recovery School District. (2013). *RSD direct-run schools 2013–2014.* Retrieved from http://lrsd.entest.org/RSD%20direct%20run%20schools%2013-14.pdf

Spalding, A. (2013, April 29). *School marketing is a-ok.* [Blog]. Retrieved from www.mackinac.org/18566?print=yes

Sugrue, T. J. (2004). *The origins of the urban crisis: Race and inequality in postwar Detroit.* Princeton, NJ: Princeton University Press.

Stone, C. N. (1998). *Changing urban education: Studies in government and public policy.* Lawrence, KS: University Press of Kansas.

3 When Policies that Impact Students with Significant Disabilities in Michigan Backfire

Mark E. Deschaine

For your consideration—a state—wanting to guarantee that all students, including those with significant disabilities, have access to a public education. Politicians and policymakers so interested in supporting educational opportunities for students with disabilities that they establish a system that competes with existing school structures. They develop separate center-based educational opportunities whereby larger educational organizations potentially become responsible for segregated schools for students with disabilities outside their local educational community. The initial program, although considered to be best practice at the time, left little opportunity for students to be educated with their peers without disabilities in their local schools. Over time, state legislative and school board policy initiatives are enacted that both strengthen segregated opportunities, while developing other initiatives to increase the likelihood that students with disabilities will attend their neighborhood schools. These conflicting policy decisions created backfire and were made in the backdrop of a national emphasis on including students with disabilities in their local community schools. As years have passed, this ebb and flow of interventions, opportunities, and regulations have caused programmatic challenges for students, families, and practitioners in . . . the Michigan Policy Zone. Deep and sincere apologies to Rod Sterling for this introduction (which attempts to parody *The Twilight Zone*), but the situation presented is reality, not fiction. Providing educational services for students with significant disabilities often feels like the requirements promulgated in Lansing have come out of the Michigan Policy Zone: a place where what appears or has been made to occur does not have the longitudinal impact expected had a consistent or logical force transpired, often causing significant policy backfire in the provision of services to students with disabilities in Michigan.

In 1971, the State of Michigan enacted PA 198 (State of Michigan [PA 198], 1971) that guaranteed students with significant disabilities access to educational systems (Michigan State School Board of Education, 1971). This chapter will explore the impact of PA 198 on programs for students with significant disabilities in light of other initiatives that have occurred since the legislation's implementation. Many different initiatives have occurred in the state since 1971. To be succinct—yet significant—this chapter takes a brief look at some of the more significant policies for students with significant disabilities in Michigan, a community of learners often overlooked when issues related to educational policy and school improvement are promulgated—policies that have often backfired and hurt the most marginalized students.

The Michigan Policy Zone—What Was the Original Intent?

In *The Twilight Zone* series, Mr. Sterling was a master at identifying salient issues, couching them within the subtleties of everyday life. Issues of importance and prominence, often overlooked at the time, had longitudinal impact that resulted in unanticipated outcomes. It wasn't until a reflective look occurred that the many moving parts could be assembled into a cohesive whole, providing flashes of insight, usually accompanied with dread and consternation. The observer leaves the session with a sense of "if I had only known then what I know now!" The Michigan Policy Zone unfortunately fits into this scheme. If policymakers knew then what appears to occur now, what changes would they make?

Public Act 198 provided access to education for all students, regardless of severity of disability, and established a system for funding and provision of services within a newly established organizational structure (Leroy & Lacey, 2010). With this legislative initiate, Michigan became one of the first states with a mandatory special education law, preceding the Federal Law PL 94–142, The Education for All Children Act (United States Department of Education [PL 94–142], 1974). When first established, Michigan was a leader nationally in ensuring that all students, regardless of the severity of their disability, had access to a public school education (Leroy & Lacey, 2010). According to LeRoy and Lacey, at the time of passage, the legislation provided state of the art best practice center-based school programs and services for students with significant disabilities. These schools provided facilities designed to support the significant educational, intellectual, emotional, cognitive, social, and medical needs students brought to the traditional educational system. Due to these extensive needs, the State of Michigan intentionally provided additional funding resources, and flexibility for programming through categorical provisions enacted within legislation and policy.

PA 198 relied upon larger instructional school districts, commonly known as Intermediate School Districts (ISDs), to provide programs and supports for Local Education Agencies (LEAs), with costs for services being shared across regions in the state, through regionalized millages (Leroy & Lacey, 2010). ISDs were given the authority to levy special education millages to pay for schools that provided specialized personnel and supports to meet individualized instructional needs. ISD millages were seen as a cost-effective way to gain an economy of scale for services, making it possible for LEAs to access specialized schools for students with disabilities closer to their home. Without such a system, it would not be financially feasible for the LEA to provide the services independently. This dual educational structure continues to this day, and has an impact on the services offered to students with significant disabilities across the state, often causing social, educational, and financial policy backfire.

Separate segregated center-based school facilities were constructed in ISDs across Michigan to meet the intense instructional needs of students with significant disabilities. The investment of ISD resources to construct center-based schools that were intentionally designed to house therapy pools, nursing office physical and occupational therapy spaces, adapted physical education facilities, offices for speech and language support, and wheelchair accessible classrooms. To provide all of these services, ISD-run programs traditionally hire specially trained staff usually not found in LEA programs. Teachers with specialized credentials and certifications, paraprofessionals with training in disabilities, occupational and physical therapists, speech and language pathologists, school nurses, transition specialists, school social workers, behavioral support personnel, school psychologists, transportation staff with specialized training to deal with disabilities, and teacher consultants often are hired by ISDs to meet the significant needs of the students within their program.

In addition to ISD millages for operational expenses, to financially assist the ISDs that established center-based facilities, state appropriation initiatives occurred that allowed ISDs to obtain a higher reimbursement rate for programs and services that directly supported ISD-run schools. In order to assist with the extensive transportation costs to school, ISDs were able to receive, and continue to receive, special funding through higher reimbursement rates to not only purchase the specialized school busses necessary to transport students, but they also receive a higher reimbursement rate for the miles incurred to transport students from home to school. Since ISDs also hire personnel with specialized credentials not often found in LEA programs, ISDs were also granted increased reimbursement rates from the State for personnel costs related to the provision of special education services within their programs.

PA 198 was, and continues to be, unique in its scope since Michigan's law provides that school systems implement appropriate educational supports and services for all students with disabilities from birth to age 25. PL 94–142, and subsequent federal revisions, mandate special education services for students with disabilities ages 3–21. Expanding the age range for students to receive special education services was intended to provide additional supports necessary to get early intervention services in place, and to provide the specialized supports necessary to help transition adult students into the world. This increase of time students can be educated beyond the federal initiative has a social impact on the center-based services selected by parents for their children with significant disabilities, and has had a financial

Table 3.1 Intents and Outcomes of the PA 198 of 1971 Michigan Policy Zone

Intent	Outcome
Access to all students with disabilities in a public education system.	Students with disabilities from birth to 25 have a right to taxpayer funded educational programs and services.
Economy of scale cost sharing for programs and services across the ISD.	ISDs have the ability to fund segregated schools through the levy of a special education millage.
Educating students with significant disabilities in segregated schools.	Many ISDs across the state built separate facilities for educational programs and supports.
Provide specially trained staff to meet the specialized educational needs of the students with significant disabilities.	ISDs provide direct instructional support of highly trained staff to students, and also provide training for staff in LEAs related to disabilities and their impact on educational functioning.
Preferential reimbursement rates and categorical funding for ISDs to provide specialized segregated schools.	ISDs have provided cooperative services to the LEAs, and provide services to students that would probably not be available without the financial inducement from the State.

impact on the ISDs offering the programs, as we will see later. Table 3.1 compares the intent of PA 198 with the outcomes of the legislation, often resulting in policy backfire.

Michigan has historically spent a great deal of energy providing legislative and policy initiatives to help local and intermediate school districts meet the needs of students with significant disabilities. The ability to access specialized schools, staffed by highly trained instructional and support staff, combined with the financial incentives of a separate millage and ability to shift costs made it attractive for LEAs to transfer the instructional responsibilities for students with significant disabilities to their ISD. However—as we shall see—policy initiatives are often dictated by financial realities of the moment, and many of these funding initiatives would be tested when an economic downturn hit the state due to the restructuring of the automobile industry.

Understanding the Successes or Failures of the Inclusion Opportunities

Michigan PA 198, mandating services for students with disabilities, was significant in its emphasis on providing all students, regardless of their severity of disability, access to educational programs and supports, across the students' lifespan into young adulthood. Promulgated in an era of civil rights initiatives, PA 198 provided the vehicle for access to students usually overlooked by educational systems due to the intensity and significance of their handicapping conditions. Unfortunately, in some parts of the state, the well-intentioned programming has longitudinally inadvertently hyper-institutionalized segregation for some students. Practice has not always been able to keep up with the social policy calls for normalization of disenfranchised groups, causing significant policy backfire from a social justice perspective.

There are many factors that potentially have a longitudinal impact on the uneven unintended backfire seen by the educational policy enshrined in PA 198. Local and intermediate school districts have been provided a great deal of flexibility to help address the needs of students with significant disabilities. Local control over the ways districts provide services has caused a great deal of disparity, even inconsistency across the state, as regional programs strive with unique issues such as geography, technology, tax base, opportunities for public transportation, weather, support of the local taxpayer, and ability to hire qualified staff. This has created uneven patterns of programming and supports. Over the lifespan of the initial legislative requirement, additional local and state policy and initiatives have provided inconsistent supports. In addition, social expectations for educational instructions have increased, and the financial stability of the state and local economies across Michigan have vacillated significantly. This section will look at a finite number of policy issues impacted by the social, financial, and educational expectations that have affected the provision of programming in segregated classrooms across Michigan.

Social Policy

Educational policy promulgation and implementation often has at its core a strong emphasis on meeting social initiatives in the community. PA 198 started as a reaction to initiatives begun during the civil rights era. Access to education for students with significant disabilities was a key feature of this legislation. With most issues related to civil rights, over time, right to access became a focus on acceptance and assimilation. Education of students with significant disabilities became a social justice issue during the era of normalization. Once access to public educational systems for students with disabilities was accomplished, social advocates soon became concerned about the segregation students in specialized schools received that did not provide access to "normalized" general education placements.

The movement to include students with disabilities into their local home school communities first started out as opportunities for "mainstreaming" into general education programs, and then was followed by calls for "inclusion" into general education classrooms. In either situation, segregated schools run by ISDs had a major societal expectation that they had to, at least initially, reactively respond to meet normalization demands. At first, calls for normalization caused some administrators difficulty: the segregated system that was designed did not anticipate the need to potentially include students with significant disabilities access to the general education setting. Initially, it was difficult for ISD and LEA administrators to respond to requests for individualized programming options for students with significant disabilities based solely upon social policy issues. With a great deal of creativity, professional development, and collegial supports, districts have been able to expand the programs and services they offer students with disabilities along all parts of the least restrictive environment continuum. As the years passed, school administrators became more open to the idea, allowing them to become abler to proactively discuss issues related to "normalization" and programming in the "least restrictive environment." School personnel in many parts of the state created opportunities where center-based students could receive their programming in self-contained classrooms within local school districts. Quite often the students from the center-based facilities educated within these self-contained classrooms were residents of the LEA district housing the classroom, and had less significant medical, emotional, intellectual, or educational needs than students left in the segregated schools.

For many parents of students with significant disabilities, incremental movement toward normalization was enough to meet the social and educational needs for their children. Many were happy with this alternative because their child continued to receive most of the extensive services offered to students educated under the ISD program. For those parents that wanted their children to be "fully included" and educated fully in the general education setting, they often had to avail themselves to the due process provisions contained within special education law. Parents had to begin a legal process against their school district to get their desires addressed. When this occurred, the district and parents—as the representative of the student—would present their side of the situation to an outside arbitrator, who would then render a decision based upon the law and the merits of the case. Both sides had the legal opportunity to appeal the decision up to and including the U.S. Supreme Court. Several situations in the state had to be resolved in utilizing this contentious process. However, with experience and change of program options, district administrators became more aware of, and better able to, meet requests for normalization and inclusion by creating linkages between LEAs and ISDs for program placement and support. Although this sounds positive, as we will see later, it created policy backfire in portions of the state.

Even with the social impetus and movement toward normalization, the majority of the parents who had their children educated in segregated schools remained committed to the segregated option. In fact, parent support for segregated programs was so high that parents often rallied to keep their center-based program options available when there was a threat of the programs closing due to financial considerations. Parents often became very strong advocates and proponents for center-based schools during two critical times during their child's life: from birth to kindergarten age, and then again from 18–25 years of age; ages where state program mandates exceeded federal mandates. Birth to kindergarten age is a critical time of educational, medical, therapeutic, social, communication, and behavioral support for infants and toddlers with significant disabilities. The supports and resources provided in center-based facilities provide opportunities for intense early intervention programs and services. Segregated schools run by ISDs are uniquely equipped to meet the myriad of significant needs students with disabilities often exhibit in their early developmental period. Federal initiatives such as Child Find have predisposed pediatricians and family physicians (often the first professional to recognize significant cognitive, intellectual, behavioral, communication, or medical needs) to contact their local ISD when they believe that their pediatric patient requires early intervention services.

Parents of young adults with significant disabilities also rely upon the services of center-based ISD programs when their children are beyond the traditional age of graduation. Young adults require significant supports through the development of transitional plans. This federally mandated service takes on added importance when dealing with the types of issues related to significant disabilities. The transition program provides a social support to students and parents through training and access to community resources in the area of vocational training, transportation, adaptive living, medical, behavioral, and financial supports.

Although no one program placement setting offers all of the elements probably needed by the student, program administrators have become defter in their approach, willing to try options on a trial basis so the efficacy of the intervention can be ascertained. Systems have been better able to individualize programs to meet the social policy needs and desires of parents, students, advocates, school boards, community members, legislators, and policymakers. Policy backfire has occurred when a larger, more systematic investigation of the program placement decision-making process occurs. Quite often there are inconsistent school options geographically across the state, and this is primarily due to financial policy disparities within individual ISDs.

Financial Policy

Since the inception of PA 198, Michigan's economy has undergone significant changes. This impacts the finances of a school system because, when first promulgated and passed, schools relied heavily upon local property taxes to fund a large portion of their costs. Municipalities, once able to count on secondary and tertiary industrial supports from the many automobile plants scattered across the state, have seen a significant decline in millage revenues when these industries closed or relocated. This statewide economic downturn had a significant impact on school districts' ability to raise operational funds through millages. Reliance on a millage to support the schools is inconsistent across districts in the state. Since millage is based on property values in the area, there are pockets across Michigan of very high end, as well as low end businesses and homes. This creates tremendous disparity in the ability of an ISD to have commensurate millage income generated based solely on property values. To alleviate this, school authorities have the opportunity to establish, and subsequently ask voters to approve, a millage rate they deem necessary to help provide income for programs. If voters approve millage increases, the initiative is passed, and increased income to help defray the costs of the center-based programs is collected. However, since millage rates and levies are a result of a popular vote, support for taxes across regions is often inconsistent due to financial realities of the electorate.

To further compound the issue, the state upended school funding mechanisms in 1994. This legislative action reduced a LEAs ability to levy millages for operational expenses. Instead, the state replaced those funds from an increase in the state sales and non-homestead property tax. At first, the funding structure change worked well. But, when the economic downturn occurred, people stopped spending money. Sales tax revenues declined, and as the economic situation worsened, the second properties that many workers owned as vacation homes went into foreclosure, thus dwindling the monies collected through the non-homestead tax. Both of these factors had an impact on school budgets across the state, causing significant financial policy backfire.

Financial policy initiatives in Michigan have attempted to align the needs of students with significant disabilities with appropriate levels of support and programming. However, reality often is different from design, and tremendous programmatic disparity exists statewide. Significant financial policy backfire occurred when funding structures were promulgated and implemented based upon, at the time, current financial realities, without taking into account potential variances in the longitudinal economic health of the state. Education continues to have to take a reactive position and attempt to offer appropriate programs, often not based upon individual student need, but based upon local financial ability to try and meet that need.

Educational Policy

Although we have primarily focused our attention on Michigan education policy up to this point, a significant legislative occurrence at the national level had dramatic impact on the programming for students with significant disabilities. Nationally, the impact of the No Child Left Behind (NCLB) Act (United States Department of Education, 2001) had programmatic implications in the area of standardized testing, Adequate Yearly Progress, and the 1.5% testing exclusion rule. It would be difficult to pin the current state of educational policy implementation on one specific factor, since so many have had a direct impact on the intent of PA 198. However, NCLB had stringent accountability provisions that required schools and districts to document the academic progress of their students on a yearly basis, and to report these findings to their community. To the greatest extent necessary, student results were published in groups, thus making comparisons across student categories more easily identifiable. Legislators and policymakers in

Washington, D.C. realized that there were a small percentage of students that would be unable to complete standardized academic tests due to their level of significant impairment. Districts were allowed to exclude their bottom 1.5% performers being provided services in special education programs from achievement calculations. This was important because schools that did not receive passing student achievement scores over a period of years had major sanctions placed upon the school, and potentially the district. In some cases, it appeared some LEAs avoided these sanctions by utilizing ISD programs to "hide" their lowest performing students, since ISD-run programs were initially exempt from the achievement requirements. Even with the best intentions at the state level when developing education policy, backfire often occurs when programs need to incorporate new provisions to meet competing, often contradictory federal legislative and policy initiatives. Table 3.2 provides a synopsis of the successes and failures related to inclusion.

Table 3.2 Inclusion Successes and Failures within the Michigan Policy Zone

Success	*Failure*
Systems have adapted to best practice calls for mainstreaming opportunities by opening classrooms for students once housed in the center-based programs into self-contained classrooms in local schools.	Providing students with disabilities from birth to kindergarten age, and from 18–25 in segregated facilities, increases the likelihood that parents will choose this educational option for their child.
Federal initiatives through No Child Left Behind Act have placed greater attention on the impact of instructional quality and student achievement.	The overemphasis on standardized assessment of student academic achievement has caused many programs and parents to opt for center-based programming options.
Students educated in local schools with self-contained classes have had the opportunity to be included in general education classrooms.	Funding realities have often overtaken initiatives toward mainstreaming and inclusion, thus making it financially untenable for some districts to move toward lesser restrictive environments.
Specialized personnel from the center-based programs have been able to play a consultant role in supporting students from the segregated facility as they transition back to their home school system.	Specially trained support personnel are not always available within each LEA in the state, and because of this, quite often the LEAs will need the support of their ISD to obtain intermittent services for students.
The initial idea of supporting LEAs through cooperative services has taken hold in many parts of the state. Services such as specialized transportation and teacher consultant support services are provided to LEAs across the state.	Often decisions about the least restrictive environments are greatly impacted by logistics. Accommodating geographic, weather, transportation, and student issues needs to be considered when options are considered and implemented.

The Michigan Policy Zone—What Did We Learn from Policy Backfire?

We have now come to the end of the Michigan Policy Zone episode, where it is appropriate to do a post-mortem investigation of the situation: looking at the big pieces of the scenario, and reflecting upon their impact on the initially less obvious aspects of the events to identify issues of policy backfire.

Current Realities

This section attempts to offer a current overview of segregated opportunities across the state, and provides insight into the collateral backfire results of the initial initiative. The review will take the perspective of both the individuals impacted by the policy, as well as the systems required by the school districts to implement this policy. This allows the reader to better identify for themselves the impact, as well as the backfire, that the development of segregated self-contained center-based programs have had on the mainstreaming and inclusion opportunities for students with significant disabilities in the state of Michigan.

Students with significant disabilities continue to present an enhanced challenge to districts, as systems attempt to provide appropriate programing to meet the students' individualized needs. Policies, funding, programmatic requirements, organizational structures, social trends, and issues related to the provision of "best practice" services within the least restrictive environment have all had transformative practical shifts, while the legal requirements for access to appropriate individualized programs have remained consistent over the years.

The establishment of, and continual funding of, a multi-level of educational systems has provided significant unintended policy outcomes and backfire. Areas such as access to programs and services, funding disparities, program delivery mechanisms, compliance and accountability structures, administrative oversight, staffing, personnel requirements and availability, transportation opportunities, lability of interpretations related to "least restrictive environments" as well as "free and appropriate education" are just a few areas where policy and practice have become disjoined across the state. These significant differences are due to geographic location, community desire to financially support center-based programs and services, local economic factors, and the percentage of students requiring specialized services: they all impact an LEA and ISD when programming decisions and opportunities are made. With the current socioeconomic conditions in the state, it is unlikely that these disparities will be solved anytime soon without an infusion of funds, which is unlikely due to the financial status of the state at this writing. In areas where ISDs are not financially or logistically able to provide the level of support to students with significant disabilities, it becomes incumbent upon the students' LEA to absorb program and services responsibility. This further leads to the disparity in programmatic options for students with disabilities, with backfire of the uniformity of policy implementation across the state.

Often, parents of students with significant disabilities, along with the educational professionals in the LEAs, have significant programmatic and financial inducements to send students with disabilities to ISD-run programs and services. However, the longer students with disabilities stay in segregated schools, the more likely they are to stay in special education through age 25, and less likely to be educated in their local school settings with peers that are non-disabled. This directly contradicts social policies of normalization and inclusion, often creating social policy backfire by offering publically supported segregated options (Michigan State School Board of Education, 1992).

Initially, the concepts of mainstreaming and inclusion were not a consideration when PA 198 was implemented: the intent was to provide appropriate educational programs and services to all students regardless of their disability. Over the years, due to financial issues, several efforts have been discussed at the state level to dismantle and slowly phase out the age coverage provision of birth to 25 for special education eligibility, and replace it with the federal mandate of 3–21. It is assumed by some that the cost savings would be significant. Others contend that the deleterious impact on students and families dependent upon the extended services makes it necessary to maintain the provision. Either way, a segregated system exists where, in some regions of the state, young adults with significant disabilities access social support structures primarily through their school district. This creates backfire in the state's community mental health system—the program responsible for supporting individuals with disabilities post-school.

From a social policy perspective, parents of students with significant disabilities often are apprehensive of the realities of general education public schools. Social issues, bullying, misunderstanding of disabilities, and acceptance often play into a parent's decision for programming and placement for their children. Even with the social push for normalization, many parents continue to choose the option of segregated schools. The extensive social, physical, medical, and recreational supports offered in center-based programs promote a sense of community and belongingness for individuals and families that often feel like they are outsiders when they are in more normalized settings. Policy backfire occurs when contradiction reigns: programs initially designed to foster independence and community integration have often become de facto vehicles for reliance and segregation.

From a district perspective, the longevity of center-based programs and supports cannot be taken for granted. Longstanding programs can quickly be dismantled or significantly reorganized due to changes in the financial, administrative, legislative, or policy landscape; locally, at the state, or national level. Competition from outside forces such as charter schools or online programming have the potential to dramatically impact the landscape for LEA and ISD programs. Alternatives are beginning to be developed that serve students traditionally considered "at-risk," incarcerated, or with discipline problems, and are appearing with greater frequency in the state. Students currently educated in segregated schools, who are not as impacted by their disabilities as some of their other classmates, have started to be enrolled in these alternative programs by the parents. Inadvertent backfire occurs when newer models for program delivery become available, often resulting in reconceptualization of the initial policy initiatives. These newer program options are slowly being recognized by legislators in Lansing.

Parents seeking the best possible programming for their children have been known to "program shop," where they move to the communities that offer the level of supports in the segregated schools they consider to be appropriate for their children. Schools of choice legislation has made this process easier for parents across the state. Unexpected increases in student enrollment due to student movement often are difficult on both the sending and receiving systems due to numbers. Planning financially, and finding qualified staff with special training to meet the specific needs of categorical programs, often leaves school districts scrambling. It is not uncommon for programs to find staff wanting to work in the programs, then provide the mentorship and support of these educators until they can meet the state certification requirements through university preparation programs. Policy backfire results on both the sending and receiving districts when consumers of a program no longer find merit or benefit to the service offered.

Students with significant disabilities often have parents that are advocacy oriented, that have a solid understanding of the prevailing political and policy issues impacting their children. The standardized testing requirements of NCLB, with extensive emphasis on traditional academic achievement, caused many parents to rethink having their children placed in a center-based program where more functional life skills were embedded in core academics. Districts running segregated school programs had to wait a great deal of time before they received guidance on NCLB provisions for their students. This caused considerable stress on the system as schools attempted to stay in compliance with state and federal mandates related to student achievement requirements, and ultimately the provisions to have their programs and schools meet the requirements for adequate yearly progress. Policy backfire often occurs when competing or contradictory policy and requirements from outside forces for new programmatic mandates are promulgated and implemented. Table 3.3 presents what we have learned from an individual and district policy perspective.

Providing appropriate educational supports and opportunities for students with significant disabilities has been—and continues to be—a challenge for educators and policymakers across the nation. Due to their potential concomitant medical, intellectual, and behavioral needs, students with significant disabilities have not always experienced the opportunity for appropriate educational programs and services offered to their nondisabled

Table 3.3 Backfires in the Michigan Policy Zone

Individual Perspective	District Perspective
Although the law states districts provide programs to meet the individual needs of students, the programs and facilities available vary considerably across the state.	The programs and services available to students are often dependent upon local features and capabilities that vary significantly across the state.
Parents have made decisions to enroll their children in programs based upon the supplemental supports provided, with little regard for mainstreaming or inclusion opportunities.	Changes in the financial situation in the district can have a rather significant impact on programs and services, sometimes rather quickly, with no guarantee that the birth to 25 provision will remain.
Parents have made decisions to keep their children educated in center-based facilities to insulate them from the social and educational realities of their local school.	Changes in policy and legislation have the potential to significantly upheave programs that have been in place for many years. Outside forces such as charter schools and contracted services have impacted the provision of services available for inclusion and mainstreaming activities for students with significant disabilities.
Parents have been willing to relocate to parts of the state that provide more extensive services. Schools of choice options have greatly increased this behavior.	The availability of qualified staff to fill open positions makes it difficult for programs to provide consistent programming options in many parts of the state.
The impact of standardized testing requirements through NCLB has caused parents to reconsider the center-based option for their child.	When NCLB was first implemented, ISD-run center-based programs had to wait a considerable amount of time before they were provided guidance on the impact the legislation would have on their programs and students.

peers in their local school setting. Michigan continues to support segregated schools for students with significant disabilities, and these often foster hyper-segregation in the minds of some. This continued support for segregated service delivery systems have caused significant policy backfire on a number of fronts. For some, segregation is welcomed, and just what they are looking for to meet the needs of their children.

The rearview mirror of policy allows "Monday Morning Quarterbacks" the luxury of hindsight. Mr. Sterling was a master at dissecting nuance, and making the implications of subtle elements clear. Unlike our situation, he had the ability to control and frame the initial narrative from the very beginning, allowing him to be directive through the entire process. Educational policy promulgation and implementation, unfortunately, is not that linear and specific. Identification of policy impact is a messy undertaking, one that relies heavily upon the perspective of the individual doing the reflective investigation. I wonder what Mr. Sterling would say about this situation!

References

Leroy, B., & Lacey, K. (2010). The inclusion of students with intellectual disabilities in Michigan. In Smith, P. (Ed.), *Whatever happened to inclusion? The place of students with intellectual disabilities in education* (pp. 101–116). New York, NY: Peter Lang Publishing.

Michigan State School Board of Education. (1992). *Inclusive education position statement*. Lansing, MI: Michigan Department of Education.

State of Michigan. *Public Act 198 of 1971*. Lansing, MI: Author.

United States Department of Education. (1974). The Education for All Children Act (Federal Law PL 94–142). Washington, DC: Author.

United States Department of Education. (2001). No Child Left Behind (Elementary and Secondary Education Act). Washington, DC: Author.

4 When Zero-Tolerance Discipline Policies in the United States Backfire

Hugh Potter and Brian Boggs

As David Cohen argues, "Once upon a time, students of American politics believed that policy turned out as intended. But they have recently concluded that intentions are an inconsistent guide to results" (1982). No greater example is there than the educational policy arena (Cusick, 1992) and many of the premises upon which action is taken in hopes of remedying a particular societal ill (Green, 1994). This is particularly true of the U.S.'s approach to zero-tolerance discipline policy. Mainly because policy is transformed as it moves through the system from its intended purpose to its actual implementation at the hands of "street-level bureaucrats" (Shulman, 1983). Using Portes' (2000) Linear Purposive Action and Alternative Sequence Framework, we analyze the unexpected, but nonetheless complex, results of zero-tolerance from its rational inception to its impact on students after implementation, and conclude with the backfire of further building the school-to-prison pipeline and making things worse for the students the policy intended to support.

Theoretical Framework

It was T. S. Eliot who once wrote that the "circle of our understanding is a very restricted area" (Unger, 1961, p. 15). It is the unrestricted area, the area that exists beyond our conceptual knowledge and rationally developed schemes—beyond our limited circle—that has caused social scientists decades of problems, misunderstandings, and misgivings (unintended side effects of interventions that make things worse). Nowhere is that more apparent, and some may argue more intrusive, than in education (Boggs, 2017). Marx had a term for this activity that is behind the appearance of things (Royce, 2015). He called it the Hidden Abode. As Alejandro Portes explains it, it is the analyzing of unexpected results of certain social events or structures (2000). Using this idea, Portes lays out a sociological framework for analyzing the implementation of a policy. This framework carries a great deal of weight and meaning when we examine the "hidden abode of education," especially as it compares and contrasts with our intentions and beliefs as they relate to zero-tolerance policies in education.

Portes explains that it is because of our complex social relationships that any kind of policy implementation is difficult (2000). This is often because policy is thought of in linear and rational relationships. Part of this stems from our training and how many social scientists view the world. Portes states, "From our first days in the discipline, we social scientists have been trained in the formulation of hypotheses about aspects of social reality" (2000, p. 2). The problem with this, he continues, is that "scientific hypotheses explicitly assume the lawfulness of the real world that makes a number of regularities predictable and observable" (2000, p. 2). As we dissect what we observe, we come to view it as part of a repeatable pattern that is both causal and linear, which means that it is also rational (it follows some form of logical beginning and sequences to a purposeful end). However, Portes suggests that we look at the "hidden abode," which he states is, "behind the appearance of things, and for unearthing the unexpected in social structures and events" (2000, p. 3).

History has shown a consistent gap between reality and theory, especially as it pertains to enacting policy. This has led to various forms of skepticism in the process. Yet, much of this can be attributed to a lack of recognition of social capital. This is defined as networks, connections, and other resources a person has beyond their actual, physical knowledge and ability (in other words, beyond their human capital) (Coleman, 1966). In part, this gap is because individuals engage in efforts of collective sense making, which involve looking out into the environment from their specific location. Part of this process, according to organizational theorists, involves gathering information, internalizing the findings, and then comparing it to what others are finding in the environment, which means it is then re-internalized and processed again in comparison to what others have found (Weick, 1979).

It becomes an evolutionary process, which can transform policy as it is implemented in a system, especially if it ignores local *metis* (Scott, 1998). By *metis*, we are referring to the local knowledge and know-how that does not directly fit with grand blueprints and designs that are intended to be universal in their approach and implemented from a high level of aggregation (e.g., federal and state level commands). This *metis* has often been ignored, and then social engineering falls short or fails in its goals (Boggs & Dunbar, 2015). Specifically, Portes outlines five areas that trigger skepticism about the existence of linear relationships, all of which impact how we view and assess the results of policy and policy implementation. These five areas, according to Portes (2000), are:

1. The "Hidden Abode"[1]: "The announced goal is not what it seems—that is, it is not what the actor or those in authority in a collectivity actually intend;"
2. The Latent Function: "The announced goal is intended by the actors, but their actions have other significant consequences of which they are unaware;"

3. The Mid-Course Shift: "The goal is what it seems, but the intervention of outside forces transforms it mid-course into a qualitatively different one;"
4. The Unexpected Outcome: "The goal is what it seems, but the intervention of outside forces produces unexpected consequences different and sometimes contrary to those intended;"
5. The Lucky Turn-of-Events: "The goal is what it seems, but its achievement depends on fortuitous events, foreign to the original plans" (Portes, 2000, pp. 7–8).

Methods

For this chapter, we utilized publicly available data from the Office for Civil Rights (OCR) regarding school punishments across the United States. These data include suspensions and expulsions on a yearly basis, broken down by gender and ethnicity. The disaggregated data was then reorganized to identify trends by state, gender, and ethnicity. Using a simple risk index calculation (number of punishments per subgroup and divided by the number of individuals in a cohort), we are able to create comparisons across time and gender/ethnicity. Following the disaggregation of the data, an analysis of the results was viewed through the lens of the risk of suspension for different ethnicities and genders of students. The results of this data analysis and the available literature related to zero-tolerance punishments comprise the structure of our chapter.

The Policy and Its Intended Audience

In the early days of the zero-tolerance approach to school discipline, the intended outcomes were clear and simple. The use of punitive measures to ward off school violence would make schools safer. It was a simple mandate, one that came from the White House in the form of the 1993 *Gun Free Schools Act*. The conceptualization of safer schools, drawing on the zero-tolerance federal drug policies, was that if students knew that they would face a mandatory, year-long expulsion from school for the possession (intended or unintended) of a weapon on school grounds, they simply would not bring weapons to school (Brownstein, 2010). Simple in theory, this policy backfired so impressively that it can be viewed as a paragon of how well-intended policies can produce horrific results.

Over the years, the rather simplistic concept of zero-tolerance toward school violence has morphed into an overarching, systematic attempt to deal with all violations to a school's code of conduct with the same heavy hand. It is possible, through research, to observe that the imposition of zero-tolerance punitive policies in schools has had considerable impact on students' interaction with the juvenile justice system. This has resulted in academic under-performance and an overall increase in the punishment of minority students. The policy once intended to provide a safe space for learning to occur has produced an environment that is neither safe nor fair for many of the very students the policy was intended to safeguard.

Origin and Transformation of Zero-Tolerance

The concept of zero-tolerance is that an organized system, such as a judicial system or a school, will employ a simple and significant policy to deal with offenders. In the 1980s, the United States' legal system developed a zero-tolerance policy toward drug offenders (Skiba & Peterson, 1999). The intent, at the time, was to establish a systematic approach to violations of drug laws that would act as a deterrent to those who violated the law, an approach that was to be clear and simple: violate the law and you will face the wrath of the legal system. It was a system that was bound and determined to punish those offenders by removing them from society. Over time, as schools became the sites of horrific violence, President Bill Clinton signed into law the 1993 *Gun Free Schools Act* (GFSA), which mandated an automatic punitive punishment (one calendar year expulsion) for the use or possession of a weapon on school grounds.

As time passed, Portes (2000) notes, the policy began to change as it was implemented or ramped up to a systems level. Schools began to apply zero-tolerance to a whole array of other violations (Brownstein, 2010). Shortly thereafter, a policy that was designed to be targeted and specific to weapons in schools (in and of itself a worthy and admirable goal) produced policies that would, for example, expel a child for possession and use of acne medicine (St. George, 2011). In retrospect, over the arc of the last 30 years, this policy that was designed to provide a safe haven for students has produced an ominous threat of life-altering punishments, without increasing school safety. The consequence is a system that looms over students like an ominous cloud with lightning ready to strike should a student so much as think about violating the school's code of conduct in any way.

The expansion of zero-tolerance policies reflected a growing desire by school leaders to send a message to students and to exert school authority when students misbehaved (Noguera, 1995; Skiba & Knesting, 2001). Over time, the design and deployment of zero-tolerance polices ultimately led to more than 80% of American schools implementing (Skiba & Knesting, 2001) harsh punitive punishments for violations of a school's code of conduct. Many times, the expansion of zero-tolerance policies was in direct reaction to high profile incidents of school violence, as can be seen following the Columbine shootings and other school shootings or acts of violence across America (Skiba & Knesting, 2001). The fact that schools responded to incidents of crisis with a knee-jerk reaction to increase the punitive nature of school codes of conduct simply shows the short-sightedness of the application of zero-tolerance policies in American schools. These policies failed to address the root causes of misbehavior and simply punished the action.

Outcomes of Zero-Tolerance Policies

As zero-tolerance began to take root and was implemented, we can identify a transformation of the policy at the local level to its unintended, but consistent consequences. The intended message being projected by school leaders who were expanding the use of zero-tolerance was that by increasing the severity of punishments, it was conceived that students would respond by exhibiting better behavior (Losen, 2013) and the entire learning environment, as a result, would improve (Brownstein, 2010; Raffele Mendez, 2003) for the students who remained. However, the theoretical "improved" learning environment that would be created for the "good students" by excluding the "bad students" from the classroom was a myth (Losen & Martinez, 2013). Classrooms did not magically get better, academic performance did not instantly rise, and the impacts of zero-tolerance were more like a tsunami upon the violators than a ripple effect for the survivors. In sum, and as will be demonstrated in the discussion to follow, the expansion of zero-tolerance policies for student misbehavior created an environment for negative outcomes for students.

Zero-tolerance policies are not just policies that push students away; they are policies that directly affect the academic outcomes for students. Zero-tolerance policies in American schools have been found to have a negative effect on students and their academic potential. Some outcomes included an increase in overall school avoidance by students, a decrease in school test scores and other academic outcomes, a ramping up of the school-to-prison pipeline, and a disproportionate effect upon minority students. Students did not benefit from the application of zero-tolerance measures because of a decrease in violent acts; students suffered because the expansion of zero-tolerance removed more and more students from the learning environment for increasingly minor offenses.

When looking into the outcome for policy implementation, one of the first questions that must be asked is whether or not the intended policy has produced evidence that its intended goals have been reached (Portes, 2000). In the case of zero-tolerance policies, the answer is no. Sadly, schools continue to be sites where violence, though rare, still occurs. It does not seem, when looking back over the litany of violent events that take place on school grounds, that zero-tolerance policies for schools have made schools safer. It could be argued, however, that zero-tolerance disciplinary problems have actually contributed to the growth in negative outcomes for students. Skiba and Peterson (1999) argue that there is a lack of evidence that harsh (zero-tolerance) policies have improved school settings, and there are other scholars who argue that school suspensions through zero-tolerance policies are not even a deterrent for future misbehavior by students (Bock, Tapscott, & Savner, 1998).

In addition, the implementation and effects of zero-tolerance policies have actually kept students from attending schools. The United States

Departments of Education and Justice, in a joint 2014 "Dear Colleague" letter, argued that the imposition of zero-tolerance policies and harsh punitive punishments have led to student disengagement and overall school avoidance, causing students to miss out on valuable learning (United States Department of Justice & United States Department of Education, 2014). Arcia (2006) posits that the more that students are suspended due to zero-tolerance policies, the more likely they are to drop out of school. In other words, students are dropping out to avoid the problems created by simply attending a school where a zero-tolerance policy might result in suspension. If the punishments dealt out by the schools result in the students leaving the school system altogether, then one must consider if the "intended" ends of the policy implementation (a safer, more educative school) justify the actual means and the collateral damage incurred along the way.

Brownstein (2010) reported that school suspensions appeared to predict higher rates of suspension further down the road in a student's academic career. As students face increased suspension time, they lose out on instructional time. While the impact on instructional time may at first seem minor, it is a precursor to cascading consequences on a student's academic outcomes (Losen, 2013).

As Dunbar (2015) noted, schools with high rates of suspension are also schools that show lower test scores for students. In addition to reduced test scores, increased exposure to school suspensions also has a negative effect on the acquisition of important reading skills. Arcia (2006) noted that the longer a student was excluded from the classroom, the lower the reading skills of the student (when compared to students with less time suspended). The overuse of exclusionary punishment has a negative effect on the cognitive capacity of students. From being forced outside of the classroom, to having fewer opportunities to gain vitally important skills in reading and reading comprehension, the impact of exclusionary punishments for students for violating the school code of conduct have lasting effects. These negative impacts on student achievement and skills are just a few that we choose to include in this analysis. The loss of opportunity to improve reading and reading comprehension skills are vitally important and could have considerable effects in the life and potential of these students who have come into contact with mandatory punishments as defined by zero-tolerance policies.

Another important aspect to consider when looking into the effects of zero-tolerance policies (and the impact of policies that backfire) is the extent to which harsh, punitive school discipline is a factor in the development of the school-to-prison pipeline. Fowler (2011) argues that the single greatest predictor of a student's future involvement with the judicial system is correlated to his/her track record of disciplinary referrals in school. At the same time as Fowler (2011) was beginning to scratch the surface in the linkage between school discipline and an individual's interaction with the judicial system, a study in Texas was about to make a stunning finding. In Fabelo et al.'s (2011) significant study of Texas's use of disciplinary tactics, it was found that for students who had been in one or more disciplinary incidents that resulted in a referral to the school's disciplinary authority, the student was 23.4 times more likely to be referred to the local justice system in the long-term. The expanded use of zero-tolerance policies, especially those policies that mandate suspension, tend to contribute to the growing school-to-prison pipeline (Potter, Boggs, & Dunbar Jr., 2017; United States Department of Justice & United States Department of Education, 2014) across American schools.

When students are removed from the classroom and school setting, students often have more time to find themselves in trouble with local law enforcement for minor, even trivial offenses. These unfortunate interactions, a product of being out of school, is the beginning of what in many cases becomes a long, rocky road of multiple interactions with the legal system. Yes, there had been suspensions prior to the implementation of the zero-tolerance discipline policy that may have also created scenarios where individuals would interact with the legal system, but not until the widely adopted zero-tolerance policies in the early 2000s did the magnitude of the problem of zero-tolerance school discipline become apparent. School suspensions grew at an astonishing rate across the board, with a disproportionate increase on African-Americans (Skiba & Knesting, 2001). So much so that one would be hard pressed not to say that the law and the embracing of zero-tolerance did not at some level have a racialized tone.

What Does the Data Say?

Speaking to the racialized tone of zero-tolerance, coupled with the concomitant growth of the school-to-prison pipeline, we explored the available data from the Office for Civil Rights (OCR) regarding student populations in the United States and the suspension rates for students within the population. The findings are a sobering reminder of the impact of school punishment. School suspensions, for whatever cause, are a product of an individual's violation of the school's code of conduct. Others have argued and shown that the school suspensions that are a by-product of the zero-tolerance school disciplinary policies encompass a wide array (not just weapons or violent acts) of actions by students. As such, we utilized the data sets made available by the OCR to assess the impact of suspension on student access to learn. In this data set, suspensions are aggregated and non-identified; therefore, we are limited in our ability to parse out individuals who may have faced multiple suspensions during the course of a data cycle.

We used the aggregate numbers of suspensions in relation to particular population groups to achieve the percentage of the population that was sanctioned by the school during the course of the academic year. In the first three (of five) data cycles, the data is categorized by a single year (i.e., 2000); however, for the last two (i.e., 2009–2010) the OCR refers to the data sets by the more common multi-year label similar to how schools label an academic school year. In the following figures, you will see that suspensions for minority populations are always greater than those for White students and that for the most part, the percentage of the population of African-American students sanctioned is roughly two to three times greater than the White population.

When looking at the data for the entire population of students, disaggregated by subgroup—African-American, Hispanic, and White—there are two critical trends to observe. First, both the Hispanic population and the African-American population are subject to greater suspensions per capita than the White population. Second, while the percentage of White students who are subject to suspension is decreasing over time, the African-American population is experiencing an upward trend over time (albeit small).

As can be identified in Figure 4.1, from 2000 to 2011–12, there was an increase in the percentage of African-American students who were sanctioned by schools across the United States, from 13.6% of the population to 15.2% of the population.[2] This means that for the entire African-American student population in 2011–2012, 15.2% of the population was suspended from the school for at least one day. Due to the limitations of the data, we cannot identify if there were individuals who accounted for more than one suspension during the course of the year or for what cause they were suspended. This would be very important to identify in a future study. However, we can identify that a large part of the student population was unable to attend school at some point during the course of the year. This is concerning from an academic and a social perspective for many reasons. Arguments made by those in the school-to-prison pipeline camp (Potter et al., 2015; Skiba & Sprague, 2008; Sprague et al., 2001) have shown that zero-tolerance policies for school discipline have had ancillary effects for students in the classroom that are negative and go far beyond the concept of making the classroom a safer place.

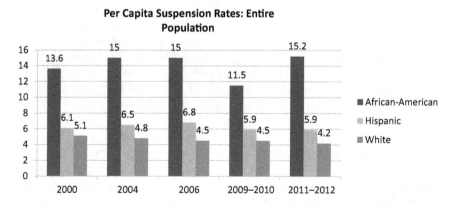

Figure 4.1 Data collected via the Office for Civil Rights

Likewise, when we disaggregate the data further by looking at school suspensions for individuals of different genders by racial identification, the data becomes even more concerning than the aggregate. For African-American males, the most heavily suspended subgroup—though not the largest subset numerically of students—the outlook is dismal. From 2000 to 2011–12, there was an overall increase in the per capita suspension rate for African-Americans, reaching 19.3% of the total population having been suspended at some point during the year (again, the same previous limitations of the data need to be recognized). Compared to the White male population (6.1% in 2011–12) and to the Hispanic population (8.1%), it is clear that the threat of suspension in schools is much higher for African-American males than for other subgroups.[3]

As can be seen in Figure 4.2, African-American males are again suspended at a much higher rate than White and Hispanic males and furthermore, Whites (who represent the largest number of actual students in American schools) are suspended at one-third the rate as African-Americans on a per capita rate. It is also evident from the data that over time, from 2000 to 2011–12, the trend for African-American males and the trend for White males are diverging. More and more, African-American male students are facing suspension in school and being denied the same access to learning that White students are.

Coupled with the fact that African-Americans represent a smaller group of individuals, but a higher per capita suspension rate (in comparison to Whites), it is a great concern how the growth of zero-tolerance punishment policies and the growth of suspension rates for African-Americans seems to coincide. Though we cannot prove causality, we do believe that there is a connection between the two that needs to be investigated in greater depth.

In much the same vein of analysis, a similar discussion of data results can be had for the female subgroup in American schools. African-American females are suspended at a rate far higher than any other subgroup, and at no point are members of any subgroup suspended less than the White

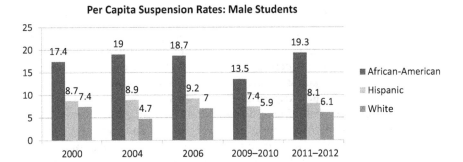

Figure 4.2 Data collected from the OCR

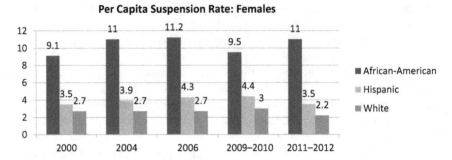

Figure 4.3 Data collected from the OCR

population of female students during the course of the data cycles. Overall, African-American females are suspended at a rate that is nearly twice per capita higher than Whites or Hispanics, and Hispanics are also consistently higher than Whites.

Regrettably, from 2000 to 2011–2012 (the same time that the expansion of zero-tolerance policies occurred), the suspension rate for African-American females (see figure 4.3) trended upward, while suspension for White females held steady over time.

The observational takeaways of the OCR data are quite telling and present an important manner to investigate the impact of suspension for students. The overall growth in suspensions from 2000 to 2012 coincides with the implementation of zero-tolerance punishment policies across the United States. It will be crucial to investigate these trends over time, as the 2013–2014 OCR data is due to be released in the latter part of 2016. At that time, we will be able to further investigate if the general outcry of the overuse of zero-tolerance punishments had any impact on the use of suspensions in American schools.

How can we Explain This Troubling Policy Outcome?

The development of zero-tolerance school discipline—a child of the "get tough" on drugs approach—has had a wide-ranging impact on schooling in general. The policy has increased the overall avoidance of schools by students, the decline in reading abilities, and the growth in student suspensions. The zero-tolerance policy toward student misbehavior was seen as a way to improve the classroom setting and to make the learning environment more beneficial for students. However, as can be seen in the data and analysis above, zero-tolerance as a positive tool to improve educational opportunities is a myth. A myth that has had deleterious effects for students across the

United States, in particular for minority students. It is a myth that has made things worse for those students it was supposed to benefit.

It is an example of policy gone awry from its intended design to its outcome as the result of large-scale implementation (Portes, 2000). The implementation of a zero-tolerance approach to school discipline is also an example of how a policy can expand and change mid-course to encompass more than the original intent due to the actions of street-level bureaucrats. It has been argued that the single greatest factor in the increase in the school-to-prison pipeline has been the increased suspensions of students, who are pushed out of school during the day. Therefore, one can logically conclude that there has been a negative impact on the ability of students to gain vital reading comprehension skills due to the amount of time a student is out of school due to repeated school suspensions. This is a direct outgrowth of this policy; albeit, an unintended consequence, as the policy transformed through its interpretation and implantation as described by Portes (2000).

Reflecting on Portes' (2000) Linear Purposive Action and Alternative Sequence Framework and the five areas that trigger skepticism, it is difficult to explain exactly why the policy transformed as it did. While the zero-tolerance policy was meant to act as a deterrent, the threat to remove students from school ran amuck. This result does not seem to align itself to the "Hidden Abode" where that would have been the goal all along or that a "lucky turn-of-events" caused this—it hasn't been lucky for anyone. There are elements of "mid-course shifts" or "unexpected outcomes," but only if we consider the school-level personnel as outside forces through their sensemaking (Spillane et al., 2002; Coburn, 2001) of the zero-tolerance policy and its implementation. However, a better explanation is the "latent function" (Portes, 2000)—the announced goal, in this case ending bad behavior to promote safe schools, was truly intended by actors, but actions at the policy level had unintended consequences at the local level that they are unaware of, in this case disproportionate numbers of minority students being suspended and increasing risk of being policed for criminal offenses. This is reinforced by Strauss's (1964) and Green's (1994) arguments that in a vain effort to force equality, the systematic approach to creating discipline policies that treat everyone the same has resulted in an inflexible, blunt instrument that restricts the administrator's decisions and forces a particular and uniform outcome (Boggs, 2017).

We need to learn that policy should not serve as the blunt instrument of exclusion for non-compliance, but should act as the lever to encourage positive classroom interactions, such as restorative justice. So, what does this mean for policy? It means we have to be cautious in our policy directions, mandates, and rules of policy implementation. Any change "must proceed in measured steps" (Portes, 2000, p. 15), which include observing interactions and pressures from both internal and external forces. This also includes knowing the actors involved in the process and "anticipating their reactions to external intervention" (Portes, 2000, p. 15). In the realm of education, Portes (2000) and Boggs (2017) believe that we need to consider three major variables when forming policy and governing its implementation:

(1) Contemplate the lens by which policy may be/is interpreted by policy actors, including parents, teachers, and administrators on the ground level. Consider the legislative intentions of the policy and consider "the possibility that one party or the other has concealed goals at variance with those overtly announced" (Portes, 2000, p. 15);
(2) Consider "unexpected consequences of increased interaction, including racial cleavages and greater awareness of the other party's shortcomings" (Portes, 2000, p. 15) that may alter the course of a policy's implementation or interpretation;
(3) Study the "external factors preventing the implementation of collectively reached decisions" (Portes, 2000, p. 15) and ask how to reach collective agreement on the purpose of the policy and adjust the policy implementation accordingly to achieve the stated goals.

After looking at these policy variables, thoughtfully consider how they may have changed the outcomes of zero-tolerance policy formation and implementation.

The initial luster of zero-tolerance school discipline policy, which at one point seemed to be a glittering example of how to improve the educational opportunities for students in the classroom, is now seen as a policy that resulted in adverse secondary effects. The policy has taken from students' precious learning time in the classroom—time that cannot be returned to these students because of the policy regarding punishment of their actions, whether minor or major. Zero-tolerance punishment was thought to be a policy that would transform unruly schools into places of calm and serenity. Sadly, zero-tolerance policies have produced significant unintended outcomes and the policy has backfired as it rippled through the system. Instead of helping the most vulnerable and making schools safe places for learning, it has in fact only exacerbated the expansion of the school-to-prison pipeline.

Notes

1 Here defined by Portes as one of the five areas and different from the broad definition given earlier by Marx.
2 The dip in the suspensions during the 2009–2010 data cycle is not identified in literature, but could be a result of early analysis of racialized disciplinary practices in schools which resulted in a one-time dip in suspensions.
3 The explanation for this differentiation is material for another study entirely, but it is possible that the traditional operational standards for schools may run in contrast to the actions of the students (i.e., schools run by White teachers and White administrators in areas of high minority student populations could be seeing a clash of cultures). Or, that schools located in areas with a high minority population are attempting to establish a harsher rule of law and order, firmness, and

adherence to stricter codes of conduct in comparison to other schools. Though the research would tell us the latter is more likely (Noguera, 1995), we are still open to other explanations, but we will not be holding our breath.

References

Arcia, E. (2006). Achievement and enrollment status of suspended students: Outcomes in a large, multicultural school district. *Education and Urban Society, 38*(3), 359–369.

Bock, S. J., Tapscott, K. E., & Savner, J. L. (1998). Suspension and expulsion: Effective management for students? *Intervention in School and Clinic, 34*(1), 50–52.

Boggs, B. (2017). The future of education: Nouveau "Pluc Que Ca Change . . ." In Ransaw, T., & Major, R. (Eds.), *Emerging issues and trends in education* (pp. 203–2014). East Lansing, MI: Michigan State University Press.

Boggs, B., & Dunbar, C. (2015). An interpretive history of urban education and leadership in an age of perceived racial invisibility. In Khalifa, M., Grant, C., & Arnold, N. (Eds.), *Handbook for urban educational leadership* (pp. 43–57). Lanham, MD: Rowman & Littlefield.

Brownstein, R. (2010, March). Pushed out. *The Education Digest.* pp. 23–27.

Coburn, C. (2001). Collective sensemaking about reading: How teachers mediate reading policy in their professional communities. *Educational Evaluation and Policy Analysis, 23*(2), 145–170.

Cohen, D. (1982). Policy and organization: The impact of state and federal educational policy on school governance. *Harvard Educational Review, 52*(4), 474–499.

Coleman, James Samuel, and Department of Health USA. Equality of educational opportunity. Vol. 2. Washington, DC: US Department of Health, Education, and Welfare, Office of Education, 1966.

Cusick, P. A. (1992). *The educational system: Its nature and logic.* New York, NY: McGraw-Hill College.

Dunbar Jr., C. (2015). *For naught: How zero-tolerance policy and school police practices imperil our students' future.* Retrieved from www.aclumich.org/blog/2015-01-27/harsh-discipline-pushes-students-out%E2%80%94-fails-make-schools-safer

Fabelo, T., Thompson, M. D., Plotkin, M., Carmichael, D., Marchbanks III, M. P., & Booth, E. A. (2011). *Breaking schools' rules: A statewide study of how school discipline relates to students' success and juvenile justice involvement.* New York, NY: My Science Network.

Fowler, D. (2011). School discipline feeds the "pipeline to prison". *Phi Delta Kappan, 93*(2), 14–19.

Green, T. F. (1994). Policy questions: A conceptual study. *Education Policy Analysis Archives, 2,* 7.

Losen, D. J. (2013). Discipline policies, successful schools, and racial justice, and the law. *Family Court Review, 51*(3), 388–400.

Losen, D. J., & Martinez, T. E. (2013). Out of school and off track: The overuse of suspensions in American middle and high schools. Los Angeles, CA: University of California.

Noguera, P. A. (1995). Preventing and producing violence: A critical analysis of responses to school violence. *Harvard Educational Review, 65*(2), 189–212.

Portes, A. (2000). The Hidden Abode: Sociology as Analysis of the Unexpected. *American Sociological Review, 65,* 1–18.

Potter, H., Boggs, B., & Dunbar, C. (2017). Discipline and punishment: How schools are building the school-to-prison pipeline. In *The school to prison pipeline: The role of culture and discipline in school* (pp. 65–90). New Delhi: Emerald Publishing Limited.

Raffele Mendez, L. M. (2003). Predictors of suspension and negative school outcomes: A longitudinal investigation. *New Directiosn for Youth Development, 2003*(99), 17–33.

Royce, Edward. (2015). Classical social theory and modern society: Marx, Durkheim, Weber. Lanham, MD: Rowman & Littlefield.

Scott, J. C. (1998). *Seeing like a state: How certain schemes to improve the human condition have failed.* New Haven, CT: Yale University Press.

Shulman, L.S. (1983). Autonomy and obligation. In L. Shulman and G. Sykes (Eds). *The Handbook of Teaching and Policy* (pp. 484–504). New York: Longman.

Skiba, R., & Knesting, K. (2001). Zero tolerance, zero evidence: An analysis of school disciplinary practice. *New Directions for Youth Development, 2001*(92), 17–43.

Skiba, R., & Peterson, R. (1999). The dark side of zero tolerance: Can punishment lead to safe schools?. *The Phi Delta Kappan, 80*(5), 372–382.

Skiba, R., & Sprague, J. (2008). Safety without suspensions. *Educational Leadership, 66*(1), 38–43.

Spillane, J., Reiser, B. J., & Reimer, T. (2002). Policy implementation and cognition: Reframing and refocusing implementation research. *Review of Educational Research, 72*(3), 387–431.

Sprague, J., Walker, H., Golly, A., White, K., Myers, D. R., & Shannon, T. (2001). Translating research into effective practice: The effects of a universal staff and student intervention on indicators of discipline and school safety. *Education and Treatment of Children, 24*(4), 495–511.

St. George, D. (2011). *Teenager suspended from Fairfax County school over acne drug.* Retrieved from www.washingtonpost.com/local/education/fairfax-schools-discipline-under-scrutiny-after-teens-suspension-for-medication/2011/03/08/ABZBiZQ_story.html

Strauss, L. (1964). *The City & Man.* Chicago, IL: University of Chicago Press.

Unger, L. (1961). *TS Eliot* (Vol. 8). Minneapolis, MN: University of Minnesota Press.

United States Department of Justice, & United States Department of Education. (2014). Notice of Language Assistance Dear Colleague letter on the Nondiscriminatory Administration of School Discipline. Washington, DC: U.S. Government Printing Office.

Weick, K. E. (1979). *The social psychology of organizing* (Topics in social psychology series). New York, NY: Mcgraw-Hill.

5   When Free Schools in England and Charter Schools in the United States Backfire

Graham Downes and Catherine A. Simon

The Academies Act (HMG, 2010) encapsulated the school reform agenda of the UK Conservative/Liberal Democrat coalition government and has continued to underpin Conservative education policy post 2015. It was one of a collection of major social policy reforms to emerge from a suite of ideologies around freedom, fairness, Big Society, and diversity of provision. Central to Coalition rhetoric was a belief that equality of opportunity and greater social mobility rested at the heart of fairness (Clegg, 2010). Enacted with astonishing speed, the Academies Act represented the primary mechanism through which levels of parental choice and competition were to be raised in the system of state schools in England. Academies—already established under New Labour—are state funded schools (maintained), yet self-governing and operating outside of direct local authority (district) control. The 2010 Act extended their scope, permitting all existing state schools, whether primary (elementary) or secondary (high), to apply for Academy status, thus radically changing the education landscape. Closely akin to United States (U.S.) charter schools, the Academies program aimed to promote an egalitarian agenda that would help turn around failing schools, draw in funding and expertise from business and philanthropic interests, and bring closer to fruition the notion of a self-improving, school-led system of education, responsive to local need.

However, it has been a policy not without criticism and one that may have fallen sway to the very excesses of hegemonic neoliberalism it sought—in part—to address. Born out of a perceived inertia within an overly centralized, bureaucratic, and alienating education system, charter schools offered the promise of a more flexible, community-based solution to the problems of compulsory schooling (Timpane et al., 2001). With reference to a halcyon era of schooling within the U.S., charter schools were an attempt to reposition the school at the center of their communities (Brouillette, 2002). Brouillette argues that undergirding this approach is a privileging of the local over the national; of individual choice over structural reform; of freedom over imposition. The key to this repositioning is in the name: "the charter." This agreement provides such schools with certain freedoms from central legislation, such as freedom from the burden to comply with state or federal requirements relating to attainment and standards. In so doing, proponents of such approaches aim to remove state imposed constraints perceived to create disenfranchised and demotivated students.

It was not unsurprising that this largely neoliberal policy initiative should gain traction within England; in 2010, the then Minister of State for Education, Michael Gove, introduced a free schools program that broadly followed the charter schools model. Similar to charter schools in the U.S., these schools could be set up by parents, community groups, or other interested parties to meet demand for new types of school (Department for Education, 2010). Indeed, demand was the central justification for creating new schools: those groups that could demonstrate demand for a new school, and the values it promoted, would be granted funding (New Schools Network, 2015). However, our research suggests that such schools actually perpetuate existing class relationships and do little to address the reproduction of existing social stratifications in education. To this end, the Academies program has failed its espoused aims of creating equality of opportunity and greater social mobility. In effect, the Academies program in England backfired and further perpetuated social and economic inequity.

The Two Communities in Understanding Policy Backfire

What follows is an account of two local communities involved in setting up a new charter in the U.S. and a free school in England; Helen's story based in Colorado USA and Sarah's story from rural England. The two cases outlined were prominent within their localities, mainly because they were amongst the first schools of their kind. As such, a range of firsthand accounts, press releases, reports, newspaper articles, online conversations, and video interviews were available. Extensive use was made of these resources in the construction of these two cases. In the case of the English free school, semi-structured interviews with governors, teachers, parents, and residents were also conducted. In the case of the charter school, use was made of existing case studies, particularly data compiled by Liane Brouillette (2002). The data was used to create thick, rich accounts of the two contexts, and data was analyzed using qualitative coding methods (Denzin & Lincoln, 2011; Silverman, 2011) and critical discourse analysis: a method of analyzing language to consider not just what is said, but why it is said (Fairclough, 2003).

Despite being in very different geographical locations, both Helen's and Sarah's experiences are strikingly similar; their comparative experiences lead to some interesting conclusions about policy backfire. Existing status relationships, predicated on class, had a significant bearing on who was involved, the reasons for setting up the school, the values that were formed and promoted, and, ultimately, the intake of pupils who attended the school. Drawing on Nussbaum's concept of thick theory of morality (Nussbaum, 2012), Rawl's interpretation of moral orders (Rawls, 2010), and May's notion of collectivist anarchism (May, 2008), we argue that the concept of community is not radical enough to deal with the issue of social stratification in local contexts. This is because social spaces go beyond the two-dimensional: they are more than relationships between the local and the national (Brenner, 2004). Without an account of the human dimension that is integral to local spaces, the values and hierarchies that are partly responsible for their formation and reproduction, policy initiatives like charter schools and free schools will always struggle to generate new social outcomes. We suggest that rather than focusing on a desire for a demand led model, policymakers need to consider whose demand is being recognized and whose is not. It is only when the values of the educationally disenfranchised are part of the process of governance that existing social hierarchies can be challenged.

History of U.S. Charter Schools

We begin first with an overview of the history of charter schools. Instigated by charter legislation, charter schools are publicly sponsored schools that, compared to public schools, have relative freedom from government control but are accountable for levels of academic performance (Brouillette, 2002; Fuller, 2009). The schools are predicated on the legal concept of "a charter": an agreement between a state or local government agency, to grant certain freedoms from central control in return for a prescribed level of performance. Although such charters vary from state to state, they do have certain commonalities: the authority agrees to withdraw its exclusive franchise over education in a given district; schools are subject to performance criteria and the charter is renewed every three to five years following a review process; the schools must be open to admissions from pupils of all backgrounds and must not use performance tests; the school can only exist through choice, no pupil can be made to attend without choosing the school and, the school is a legal entity with its own board (Kolderie, 1990).

Although the majority of charter schools are still independent (National Alliance for Public Charter Schools, 2016), the ratio varies from state to state. Colorado has a relatively low number of multi charter school providers at less than a quarter of the overall provision (Baker, 2015), whilst for other states, such as Illinois, the same figure is above 75% (Baker, 2015). It is also true that the number of not-for-profit multiple providers (EMO) and for-profit providers (CMO) is growing year on year (National Alliance for Public Charter Schools, 2016) and that there has also been a tendency for a concentration of providers, as certain actors start to dominate the market, particularly amongst CMOs (National Alliance for Public Charter Schools, 2011). One of the distinct issues that independent charter schools face is developing and maintaining a distinctive identity. A number of case studies (e.g., Brouillette, 2002; Fuller, 2009; Wells, 2002) demonstrate the difficulties many of these schools encounter after setting up; often morphing into very different organizations as they seek to expand their expertise and shared understandings in response to unforeseen challenges. However, it should also be noted that most EMO/CMO charter schools are not created as the result of takeovers of independent schools, with 95% of charter schools historically created as start-ups (National Alliance for Public Charter Schools, 2011)

Helen's Story and the Core Academy in Colorado

Helen was a parent who lived in a relatively affluent part of Douglas County District, Colorado. Brouillette's (2002) account of Helen's story suggests the although the schools in the area performed well relative to national averages, she was frustrated by the "don't worry be happy" approach of the local education system: an approach that placed too much emphasis on self-esteem, rather than academic rigor (Brouillette, 2002, p. 44). Her frustration was driven by global discourses that revealed U.S. pupils were not performing well internationally, and this, she felt, would negatively affect her own children's employability within a global market (Brouillette, 2002, p. 225). Helen and four friends were amongst the first to take advantage of the Colorado Charter School Act (1993), and they successfully set up a new charter school: Core Academy, in the same year the Bill was passed. The vision was to create a school based on the Core Knowledge Curriculum developed by E.D. Hirsch (Core Knowledge, n.d.). Hirsch's curriculum places an emphasis on the learning of key factual knowledge, and the parents felt this was an approach that would push their children to produce better results and compete with children anywhere (Brouillette, 2002, p. 226). The school was swiftly approved by the Board of Education and opened its doors to 117 students in September 1993. The Academy was designed around different themes that reflected different parents' areas of concern (curriculum, student/teacher ratio, dress code), with each parent taking responsibility for one of these areas (Brouillette, 2002, p. 44).

Helen and the other members of the group came up with the school's original mission statement: "Strive for Knowledge and Truth in all you do" (Brouillette, 2002, p. 44). This somewhat ambiguous statement covered a multitude of tensions between Helen and the other parents, which created a hostile culture. Counter culture is often defined by what it is not rather than what it is (Roszak, 1995). In reality, there was a paradox at the heart of the project: on the one hand the group were united in their antipathy toward the education system; on the other hand, the parents were disunited in their sense of what the school should be (Brouillette, 2002, p. 4). This led to a degree of inertia, as Helen and the other parents felt unable to trust educators with the leadership of the school whilst also being unable to agree amongst themselves about a way forward (Brouillette, 2002, p. 45). As a result, the school had a difficult start with a high turnover of principals and teaching staff (Brouillette, 2002). This turnover was undergirded by tensions between the parental group, the leadership team, teachers, and the district education board. These interrelationships proved to be highly destructive, as each fought to set the agenda for the school based on their own preconceptions, values, and constraints (Brouillette, 2002). Whilst Helen's, and most of the other parents', aim went little beyond maintaining a degree of involvement in the school, the principal occupied a much more conflicted position, caught between a desire to appease the parental group and a need to create cohesion amongst teaching staff. The high turnover of both principals and teaching staff reflected this conflict, as different leaders veered between authoritarian and weak forms of leadership (Brouillette, 2002).

At times, this tension also included the local education board. As the district expanded its number of charter schools, the Board initiated moves to mediate governance between it and the schools, primarily through the appointment of a school liaison officer (Brouillette, 2002, p. 49). At this juncture, the school's principal openly desired more autonomy. The ensuing power struggle meant the principal's contract was not renewed (Brouillette, 2002, p. 49). The upshot of these protracted struggles was a gradual move away from a school characterized by its need to be different and to reflect parental values, to one that became a more formal institution, characterized by more commonly accepted practices. Today the school occupies a purpose built campus, a long way from the strip mall and grocery store that were its genesis (Speer, 2013). Core Academy retained some aspects of the original school set-up: the school website for example emphasized the "unique educational opportunities (offered) through our Core Knowledge Curriculum" and referred to "Core Virtues, and rigorous academics" as well as the importance of "Our parent community" ("About Academy Charter School," n.d.). This aspect was foregrounded further in a promotional video produced by Douglas County Schools, which began by highlighting the fact the school was run by parents (Douglas County Schools, 2014). However, what had waned was the "do it yourself" aspect of the free school movement, that is, the need for parents to both set up the school and to keep it upright. As Helen stated:

> It was parents who did the dry walling, painting, laying the carpet, doing all of the remodeling of the strip mall and almost from day one there was a huge waiting list.
>
> (Speer, 2013)

The current requirement of parents to do 20 hours of volunteering a year ("About Academy Charter School," n.d.) is somewhat pallid by comparison; an act of remembrance to the endeavors of the founding members. Indeed, it is difficult to see what separated the school from other public schools. The core knowledge curriculum was distinctive but not unique; indeed, it has been exported all over the world and has gained significant traction in English schools. Furthermore, the demographic data on the school revealed little of the choice that was supposedly a distinctive element of charter schools (Kolderie, 1990). Although the school intake was not very different from nearby schools (those within walking distance), it is difficult to make the claim that it was more diverse. In fact, its intake of children from ethnic minority backgrounds represented the lowest of all neighboring elementary schools (17% of the intake [728]). A nearby school, for example, had 30% of the intake (400) from ethnic minority backgrounds (Colorado Department of Education, 2016b). Furthermore, of all the schools in the area, Core Academy had a significantly lower intake of children who were eligible for free or reduced fee meals (6.6%). This compares with another local school where the figure was 29.8%. In fact, the next lowest school had nearly twice as many children eligible for free or reduced fee meals (10.6% of 506 pupils) (Colorado Department of Education, 2016a). Thus, Core Academy was in reality only offering choice for those in a relative position of privilege within the immediate area. It should also be noted that within Colorado, the area itself was one of relative wealth and privilege. For example, data produced to map out inequality in the district reveals that a school 26 miles away had 70% of its intake eligible for free or reduced fee meals (Colorado Department of Education, 2016a).

What emerges from Helen's story in setting up Core Academy is a charter school policy undermined by the very ideologies of choice, autonomy, and freedom upon which it was based. Freedom *from* is not the same as freedom *to*; a lesson also writ large in the English experience of free schools.

Background to Free Schools in England

Largely the outcome of policy borrowing from the charter school program in the U.S., English free schools were volunteered as the answer to some of the perceived social and economic problems associated with state education in England (Gove, 2010). Based on a similar charter style arrangement, free schools policy created opportunities for actors other than the state to engage in educational provision (Department for Education, 2010). Justification for setting up a free school rested on a number of factors: a need for places not currently met by state schools, the want of or desire for something different, or a school focused upon meeting the needs of a particular cohort of children (New Schools Network, 2013). As such, free school funding is provided where the local authority (school district) does not provide sufficient school places, or school places of an adequate standard (New Schools Network, 2013). The schools' legal status rests on a funding agreement enacted between the Secretary of State and the individual school. This is a direct translation of the charter agreement used for charter schools. However, this agreement is no different from that offered to the long-established academies—schools independent from the state but not newly established as a response to local, community, or parental pressure. Unlike charter schools, there is also no periodic review of the funding agreement; thus the initial values of the free school have greater potential to become lost over time.

Like their charter school counterparts, free schools operate as stand-alone schools or as part of chains run by both not-for-profit and for-profit organizations. However, unlike the U.S. experience, the proportion of stand-alone schools is much smaller. Bidding groups are encouraged to enter into a memorandum of understanding with a service provider from the outset. Increasingly, such stand-alone schools have been the subject of much debate and are under mounting pressure to conform to existing practices. The Al Madinah School in Derby, for example, provided an education based upon a Muslim ethos, but was shut down following a damning Office for Standards in Education, Children's Services and Skills (Ofsted) inspection. Their closure was set against a background of media hype, controversy, and fear, mainly because ethnicity and religious ethos were significant aspects of the school's character (Gye, 2013).

Sarah's Story and the Trinity Academy in England

Sarah and her family lived in a remote rural area of England. Their nearest secondary school was large—almost 2,000 pupils—and was situated over 10 miles from the family home. Sarah had a history of local activism: she had written a book and a number of articles on the importance of people taking control of their communities. In many ways, her qualities mirror those of Helen: she was driven, had a clear sense of how things should be, was articulate, and she was well connected. Sarah felt the local secondary education offering was inadequate—a large rural school some distance away was not appropriate for children attending small primary schools in a rural setting. Not only was the size of the school an issue for Sarah, their curriculum would not recognize the specific experiences of children in rural settings. Sarah persuaded friends to bid for a new free school as her children approached secondary school age.

One of the requirements for a bid was to demonstrate sufficient local support to warrant a school (New Schools Network, 2013). Sarah set about promoting the idea with considerable energy: she knocked on doors, attended council meetings, and even stood at the gates of existing secondary schools to garner support. It was the intervention of a local theme park owner that really helped. He provided free access to his park for a day. As parents entered, they were invited to pledge their support for the school, thereby adding a considerable number of signatures to the supporting documentation.

However, the strategy was not without its issues. Although Sarah demonstrated support in terms of the number of signatures, her strategy did not highlight potential resistance to the project, which turned out to be significant on a number of fronts. First, existing state schools, angered by the lack of consultation, believed there was already enough provision in the area, and the proposed new establishment was therefore a threat to existing schools and staffing. Second, private schools in the area were worried that a free school would damage their own intake and threaten their survival. Third, the proposed site for the new school, beside a small and picturesque village, angered residents, particularly as they felt they had not been consulted properly. Many only found out about the proposed development *post hoc* and felt that—although there was an attempt to consult—this was precursory ("No to Route 39 Academy," n.d.).

Finally, as in the case of Core Academy, the school struggled to find a shared vision amongst its steering group. Sarah had been keen to create a school with an environmentalist ethos, whilst others wanted to develop a creative curriculum. The issue was further complicated as the group expanded to incorporate educational expertise, a requirement of the bid (New Schools Network, 2013). The group worked with Pearson Publishing on the bidding process, but the partnership was not based on mutual interests. The school wanted Pearson's inside knowledge of education to help with the bid whilst Pearson saw the project as a test bed, primarily for its digital resources. The group placed an increasing number of demands on Pearson, who eventually felt their involvement was not cost effective and withdrew. The group had also continued to expand in number as the demands of the bid grew. A retired head teacher and his partner (also a teacher) became involved through informal conversations with "friends of friends." This pair, in particular, added a forceful dynamic, and this new impetus was to take the group in a new direction. Rather than emphasizing "alternative education," the discourse tended toward more traditional justificatory rhetoric associated with education: equal opportunity and aspiration for the poor, teaching standards, competition, leadership, and vision. The purpose of Trinity Academy also shifted; it was now justified in terms of addressing the deficit in the existing provision. As one member of the steering group put it, local schools needed to be given "a kick up the backside."

These new justifications were very much in tune with national Government rhetoric on free schools (Department for Education, 2010). Rather than being a local school for local children, the school shifted its focus in favor of those from lower socioeconomic groups who tended to live in urban areas, thereby bringing it into line with existing schools in the urban areas. Competing with these schools meant competing for the same pupils. In truth, a class dimension emerged from the project: cheaper housing tended to be available in the towns whilst the housing in the remote areas was more exclusive, more expensive, and therefore more likely to be occupied by aspiring middle class families. Those setting up Trinity Academy were dependent upon families, ostensibly from a different social class, to buy into their middle-class values and have the economic wherewithal to travel out of town to the rural setting.

The group's bid was successful, and Trinity Academy opened in autumn 2014; however, its continued existence was fraught with difficulties. As well as resistance from other schools in the area, the main issue was with local residents. Although small in number, this group had been extremely effective in subverting Trinity Academy's development. Part of the bid had been for a new purpose built school to accommodate 700 pupils. However, the short timescales involved meant the school first opened in a nearby village hall with just over 60 pupils. Originally intended as a temporary measure, deputations from local residents resulted in the district council rejecting the necessary planning permission for the new premises. National government eventually overturned this judgment ("No to Route 39 Academy," n.d.). Added to this uncertainty, the school received a "requires improvement" grading from Ofsted in its second year, leading to the resignation of the Principal.

Trinity Academy therefore developed in an *ad hoc* manner. Despite the aim of improving opportunities for all, the number of children on free school meals remained broadly in line with other schools in the area. Furthermore, evidence from parents' and prospective parents' interviews indicated a tendency to see Trinity Academy as an alternative to state provision that was also exclusive. All of those who expressed a desire to send their children to the school, for example, referred to its small size. One parent stated that their child "would not be able to cope in a large school because of their specific emotional needs," a view indicative of many parents' attitudes: the school was considered an appropriate place for pupils with emotional issues who could not cope in a larger school. In addition, the notion of bullying came up consistently: the school was perceived as a good place for children who might otherwise be bullied. The class dynamic was also evident here: those from wealthier backgrounds used the word "bullying," and there was a strong perception that children from more deprived backgrounds would not attend the school. To quote another parent, "they would be too lazy to catch the bus in the morning." Indeed, parents interviewed from a local housing estate did not want to send their children to the school.

One of the freedoms enjoyed by academies and free schools is the ability to remove pupils with little or no recourse. The principal of Trinity Academy was forthright in her assertion of this right, stating that pupils who did not work within the school's values would be asked to leave. The travel time and the extended school day were further elements that deterred parents from the housing estate, but there was also a clear sense that Trinity Academy was not for them. One parent commented that a child from the estate had gone to the school, to which the reply came: "not for long," followed by laughter from the rest of the group.

Toward a More Progressive Communitarianism

The reading of these two cases suggests there are deeper, more manifest tendencies within the process of social reproduction. As Roger Dale observes, this process of education centers on three questions:

1. Who gets taught what, how, by whom, and under what conditions and circumstances?

2. How, by whom, and with what relations to other sectors and through what structures, institutions, and processes are these things defined, governed, organized, and managed?
3. To what ends and in whose interests do these structures and processes occur, and what are their social and individual consequences? (Dale, 2000, p. 438).

What is foregrounded in these questions is the issue of power. Steven Lukes defines power as: *A exercises power over B when A affects B in a manner contrary to B's interests* (2005, p. 47). Based on the examples of Core Academy and Trinity Academy, *A* can be defined as the parents who founded the schools. Although the groups are heterogeneous in their motivations, they can be seen as single groups in that they are colonizing a pre-determined space through a process of legitimation and mutual agreement. In other words, the group is able to make decisions about where the school will be, who can and cannot get in, and the expectations placed upon pupils and their parents. By contrast, *B* is the group that can try and attend the school, but they cannot decide the rules to which they are to be subjected. Of course, this does not necessarily preclude the notion that all prospective parents are subjected to an asymmetrical power relationship—using Lukes' criterion, it can be argued that this arrangement is in the interests of some pupils and parents and not in the interests of others. Indeed, gaining an advantage was often a motivating factor amongst the wealthier parents who sent their children to the prospective schools. These parents viewed school as a positional good, that is, a good that can only provide utility through negative consumption by others. For example, the participants from the Trinity Academy were keen to present themselves as knowing, active consumers in the education market. They wanted an education that enabled their child to "reach their potential" whilst realizing that this potential had limits. They liked the idea of an extended school day and were keen to highlight the fact that the parents of poorer children would not be prepared to make the effort to get their offspring into school for an early start. Similarly, the parents who were initially engaged in creating the Core Academy were keen to develop a school that offered more than what was already on offer. In fact, many of the original parents who sent their children to Core Academy were drawn from a vocal group of middle-class parents who had previously demanded the setting up of "schools within schools" so that a more aspirational approach to education could be provided for their children and others like them (Brouillette, 2002, p. 44). In the case of Trinity Academy, the participants' reference to bullying reveals a strategy to align themselves with a more favorable social group than was otherwise afforded to them. Here, the participants only referred to bullying as a problem that is unique to existing state provision. By placing their children in the new school, they were taking them away from the threat of bullying. Although the small size of the school was identified as a factor, the school's values and creative curriculum were also mentioned. As discussed earlier, these are factors that are historically engrained within the social fabric of the English education system: creative moral education can be placed in an advantageous, hierarchical, discursive relationship with the basic skills approach attributed to the lower orders.

Both cases thus illustrate a process of differentiation by the middle classes so that education is constructed as a positional good. By contrast, the participants from the poorest backgrounds do not necessarily share the same values. For example, parents interviewed from poorer areas near Trinity Academy said they would not send their children there because the school day was too long and they believed it was important for children to spend time at home with their families. They also presented themselves as consumers and foregrounded the notion of choice, but it was evident that these choices were framed negatively and were not related to the notion of education as a positional good. For many, choice was a strategy for survival: they moved their children from school to school to try and find a place where they would fit in enough to get through the education system. Many had been "diagnosed" with behavioral or learning difficulties, and choice had more to do with ensuring their children could cope rather than the idea that their children could attain excellence or reach their potential.

Amongst this group there was also a strong sense of exclusion, not just from Trinity Academy, but the education system writ large. One parent spoke emotionally about her attempts to join a school's parent group, only to be provided with rebuttals or told the wrong meeting times. In his book *Relations in Public*, Erving Goffman outlines the ways in which individuals and groups territorialize spaces through a process of claims (1971). Following through Goffman's framework, it is the parents from the lower socio-economic groups who are clearly excluded from the creation and habitation of the new space; in other words, the new school. Given that there is a strong tendency for children from such backgrounds to do badly at school, there is a strong case that they are at the wrong end of an asymmetrical power relationship. However, whilst the wealthier parental group gain an advantage over the poorer parents, it is also possible to make the case that they too are disadvantaged in relation to Sarah and her friends because they still have to comply with the wishes of the school's founders. We describe this process as *resonance*: the more one is able to resonate with the values of the agenda setting group, the more one is attracted to, and able to access, the space being created. The statistics outlined from the Core Academy and surrounding area add additional detail of this process: the school's intake is very much in line with those of the immediate surrounding area, which, in turn, has markedly different intake characteristics to schools in adjacent poorer areas (Colorado Department of Education, 2016b).

It should be noted at this point that the founding members of both schools were united in their desire to get parents involved in the running of the school, but they were also frustrated by the lack of a response from parents.

In the case of Trinity Academy, some of this can be attributed to material considerations: Sarah and her friends were able to take time out of working to set the school up, whilst prospective parents are not always able to do this. The school is also over 10 miles from other parents' homes, whilst it is close to Sarah's. However, this alone does not explain the entirety of the problem. In the case of Core Academy, the school does have a higher level of parental participation but only because the 20 hours of volunteering is an entry requirement of the school (Douglas County Schools, 2014). Some of this willing lack of participation is due to social stratification. Here we argue, with reference to Jacques Ranciere's work, that once the school was imagined with a certain set of values, the gatekeepers of those values are in the ascendency: it is only through their acceptance that an individual can join this group, and they can only be accepted if they adhere to the group's values. Of course, over time, it might be possible to exact some change on the group, but this is a high-risk strategy for any prospective incumbent.

Active and Passive Equality in the Backfire Process

At this point we want to emphasize that the process of policy backfire is not down to the moral limitations of people like Sarah and Helen. Both were committed to the common good and both were trying to improve opportunities for their own children and others. Instead, we proffer that the problem is with the system of education, and particularly the discursive structure that undergirds it. Here, we use Jacques Ranciere's theory of "policing" (Ranciere & Corcoran, 2010) and Todd May's concepts of "active and passive equality" (2008) to provide explanations and possible solutions. For Ranciere, the problem of policing (a group's ability to decide whilst others' lack of ability to make decisions goes unrecognized) is at the heart of social injustice. The argument that Sarah is in a privileged position here has already been documented, but it also is necessary to acknowledge the fact that asymmetric power relationships do not end with Sarah and the steering group; they are also operating within a predetermined structure created by others. Sarah, in particular, felt a deep sense of frustration toward the Department for Education for the lack of support and guidance. On the one hand, the school had to follow predetermined rules and regulations laid down by successive governments; on the other, the group began with little or no experience of the education system. This sense of alienation was compounded by a negative Ofsted inspection in the school's second year; thus, the excluding were also the excluded.

For May (2008), this situation can only be addressed through a closer look at the process of interaction. In the education system on both sides of the Atlantic, it is an existing group who decide what inequality looks like and how it should be addressed. In other words, the problem is reduced to one of distribution rather than formulation: one group decides what is of value and then what each group is entitled to; those who are without are only acknowledged in terms of what they should receive. This is an example of passive distribution: one that is particularly prescient in the case of education. For May, the issue can only seriously be addressed through a process of active equality: one that begins with an assumption of equality between people rather than ends with equality as an outcome (May, 2008, p. 38). This means that equality can only happen when people are able to interact and negotiate around the issues raised by Dale. In the case of community schools, it is, therefore, necessary for all interested parties to be represented in the formulation of the school from the outset.

One solution here would be to ensure that the bidding groups demonstrate that they are representative of the people who will use the school. Of course, this would not exclude the problem of uneven funding provision at a government level—people like Sarah will always be more successful in gaining provision from people "like them." Therefore, representation and negotiating mechanisms are required at all levels of the education system. This requires a privileging of democratic process over economic discourses; it requires the promotion of fairness over productivity, and it requires the placement of social diversity over meritocracy. It is only by doing these things that society will be able to truly flourish at all levels. As Martha Nussbaum also observes, although the rhetoric appears diametrically opposed to existing approaches, it need not be mutually exclusive (Nussbaum, 2012). It is possible for a more inclusive education system to be more, rather than less, productive.

References

Baker, B. D. (2015). *Follow up on who's running America's charter schools*. Retrieved June 20, 2016, from https://schoolfinance101.wordpress.com/2015/12/07/picture-post-week-follow-up-on-whos-running-americas-charter-schools/?utm_content=buffer0175a&utm_medium=social&utm_source=twitter.com&utm_campaign=buffer

Brenner, N. (2004). *New state spaces: Urban governance and the rescaling of statehood*. Oxford: Oxford University Press.

Brouillette, L. (2002). *Charter schools: Lessons in school reform*. Abingdon, UK: Taylor & Francis.

Brown, Y. (n.d.) About Academy Charter School. Retrieved June 20, 2016, from www.academycharter.org/about-acs

Clegg, N. (2010) Hugo Young Lecture. Retrieved 28 January, 2014 from https://www.theguardian.com/politics/2010/nov/23/nick-clegg-hugo-young-text

Colorado Department of Education. (2016a). *2015–2016 PK-12 Free and reduced lunch eligibility by County and District (XLSX)*. Retrieved from www.cde.state.co.us/cdereval/2015-16-pupilmembership-pk12-frl-bycountydistrict-excel

Colorado Department of Education. (2016b). *2015–2016 Pupil membership by County, District, ethnicity, and gender (XLSX)*. Retrieved from www.cde.state.co.us/cdereval/2015-16-pupilmembership-bycountydistrict-ethnicitygender-excel

Colorado State Department of Education. (1993) Colorado Charter School Act. Denver: Colorado State Department of Education

Core Knowledge. (n.d.). *Learn about Core Knowledge Schools*. Retrieved June 24, 2016, from www.coreknowledge.org/core-knowledge-schools

Dale, I. R. (2000) Globalization and Education: Demonstrating a 'Common World Educational Culture' or locating a 'Globally Structured Educational Agenda'? *Educational Theory 50*(4), 427–448.

Denzin, N. and Lincoln, Y. (2011) *The SAGE Handbook of Qualitative Research, 4th Edition*. Thousand Oaks, CA: Sage Publications Inc.

Department for Education. (2010). *The importance of teaching white paper*. London. Retrieved from www.education.gov.uk/publications/eOrderingDownload/CM-7980.pdf

Douglas County Schools. (2014). *Academy Charter School in Castle Rock, Colorado*. YouTube. Retrieved from https://youtu.be/gR6lIRCtC3g

Fairclough, N. (2003) *Analysing discourse: Textual analysis for social research*. London: Routledge

Fuller, B. (2009). *Inside charter schools: The paradox of radical decentralization*. Cambridge, MA: Harvard University Press.

Goffman, E. (1971). *Relations in public microstudies of the public order*. New York: Basic Books.

Gove, M. (2010) *Michael Gove's speech to the Policy Exchange on free schools*. Retrieved 29 January, 2014, from https://www.gov.uk/government/speeches/michael-goves-speech-to-the-policy-exchange-on-free-schools

Gye, H. (2013). Muslim Al-Madinah free school slammed as "dysfunctional" in Ofsted report. *Daily Mail Online*. Retrieved September 22, 2015, from www.dailymail.co.uk/news/article-2464351/Muslim-Al-Madinah-free-school-slammed-dysfunctional-Ofsted-report.html

HMG. (2010) Academies Act 2010. London: HMSO

Kolderie, T. (1990). *The States will have to withdraw the exclusive*. Minneapolis. Retrieved from www.educationevolving.org/pdf/StatesWillHavetoWithdrawtheExclusive.pdf

Lukes, S. (2005). *Power, second edition: A radical view*. New York, NY: Palgrave Macmillan.

May, T. (2008). *The political thought of Jacques Rancière: Creating equality*. Edinburgh, UK: Edinburgh University Press.

National Alliance for Public Charter Schools. (2011). *CMO and EMO Public Charter Schools: A growing phenomenon in the Charter School Sector public charter schools dashboard data from 2007–08, 2008–09, and 2009–10*. Retrieved from www.publiccharters.org/wp-content/uploads/2014/01/NAPCS-CMO-EMO-DASHBOARD-DETAILS_20111103T102812.pdf

National Alliance for Public Charter Schools. (2016). *A closer look at the Charter School movement*. Retrieved from www.publiccharters.org/wp-content/uploads/2016/02/New-Closed-2016.pdf

New Schools Network. (2013). *Free schools 101*. Retrieved from www.newschoolsnetwork.org/sites/default/files/Free Schools 101.pdf

New Schools Network. (2015). AP schools opening in 2017 and beyond Free school application guidance. Retrieved 3 February, 2016, from http://www.newschoolsnetwork.org/sites/default/files/Mainstream%20Free%20school%20application%20guidance%20-%20December%2015.pdf

No to Route 39 Academy. (n.d.). Retrieved June 10, 2016, from www.dispute39.co.uk

Nussbaum, M. C. (2012). *Not for profit: Why Democracy needs the humanities.* Princeton, NJ: Princeton University Press.

Ranciere, J., & Corcoran, S. (2010). *Dissensus: On politics and aesthetics.* Bloomsbury Academic. Retrieved from https://books.google.co.uk/books?id=mXPSsMk-71cC

Rawls, A. (2010) Social order as moral order. In: Steven Hitlin & Stephen Vaisey (eds). *Handbook of the sociology of morality.* New York: Springer

Roszak, T. (1995). *The making of a counter culture: Reflections on the technocratic society and its youthful opposition.* Berkeley, CA: University of California Press.

Silverman, D. (2011). *Interpreting qualitative data: A guide to the principles of qualitative research.* London: SAGE

Speer, J. (2013). *CO Charter Schools 20th anniversary Documentary (2013).* Colorado League of Charter Schools. Retrieved from https://youtu.be/WxBMPrBNbEM

Timpane, M., Brewer, D., Gill, B. and Ross, K. (2001) *Rhetoric vs. reality: What we know and what we need to know about vouchers and charter schools.* Santa Monica, CA: RAND Corporation

Wells, A. S. (2002). *Where charter school policy fails: The problems of accountability and equity.* New York, NY: Teachers College Press.

6 When High-Stakes Accountability Measures Impact Promising Practices in an Indigenous-Serving Charter School

Vanessa Anthony-Stevens

Over the past two decades, school choice in the United States has been hailed as a leading educational policy reform to address the persisting "achievement gap" between Black, Latino/a, Native American, immigrant students, and their White counterparts.[1] Choice, as school reform, is argued to offer "equal opportunity" to poor and minoritized youth constrained by underperforming and under-resourced neighborhood schools (Andre-Bechely, 2013; Murphy & Shiffman, 2002).[2] Policymakers argue that choice empowers the families of minoritized students' to circumvent the bureaucracy of traditional neighborhood-school linkages in U.S. school districting by self-selecting educational environments that offer a high quality education (Cullen, Jacob & Levitt, 2005). The ideology of choice is historically associated with magnet schools and alternative schools; however, charter schools have become the most visible school reform proposal to be included in the Elementary and Secondary Education Act (ESEA), through No Child Left Behind and Race to the Top (Powers, 2009). Overwhelmingly, charter schools have been promoted as *"the* answer to class and race opportunity gaps" (Fabricant & Fine, 2012, p. 2).

In this chapter I tell the story of an Indigenous-led, Indigenous-serving charter school to examine the failure of choice policy to meaningfully improve the educational options in poor and minoritized communities. Through the experience of Urban Native Middle School (UNMS), a charter middle school in Arizona designed to serve our nation's most underserved youth—American Indians—I make two key critiques of charter school policy as *the* answer to class and race opportunity gaps in American public schools: 1) charter school policy frameworks fail to address root issues contributing to educational inequity, locally and systemically, and reduce the "achievement gap" to individual choice; 2) the shallowness of high-stakes accountability measurements fails to offer the local and systemic support needed for sustainable, equitable educational reform.[3]

Charter Schools and Indigenous Communities

Although school choice was a central component of the federal No Child Left Behind Act (NCLB), and the current Race to the Top initiative, choice precedes recent policy by nearly 40 years as a strategy to remedy a variety of social ills in education (Fuller & Elmore, 1996; Meens & Howe, 2015). Introduced in the 1960s *War on Poverty* platform, presented under the terminology *family-choice,* choice was hailed as a vehicle to (1) desegregate southern and urban schools, (2) empower poor and working-class families to challenge centralized government, and (3) boost religious freedom among political conservatives (Fuller & Elmore, 1996). In 2001, the NCLB Act launched accountability through one-size-fits-all high-stakes accountability testing in reading and writing to remedy what was described as the "crisis" in American education: the failure of brown and poor children in schools (McCarty, 2012). Standardized, high-stakes accountability tests coupled with school choice have offered the public an educational reform narrative of increased local autonomy with a hard-bottom line, ingredients which purport to ameliorate the educational disparities among schools serving poor families and families of color (Wells, 2002). This "autonomy-for-accountability" framework is the driving force of market-based "boot straps" social reform, at little cost to the tax payer (Powers, 2009). Charter schools continue to dominate much of the recent Race to the Top reform discourse, yet little to no evidence exists that charters or school choice address the achievement gap, or offer greater educational equity to the most underserved communities across the U.S. (Fabricant & Fine, 2012; Meens & Howe, 2015; Wells, 2002). With respect to this chapter, I concentrate on the experiences of Indigenous communities and charter schools.

Schooling in American Indian communities has a history of homogenizing and racializing practices, denying the legitimacy of Native language(s) and identities, and devastating Indian children and communities (Brayboy, Faircloth, Lee, Maaka & Richardson, 2015; Lomawaima & McCarty, 2006). The historic struggle for self-determination and educational equity motivate many Native communities to see charter school policy as an "option for mediating the pressures of the standards movement and exerting local control" (Lomawaima & McCarty, 2006, p. 162). Indigenous-led charter schools are described among the "ethnocentric schools" and feature tribal traditions and values with the goal of improving the academic performance of students underserved by traditional schools (Buchanan & Fox, 2003). Many Indigenous-led charter schools incorporate Native languages and promote pedagogical practices geared toward the specific Indigenous populations they serve (Fenimore-Smith, 2009). The Hawaiian charter school movement is among the most documented of these efforts (Buchanan & Fox, 2003; Goodyear-Ka'ōpua, 2013); however, many other independent Indigenous-led charter schools have also experimented with charters but not without struggle (Lee, 2015).

The UNMS community was similar to other documented Indigenous and marginalized communities who desire to redefine educational opportunities through the creation of separate spaces to address educational inequity (Wells et al., 1999). However, community use of charter school legislation to better local schooling butts up against a hard reality: policy never intended to allocate the necessary infrastructure to support sustainable educational innovation for *all* students; neither did it intend to be flexible enough to support the local needs of Native American communities. The case of UNMS brings into relief the subtle ways policy constraints reduce the accumulated effects of systemic discrimination to a matter of individual choice and high-stakes standardized test scores. The following offers a detailed look at one community's struggle, and untimely failure, utilizing charter policy to improve the educational experience of its youth.

Understanding the Community and School Through Their Voices

This portrait is told through the reflections of its students, teachers, and families.[4] I was a participant and observer of the daily life of UNMS as a science teacher for three years. With school board approval, I led a multiyear effort to document the school's practice from the perspective of its students and their families. The experience was sobering. As UNMS students and their families detailed the impacts of the school on their educational trajectories, the school itself fell under increasing pressure from the state board of education for not making Adequate Yearly Progress (AYP) on the state standardized assessment test, as mandated by NCLB. Over the course of four years, UNMS moved on a scale from being labeled underperforming to failing. In order to understand the school and its untimely closure, I offer its description from the point of view of its stakeholders, with a concluding emphasis on the importance of bi-cultural integration.

The Public Charter School

UNMS opened in 2006. Its charter agreement allows it to serve 60 students in grades six through eight. As a public charter, the school was state funded, was required to comply with state-mandated curricular and assessment guidelines, and was non-discriminatory in its enrollment. The school, built upon the success of its sister high school (founded in 1998), served a majority Tohono O'odham[5] tribal member students, and nearly all of its students were enrolled members of federally recognized tribal nations, most of which were tribes located in the state. The culturally and linguistically sustaining and revitalizing pedagogy (McCarty & Lee, 2014) practiced at UNMS is captured in its mission statement:

> [Urban Native Middle School] is designed to serve as an academically rigorous, bicultural, and community-based middle school for Native youth. By infusing all aspects of the educational experience with elements of O'odham language and Native history, the school will nurture individual students, helping them become strong and responsible contributors to their communities.

The school itself was located outside of the students' home community. Due to limited infrastructure and political debates on the impact of charters on the reservation district funding, UNMS's sponsoring not-for-profit agency purchased a former adult education facility in an urban center, between 20 and 70 miles from the students' home communities. The majority of the students qualified for free and reduced lunch, and did not have access to personal transportation. The school provided bussing for students from the main reservation, closer reservation districts (including the Pascua Yaqui Reservation), and urban neighborhoods at little or no charge to families. Roughly 60% of the students attending came from a rural reservation main town (70 miles away) and 40% came from semi-rural reservation communities/districts (20 miles away).

The Students

Students arrived at UNMS with similar narratives: schools around them were unchallenging, unsafe, culturally isolating, and did not offer an academically rigorous curriculum. Since no one accidentally ended up at UNMS due to its distance from their home communities, families had to invest time and energy into choosing UNMS. Alisha, who came to UNMS as a 6th grader in 2006, shared this reflection in her 8th grade, recalling why she came from her home town on the reservation to attend middle school:

> . . . my mom wanted me to come out here [to UNMS], but—well she told me for sure I was gonna come out, but then I wanted to come out here to come to a different school, [. . .]cause I kinda didn't like the school down in [reservation], they don't really teach that much. Um, everything they say, they repeat over, and over and over, so like we were learning the same thing in one year.
>
> *(Alisha, class of 2009)*

UNMS's students regularly expressed their desire to be in an academically challenging environment where teachers supported them as reasons for enrolling in UNMS. The desire to escape what were seen as dead-end opportunities in the schools close to their homes is captured in Kelly's reflection on why she came to UNMS at the beginning of her 8th grade year, after being on the UNMS waitlist for two years:

> . . . a lot of the kids I went to school with [on the rez] they weren't like getting challenged and they just like would say 'oh I'm not promoting' or 'I'm not gonna go to college because this [previous school] place doesn't care what I do.'

While many UNMS students felt pushed out or limited by the educational options immediately around them, their family, and their peers, they expressed a sense of comfort and opportunity offered to them through the curriculum and student-teacher relationships encountered at UNMS. Two students capture the academic and relational factors significant to them about attending UNMS by comparing UNMS with the schools in their local district:

> [At the reservation middle school,] they just let anyone pass even if they have a bad grade or not. They just let them go [. . .] here [at UNMS], you get like more into details, like more—more information than out there [at the reservation school]. And to learn more deep into like other subjects.
>
> *(Nolan, class of 2009)*

> "[At UNMS] we're asked for our point of view from the school unlike the schools on the reservation . . . [at UNMS] they are really supportive and care.
>
> *(James, class of 2011)*

The Teachers

UNMS employed a 1:4 ratio of non-Indigenous to Indigenous teachers, a highly uncommon feature in Native serving schools.[6] A third of the teachers came to the school with teacher certification, while the other two-thirds benefited from the flexible timelines offered in charter policy to acquire teaching credentials gradually. Four of the eight-member teacher staff had master's degrees, of which three were pursuing doctoral degrees (myself included), one teacher had two Bachelor's degrees (history and secondary education), one had a Bachelor's in elementary education with middle school endorsement. The O'odham language teacher was working on finishing her Bachelor's degree to supplement her O'odham expertise with mainstream pedagogical expertise.

The school's small size (60 students and 11 regular faculty and staff members) facilitated close relationships with teachers, students, and their families. Many of the Indigenous teachers/staff were extended family to students. Cultural responsiveness took on many forms in UNMS teacher-student-parent interactions. To be responsive to parent realities, the school took parent-teacher conferences to the students' home communities, alternating quarterly between holding conferences in the main reservation town, the semi-rural reservation district town, and at the school itself. Many of the teachers experienced marginalization as Indigenous people in their own schooling, and drew lessons from those experiences to counteract discrimination in their work with UNMS youth. Their approaches, while varied, sought to engage students in classroom learning where Indigenous cultural practices previously marginalized in other school environments took on center stage. Mr. Molina, the Social Studies and Native History and Culture teacher, reflected on how he enacted cultural responsiveness to engage students in state-mandated social studies content,

> . . . I would always do my best to get them to realize and tell [the students] to remember and question, what were Native people doing? Where were the Native people at this time? And then especially for the O'odham students, what was happening to the Tohono O'odham people? . . . at every opportunity I got, I would remind them. . . .

Teachers' involvement in the lives of their students facilitated a disposition to center on the dynamic reality of the students themselves. Mr. Kewa (6th-8th Math and Art teacher) reflected this approach as he described how he brought predominantly oral cultural practices into the classroom curriculum,

> . . . we always bring the students back to their families and their communities to find out what it is that you do, because there's no one ultimate way that, uh, culture is taught or learned or practiced.

High levels of teacher investment in students was particularly important, as students often left underperforming and under-resourced districts to attend UNMS. This did not mean that all students were testing academically behind grade level; however, many were, and as seen from the previous student reflections, students came to UNMS with a history of negative school experiences. To interrupt negative histories of schooling, teachers at UNMS treated teacher-student-family relationships as critical elements for student success.

The Parents

Because UNMS was a choice school, it required parent agency to pursue choice. Choice generally resulted in positive parent feedback toward the school. Similar to the students' observations, parents hoped that UNMS would get their children away from what one mother described as an "ABC's education," or "drug infested schools." With little resources for private education, UNMS was a sought-out alternative. It was not uncommon to hear parents share the responsibility of protecting UNMS as a productive academic alternative for community youth. Parents would voice to teachers and school staff behaviors they wanted to see kept out of UNMS, for example, visible displays of gang affiliations, or disrespect for tribal traditions. Many parents made it known that they selected UNMS for their children in part because it separated them from social influences they found harmful or unhealthy.

There was a discourse of "opportunity" associated with the school. One mother's reflection on her then 7th grade son's moments of academic apathy underscores a common perception among parents.

> Leon's mom says she reminds [Leon] that he does not have to go to UNMS, he can be enrolled at Mountain Middle School.[7] She says she

would gladly go to any kid at Mountain and offer to sponsor them and pay their transportation fee to UNMS. She says that she knows most of those kids would love to go to UNMS. The waiting list is long and it is a privilege that her son gets to attend the school. So she reminds him of this because it is not easy for her or him to have such long days or travel so far to get to the school.

(Field notes, 4/13/08)

Due to the distance between parents and the school itself, it was not common to see parents at school during the regular school day. However, outside of school events were well supported and attended by parents.

Bi-Cultural Curriculum

UNMS's bi-cultural curriculum aimed to articulate connections to local Indigenous knowledge across the state-mandated content areas. Classes were on block scheduling to facilitate more time for bi-cultural integration. Additionally, Native History and Culture, O'odham Language, and Native Arts were taken by all students across grade levels alongside state-mandated courses such as English Language Arts, Mathematics, Science, etc. UNMS's bi-cultural focus is captured in this statement from its charter application,

> We believe that with a firm base in cultural heritage students can meet the highest expectations both academically and socially. Cultural knowledge alone, however, is not enough in today's globalizing world. Students must also know how to interact with and learn from diverse cultures.
>
> (UNMS Charter application)

The school's emphasis on academic rigor was met through a higher grading scale (below 70% was considered failing), as well as through collaborations with the local university and academic tutoring to support student development of academic skills.

As an example, the 6th, 7th, and 8th grade science classes which I taught featured regular collaboration with the school's O'odham language instructor. We worked together to integrate Western science concepts alongside O'odham ways of knowing the natural world. Feedback solicited from students during the 2009–2010 school year captured ways students themselves made sense of the bi-cultural curriculum. When asked to reflect on the utility of bi-cultural content, students shared statements like these:

> It was helpful to [have O'odham language and science integrated] because I know now that there is always some way I could connect the O'odham culture to the modern world.
>
> *(8th grade student)*

. . . O'odham culture connects to language then to science. And if you put all these together you're just learning more.

(8th grade student)

Experiential learning trips were also hallmarks of UNMS's bi-cultural curriculum. Experiential learning trips occurred two to three times annually, and included activities such as hiking, archery, gender divided talking circles, and cultural lessons. The mandatory trips received support from families and community members. The trips took students to places connected with Tohono O'odham heritage, both sacred and historical, and incorporated tribal community members and oral traditions. UNMS staff consciously selected community leaders, elders, and tribal entrepreneurs to speak with students about building a strong sense of local identity and academic knowledge in order to persist through school.

The school's bi-cultural curriculum was a dynamically evolving local process which improved each year the school was open. Building comprehensive bi-cultural units was a ground-up effort, requiring a great deal of collaboration, which could not be purchased in boxed curriculum.

Why Close the School Despite Promising Practices?

Despite evidence that UNMS offered its students improved school experiences, academically, socially, and culturally, UNMS closed in June of 2010. What happened? And why?

According to AZ Learns, the Arizona Department of Education's accountability measurements that assessed school performance through state sanctioned standardized test scores, UNMS was labeled an "underperforming school" in the fall of 2007, after being open only one school year (2006–2007). The school leaders were under the impression that the first year's Arizona Instrument for Measuring Standards (AIMS) scores would serve as the baseline from which to measure the next year's student progress, or Adequate Yearly Progress (AYP). This was not the case, and although there was no baseline to decipher UNMS student growth, UNMS began its life from behind.

At the end of the 2007–2008 academic year, UNMS did not make AYP and was labeled "second year underperforming." Under mandate to develop a school improvement plan, UNMS teachers spent the beginning of the 2008–2009 academic year studying the individual test scores of students to identify trends of strength and areas for improvement. Through a composite analysis of AIMS test data, teachers were shocked to discover two trends: 1) when examined individually, students at UNMS demonstrated improvements on standardized tests from year to year; and 2) due to the school's small class sizes (no more than 20 students in a grade level), the Arizona Department of Education's (ADE) assessment formula was drawing from previous years' AIMS scores to create data sets of 30 students per grade level to calculate AYP growth. This inaccurate information was used to find the class test score average for the current year, and consequently used to calculate AYP. Not only did UNMS draft an improvement plan, but it did so while struggling to see how such faulty test score analysis on the part of the state could serve as the basis for judging its success with students.

The national financial crisis of 2008 prompted major budget cuts to the state's public education programs, a reality which impacted UNMS's ability to receive support from a school improvement coach (a mandate of NCLB). Statewide cutbacks to education and bureaucratic personnel shifts obscured how and to whom the school's administrators needed to document the implementation of its improvement plan. This circumstance was not helped by the school's turnover in leadership: in four years, the school saw three directors. While leadership turnover may appear surprising, it is not an uncommon circumstance in the early years of school growth and change in high-need schools (Orr, Berg, Shore, & Meier, 2008)

The circumstances of AYP did not improve, and regardless of changes made during the 2008–2009 school year, in the fall of 2009, UNMS was labeled a "failing" school by the ADE. The Arizona State Board for Charter Schools (ASBCS) scheduled a failing school site visit in November of 2009. Four state representatives arrived from the state capitol, and spent one day on the UNMS campus. The majority of the representatives' time was spent in small rooms with the school's leadership team and reviewing binders of administrative and curricular documentation. The one-day visit culminated in a public meeting with parents at the school site in order for the ASBCS to make clear to parents/guardians the implications of UNMS's failing status— potential school closure. Ten families, some of whom had multiple children enrolled at UNMS, traveled distances, borrowed cars, or took public transportation to attend the late afternoon meeting.

I attended the meeting with parents, an opportunity I leveraged in my role as a graduate student (the state representative said "no teachers allowed"). The ASBCS representative shared that the state would spend the following months deciding if UNMS would be allowed to stay open with a school improvement plan, or be closed completely. Upon hearing the implications, parents voiced their concerns with questions pregnant with emotion: "If the school closes, how will I find a new school that meets my daughter's needs like this one does?" Parents also shared statements such as, "I don't know what the school has done to not meet the state's expectations, but I do know that my child has learned a lot here . . . more than they learned at other schools." The ASBCS representative offered little response, except to direct parents to lists of other available public schools in the region.

Teachers went about the 2009–2010 school year focused on systematizing the bi-cultural curriculum and pedagogy, and focused on improving students' high-stakes standardized test scores using state endorsed standardized test study kits (e.g. on-line sample tests, and other pre-packaged benchmark assessment tools). Lawyers retained by the school's sponsoring not-for-profit agency negotiated the case of UNMS with the Department of Education. In efforts to "standardize" the school's practice, three of the teachers, including myself, passed the state's teacher credentialing exams to demonstrate progress toward gaining "highly-qualified" certification in our content areas. The school's principal issued all the teachers a standard lesson plan rubric. The school's leadership team drafted a plan to move away from block scheduling and limit the contact hours for O'odham language and culture classes. However, in March of 2010, the ASBCS sent UNMS, via email, a report from its November site visit. The ASBCS announced it intended to revoke the school's charter at the end of the academic year.

The school was given the option to relinquish the charter, or attend a hearing in late May to attempt to plead the case of UNMS before the ASBCS. Ironically, the date of the hearing was scheduled two weeks before the statewide release of the 2009–2010 AIMS scores. In hopes of positive AIMS test results, the UNMS school board requested, through its attorneys, a hearing extension until early June of 2010. The request was denied. With limited funds, a lack of Native American advocacy/representation on the ASBCS board, and a fear that revocation of the school's charter would impact the status of its sister high school charter, the school board held a closed-door session which resulted in a vote to relinquish the UNMS charter. At the time of this decision, the school board had lost significant community representatives and was in the process of filling the school board seats. The board subsequently had difficulty making quorum for its meetings, causing the burden of the charter's future to fall on the shoulders of four board members, all of whom were employees (teachers) at UNHS.

In the early days of June 2010, UNMS closed out its fourth and final school year. UNMS teachers, disappointed and frustrated, maintained resolve to work through closure in the most productive way with students. The last day of school closed in a celebration led by teachers, students' families, and invited community members. Arranged in the school's parking lot, site to years of weekly prayer circle gatherings, UNMS students danced a traditional give-away dance to end their time together. Students, teachers, families, and friends sang, cried, and prayed under the blazing Arizona sun. Balancing years of accomplishment with the temporal disappointment of closure, teachers and staff watched the bus pull away from the school building for the last time. Exhausted, teachers spent the next two to three days packing up rooms in relative silence, and semi-disbelief that the materials painstakingly collected and developed over the course of years would no longer have a home or an audience. All solemnly parted ways, turning in keys, and leaving the small unconventional school building in search of needed respite and future employment.

Throughout the battle to justify the promising practices of UNMS in the face of state scrutiny, staff compiled charts and graphs of high-stakes test data. These comparisons, even when using such a limited tool as standardized assessment tests, showed that UNMS's test scores were higher than those of other schools serving a similar population, both urban and rural. This evidence did not prove compelling enough for the state at the time. In early July of 2010, the state released the results of the 2009–2010 high-stakes accountability testing, and UNMS was labeled a "performing" school according to AZ Learns assessment standards. The painful irony of this label came too-little-too-late, for UNMS had already relinquished its charter.

How Context-Blind Policy Results in Failures

What do we learn from the complicated case of UNMS? During its four years of operation, UNMS cultivated a locally meaningful approach to education as characterized by its students, their families, and its educators (Anthony-Stevens, 2013). The school was in a constant process of negotiating and articulating the meaning of bi-cultural schooling to best serve the complex lives of its students. This process was far from perfect, yet it offered much needed opportunities to its students. The impacts of the school on the educational trajectories of its students are not easily quantifiable on standardized tests or in snap-shot measurements, and surly could have benefited from more participatory support for improving areas of weakness and drawing on areas of strength. The school's birth and closure demonstrates the catch-22 of policy and offers a nuanced portrait of deep-rooted inequities which continue to deny Indigenous and minoritized youth educational opportunity in the U.S., even as minoritized communities strategically take up choice options in hopes of interrupting intergenerational educational disparities.

The appropriation of charter funding by Indigenous communities to develop education programs that serve the unique circumstances, needs, and aspirations of Native students within school climates of respect for local identity, high levels of student engagement, and negotiations of bi-cultural knowledge, offered the promise "for Indian communities to restore educational governance and decision making to the local level and to change the course of history in Indian education" (Belgarde, 2004, p. 119). To be clear though, the "opportunity" in charter policy has to be interpreted against the deplorable educational experience afforded to Native students across the United States (McCarty, 2009). Generations of school violence through government sponsored boarding schools (Adams, 1995), and a half-century of institutional racism projected through deficit ideologies and remedial courses meted to Native students on and off reservations (Lomawaima & McCarty, 2006) fail to be captured in the policy narrative which presents charters as *the* answer to class and race opportunity gaps in public schools. The desire of communities like UNMS to increase academic achievement, a desire for accountability, and a desire for increased educational relevancy and innovation are minimal opportunities which should be afforded all children, and arguably are processes to be taken up *with* communities, not in spite of them.

A significant factor in charter policy is a short timeline of closure if schools do not demonstrate academic improvement (Powers, 2009). School closures disproportionally impact communities of color, and rest on very little evidence that closure results in increased academic performance among poor students and students of color (Kirshner, Gaertner, & Pozzoboni, 2010). UNMS represented an alternative to entrenched educational opportunity denial, and although these perspectives were voiced and documented, the needs of its community were disregarded by policy enactors. The slow violence of educational reform thus can be seen to build on decades of community abandonment (Aggarwal, Mayorga, & Nevel, 2012). The violence began well before UNMS was labeled underperforming and was not offered sustainable support from the state to structure multiple levels of success for and with its students. Rationalizing closure based on snap-shot standardized test scores avoids acknowledgement of a century of race-based, class-based inequity, and if that is not enough, ignores the contemporary voices of UNMS stakeholders (parents, teachers, students). Community-driven not-for-profit charters attempting to address root issues of educational inequity must contend with policy which perpetuates educational inequity (Goodyear-Ka'ōpua, 2013), a reality exacerbated within a neoliberal policy landscape forcing public school closures in our nation's most underserved communities, and turning over the current and future efforts to address race and class-based inequities to profit-drive charter corporations, with ineffective results (Fabricant & Fine, 2012) Charter schools as a vehicle for curbing persistent inequity "moves us toward short-term solutions that are unlikely to address the long-term underlying problems" (Ladson-Billings, 2006, p. 4), leaving the longstanding "achievement gap" untraversed in the greater educational landscape.

The failure of policy to offer better school options to its targeted demographic is at best an unintended consequence, and at worst masked hegemony. The portrait of UNMS challenges policy to see that choice coupled with shallow assessment measurements unfairly reduce systems of inequity into burdens of individual communities and silence the daily perseverance of families as they fight on unequal terms to access schools which support the well-being of their children.

Notes

1 "Achievement gap" is in parentheses to refer to Ladson-Billings' (2006) uses of the term. I concur with Ladson-Billings that a focus on "the gap" is misplaced. Instead, we need to look at the "education debt" that has accumulated over time, comprised of historical, economic, sociopolitical, and moral components.
2 *Minoritized* is used to refer to groups and identities often referred to as "minority" groups. Minority status is a socially constructed concept, thus use of the term *minoritized* allows for emphasis on minoritization as a product of social interaction and social structures.
3 Urban Native Middle School is a pseudonym. All specific names of places and schools are pseudonyms in order to protect the identity of the research participants.

4 This research is part of a four-year ethnography which documented three years of UNMS's operation (2007–2010), and one-year post school closure (2010–2011). See Anthony-Stevens (2013).

5 The Tohono O'odham Nation is among the largest American Indian tribes, with its contemporary land base beginning roughly 20 miles outside of the urban area where UNMS was located.

6 The majority of Native-serving schools in the U.S. are dominated by White/non-Native teachers (Lee, 2015).

7 Mountain Middle School is a pseudonym.

References

Adams, D. W. (1995). *Education for extinction: American Indians and the boarding school experience 1875–1928*. Lawrence, KS: University Press of Kansas.

Aggarwal, U., Mayorga, E., & Nevel, D. (2012). Slow violence and neoliberal education reform: Reflections on a school closure. *Peace and Conflict: Journal of Peace Psychology*, 18(2), 156.

Andre-Bechely, L. (2013). Could it be otherwise? Parents and the inequalities of public school choice. New York: Routledge.

Anthony-Stevens, V. E. (2013). Indigenous students, families and educators negotiating school choice and educational opportunity: A critical ethnographic case study of enduring struggle and educational survivance in a Southwest Charter School. (Unpublished dissertation). The University of Arizona, Tucson, AZ.

Belgarde, M. J. (2004). Native American charter schools: Culture, language, and self-determination. In Rofes, E., & Stulberg, L. (Eds.), *The emancipator promise of charter schools: Toward a progressive politics of school choice* (pp. 107–124). Albany, NY: SUNY Press.

Brayboy, B. M. J., Faircloth, S. C., Lee, T. S., Maaka, M. J., & Richardson, T. A. (2015). Sovereignty and education: An overview of the unique nature of indigenous education. *Journal of American Indian Education*, 54(1), 1–9.

Buchanan, N. K., & Fox, R. A. (2003). To learn and to belong: Case studies of emerging ethnocentric charter schools in Hawai'i [Electronic Version]. *Education Policy Analysis Archives*, 11(8), 1–23.

Cullen, J., Jacob, B., & Levitt, S. (2005). The impact of school choice on student outcomes: An analysis of the Chicago Public Schools. *Journal of Public Economics*, 89, 729–760.

Fabricant, M., & Fine, M. (2012). Charter schools and the corporate makeover of public education: What's at stake? New York: Teachers College Press.

Fenimore-Smith, J. K. (2009). The power of place: Creating an indigenous Charter School. *Journal of American Indian Education*, 48(2), 1–17.

Fuller, B. F., & Elmore, R. (1996). Who chooses? Who loses? Culture, institutions and the unequal effects of school choice. New York, NY: Teachers College Press.

Goodyear-Ka'ōpua, N. (2013). *The seeds we planted: Portraits of a native Hawaiian Charter School* (Vol. 26). Minneapolis: University of Minnesota Press.

Kirshner, B., Gaertner, M., & Pozzoboni, K. (2010). Tracing transitions the effect of high school closure on displaced students. *Educational Evaluation and Policy Analysis*, 32(3), 407–429.

Ladson-Billings, G. (2006). From the achievement gap to the education debt: Understanding achievement in US schools. *Educational Researcher*, 35(7), 3–12.

Lee, T. S. (2015). The significance of self-determination in socially, culturally, and linguistically responsive (SCLR) education in Indigenous contexts. *Journal of American Indian Education, 54*(1), 10–32.

Lomawaima, K. T., & McCarty, T. L. (2006). "To remain an Indian": Lessons in Democracy from a century of Native American education. New York, NY: Teachers College Press.

McCarty, T. L. (2009). The impact of high-stakes accountability policies on Native American learners: Evidence from research. *Teaching Education, 20*(1), 7–29.

McCarty, T. L. (2012). Enduring inequities, imagined futures—Circulating policy discourses and dilemmas in the anthropology of education. *Anthropology & Education Quarterly, 43*(1), 1–12.

McCarty, T., & Lee, T. (2014). Critical culturally sustaining/revitalizing pedagogy and Indigenous education sovereignty. *Harvard Educational Review, 84*(1), 101–124.

Meens, D. E., & Howe, K. R. (2015). NCLB and its wake: Bad news for Democracy. *Teachers College Record, 117*(6), n6.

Murphy, J., & Shiffman, C. D. (2002). *Understanding and assessing the charter school movement* (Vol. 6). New York, NY: Teachers College Press.

Orr, M. T., Berg, B., Shore, R., & Meier, E. (2008). Putting the pieces together leadership for change in low-performing urban schools. *Education and Urban Society, 40*(6), 670–693.

Powers, J. M. (2009). *Charter schools*. New York: Palgrave Macmillan.

Wells, A.S. (Ed.) (2002). Where charter school policy fails; The problems of accountability and equity (Vol. 12). Teachers College Press.

Wells, A.S., Lopez, A., Scott, J., & Holme, J.J. (1999). Charter schools as postmodern paradox: Rethinking social stratification in an age of deregulated school choice. *Harvard Educational Review, 69*(2), 172–205.

7 How Public-Private Partnerships Contribute to Educational Policy Failure

Frank Fernandez, Karla I. Loya, and Leticia Oseguera

Introduction

In recent years, new public management has started to shape educational policy. Tolofari (2005) observed that governments around the world are using public-private arrangements including "more contracting and out-sourcing" to run schools (p. 83). O'Toole and Meier (2004) examined more than 1,000 school districts in Texas, which contracted out for "a wide variety of activities, including services for students with special needs, cafeteria management, security, professional development, and so forth" (p. 345). According to O'Toole and Meier, the school districts that adopted public-private partnerships did not spend more on instruction or improve student outcomes, such as performance on state tests or college entrance exams (ACT and SAT). O'Toole and Meier's work identified problems with public-private partnerships by showing that they do not improve academic achievement. As external evaluators, we set out to determine whether a college access program, which was delivered through a public-private arrangement, increased college access and college-going among low-income underrepresented minority students. In this chapter, we share a case study that builds on O'Toole and Meier's work by showing that public-private partnerships are also not necessarily a reliable way to improve college access for low-income and underrepresented racial and ethnic minority students.

We began a series of interviews to evaluate a partnership between a federal agency (i.e., public partner) and a national non-profit organization (i.e., private partner) resulting in a college access program that we call Project GROW.[1] During one of our interviews, a coordinator proudly told us, "Nobody treats me like an outsider . . . I get full cooperation from anybody." For the coordinator, it was a statement of satisfaction—a sign of how deeply a grant-funded employee (i.e., private partner) was able to immerse himself in the local high school. At this particular site, the coordinator worked hard to tutor students with homework assignments. Along the way, he reached out to school principals, counselors, and teachers to build relationships and in his words "get their trust." Evidently those efforts worked, but another statement suggested that his efforts to cooperate with school officials may

have worked too well: "You almost don't know we're [Project GROW]."
On face value, the dynamic of the public-private partnership was evidently
not clearly structured.

Project GROW was funded by the federal government to deliver specific
services to improve college access, such as helping students apply for financial aid, providing tours of college campuses, and sending letters to parents
about the college admissions process. The Project GROW services were supposed to be separate from the work regularly performed by school officials.
As we continued our series of interviews, a pattern emerged. The coordinators worked hard and wanted to help students succeed. For example, one
coordinator told us that he would arrive at campus before the school day
even started to use his pickup truck to help plant flowers around campus.
On schoolwide testing days, he volunteered to carry staplers from classroom
to classroom. The coordinator found ways to keep busy and was appreciated by school principals, but many of his efforts were tangential to Project
GROW's core mission of improving college access.

We learned that in the early days of Project GROW, the coordinators
received training from the national office, and they held monthly meetings
or conference calls to share best practices. After several months, the professional development stopped due to budget cuts. The lack of training had
immediate and future impacts on the coordinators' practices and the documentation of their work that would eventually affect the program evaluation. When site coordinators encountered challenges (such as difficulty
using an online database for recording the number of students they helped),
the coordinators improvised and made judgment calls, which led to Project
GROW being inconsistently implemented across school sites. After the first
year, many program coordinators left to other jobs. The departing coordinators were sometimes replaced by new hires—all of whom were eager to help
students, but none of whom had received formal training to carry on and
document their work.

As outside evaluators, we found that despite good intentions and hard
work, Project GROW was poorly implemented in large part due to lack
of communication from the national office to the local coordinators about
which types of tasks were supposed to be completed, how they were supposed to accomplish those tasks, and why the tasks were important to the
success of the program. The federal government awarded several million
dollars to a national non-profit organization that spreads Project GROW
from state to state. Then the national Project GROW office selected state
partners who, in turn, identified local high schools that tended to serve low-
income and racial or ethnic underrepresented students. Each school site
hired program coordinators to work with students and reach out to parents
to improve access to higher education and build a culture that encourages
young students to attend college.

The national office for the non-profit organization (private partner)
encouraged a range of services that program coordinators could use to

prepare students for college, such as test prep for students to do well on college admissions tests or hosting information forums for parents. Additionally, program coordinators were told to keep track of their work using an online database (such as recording the number of times they interacted with students, the dates and durations of their interactions, and the types of assistance they delivered). Program coordinators worked diligently, but without regular communication about their progress, they lost their focus on delivering Project GROW services and implementing accountability measures. Often Project GROW staff were asked to take on duties ordinarily assigned to "regular" high school staff, so their roles on campus were blurred. Additionally, each partner (e.g., national office, state department of education, school principals, and program coordinators) was supposed to provide data to the program evaluation team to determine whether Project GROW was successful. However, the groups were not communicating, and most erroneously assumed that some other entity was collecting or had access to data.

In this chapter, we present a case study of policy failure resulting from poor public-private partnership communication based on our evaluation of Project GROW. We draw on our experiences and field notes from on-site interviews and what we learned in analyzing quantitative data from the Project GROW database that project coordinators used to record their work (for the purposes of this chapter, we focus on the qualitative parts of the program evaluation). Many people argue that public-private partnerships (i.e., state and federal agencies working together with non-governmental groups) can make educational policy initiatives more efficient and effective (e.g., Brodkin, 2007). However, our case study shows that without sufficient communication, there are several ways that public-private partnerships to improve educational equity can fail. All federally funded projects must include program evaluations, but our case study demonstrates that public-private partnerships are not able to oversee the collection of high-quality data without communication between multiple parties. Without good data, evaluators cannot perform the types of analyses that show whether policy interventions achieve their intended outcomes. Thus, poor record keeping and data tracking represents a second failure in that the public-private partnership cannot be shown to be effective or efficient at meeting policy goals. We end the chapter by offering suggestions to improve educational policy and school success.

School Reform and Public-Private Partnerships

We draw on studies of public administration and analyze Project GROW as a public-private partnership. Traditionally, governments allocated money to state agencies and local schools that hired and managed public employees. However, under the "new public management" approach, government leaders privatize programs or contract with third parties to deliver services (Brodkin, 2007). Public-private partnerships are meant to reduce costs and increase efficiency, but researchers have pointed out that new public management reforms rarely live up to such expectations (e.g., Hodge, 1999; Lowery, 1998, 1999; van Thiel, 2004).

Scholars of public administration have argued that several issues prevent public-private partnerships from being effective. Kirkpatrick (1999) examined the ways that networks of public agencies and private actors work together to deliver services. Based on his review of the literature, Kirkpatrick concluded that public-private partnerships suffer from "long-term instability" because many actors view their networks as "purely temporary phenomena" (p. 10). Moreover, public and private organizations must establish "trust-based relationships in a context where there is relatively limited trust between parties" (Kirkpatrick, 1999, p. 10). Additionally, partnerships are strained when there is uncertainty about whether government funding will continue to be available or whether employees will be able to keep their jobs (Kirkpatrick, 1999).

Kirkpatrick also acknowledges that trust is a necessary, but not sufficient, component of a successful public-private partnership. Paradoxically, there are "unintended consequences of trust" (p. 10). Public-private partnerships are supposed to reflect structured agreements between independent organizations with complementary goals. However, partnerships can begin to break down if people develop such strong relationships that employees from one organization essentially go to work for the partner organization. In such a case, employees may stop fulfilling their original job duties and be less effective at working toward the outcomes that inspired the public-private partnership. In other words, public-private organizations can focus too much on developing trust and not enough on accountability or communication.

In the sections that follow, we suggest that Project GROW implementation can be understood according to new public management principles. We draw on Kirkpatrick's work to illustrate why the public-private partnership was ineffective. Kirkpatrick highlighted several challenges that prevent public-private partnerships from being successfully implemented, and we find that each of the challenges applies to different partners or stages of the case study. We explain that a network of governmental (i.e., public) and non-governmental (i.e., private) actors failed to properly implement Project GROW, including its evaluation component, and argue that educational innovations, which rely primarily on new public management principles, may not be sufficient to create more successful schooling that can improve equity. We draw on our experiences as external evaluators to describe how new public management principles may contribute to educational initiative failures.

Project GROW as a Public-Private Partnership

Project GROW is a federally sponsored college access program that was implemented at several school districts in a Mid-Atlantic state. The federal government and a state department of education established a public-private partnership with a non-profit organization, which we refer to as the Project GROW national office. The federal government awarded several million dollars to provide programs and services to low-income and racial or ethnic underrepresented high school students, who for a variety of reasons tend to be less likely to attend college than students in affluent schools (e.g., Sólorzano, Villalpando, & Oseguera, 2005). The Project GROW national office accepted the federal money and found a state partner (i.e., department of education) that would help identify schools that enrolled Project GROW's target population. Additionally, the state department of education had to agree to provide matching grants to help offset the costs of hiring Project GROW program coordinators for each school site. Together, the federal and state governments committed to providing three years of funding to promote college access and reduce opportunity gaps at some of the state's most racially diverse and low-income high schools.

The state department of education also allocated a six-figure sum to pay for a mixed-method evaluation of Project GROW. The Department of Education's investments were significant because at the time the program started, the state budget was still strained from the Great Recession. At the local school sites, districts contributed staff time and school space to host the college access program. Although the program coordinators worked in local schools, they were hired to provide Project GROW services that offered something new and different than other school counseling or after-school programs.

The Mid-Atlantic program was part of a national initiative to create college access centers, separate from existing academic counseling offices, where students could receive personalized services in welcoming environments. Project GROW focused on providing services that were supported by empirical research on college access. In addition to helping students complete homework assignments, Project GROW coordinators were to offer services such as: help students apply to college, seek financial aid, tour college campuses, and prepare to take standardized college entrance examinations (e.g., ACT/SAT tests). Researchers have argued that educational programs should draw on "community cultural wealth" to help racial or ethnic underrepresented students; therefore, Project GROW was also designed to engage parents and communities in the success of their children and local schools (e.g., Yosso, 2005).

Project GROW received support from public partners at different levels, ranging from the federal government to the state department of education and down to local school sites. Although several public entities had stakes in the successful implementation of Project GROW, the program coordinators were primarily accountable to the national office, which facilitated the partnership. In the subsections below, we draw on Kirkpatrick's (1999) work to describe how three different sets of challenges affected the public-private partnership.

A Lack of Long-Term Stability and Trust Among Program Partners

Even though several stakeholders were invested in the success of Project GROW, the policy innovation failed because the partnership was viewed as temporary by the various partners. Even though Project GROW was funded as a multi-year program, three years was a relatively short timeline considering that it takes four years for most students to complete high school. Furthermore, 12 schools were selected as Project GROW sites, but not all the sites had services for the duration of the public-private partnership (and one of the 12 school sites that was to serve as a control site ended up not participating in the evaluation). Due to funding challenges, only five sites received Project GROW services during the third year of the program, and even these services were reduced. In reality, the three-year public-private partnership had a much shorter horizon across sites.

The partnership was championed by leaders in the national program office and the state department of education. After early enthusiasm subsided, the trust and relationships that underpinned the public-private relationship were lost when the state department of education's grant manager left the position. It took the state department of education more than half of one year to hire someone to fill the grant coordinator role, and that person was assigned to work on the partnership with Project GROW as one of many other job duties. Within the first year, most sites experienced Project GROW staff turnover as well as turnover in leadership for the local school sites. Before the grant funds were expended, there was also change in Project GROW leadership. Thus, the public-private partnership experienced setbacks at the upper levels due to a lack of permanent staff who could build trusting, cooperative relationships for the duration of the policy initiative.

In practice, the lack of a trusting, long-term relationship resulted in poor communication between the public and private partners. For example, when it came time to determine the extent to which Project GROW was delivering services and improving college access, the various partners were unable to provide data to the evaluation team. Originally, the evaluation component, which had been vetted and approved by both the private and public partners, was supposed to be a short-term capstone that would only last a couple months. It was relayed to the evaluation team that the necessary data was already being collected and was available or could be easily accessed through the state department of education, local school district offices, or through the Project GROW national office. However, when the external evaluation team (including the chapter authors) requested school- and student-level data, we found that the state department of education and the Project GROW national office were not communicating about data collection or storage.

The data sharing issue demonstrated that public and private organizations entered into a partnership to implement an educational innovation, but they did not have protocols in place to share information. The partnership was a short-term arrangement, and the program ended before the partners resolved the data sharing problems. The evaluation team was invited to be the final partner in the collaboration, and the principal investigators prepared a proposal to analyze data that were said to be available from the primary partners. Both public and private stakeholders were involved in reviewing the program evaluation proposal and data access requests, so they were aware that multiple data sets were needed to address the evaluation questions in the final, funded evaluation proposal. However, we found that the Project GROW national office had not requested or received data from the department of education or the individual school districts.

After both the evaluation team and Project GROW staff requested data for the program evaluation, they found that their public partners were not willing to share data with the non-governmental organizations because they were concerned about data security. Although the decision not to share data may seem understandable, there were many ways that the state and local districts could have made the data sets anonymous to protect the identities of the participants. The data issues were further exacerbated by the fact that different software programs were being used at various school sites. Moreover, each partner used different student identification numbers for record keeping; however, most partners thought there was a unique common identifier across data sets. In most instances, public partners were unaware that they would be asked to provide data to the evaluators.

The evaluation team began communicating with the public and private partners to retrieve and analyze the data that were needed to complete the program evaluation. The evaluation team then utilized their own relationships and resources to try to gather data that would be beneficial to understanding Project GROW service delivery and college access outcomes. We found that the public partners did not have the technical capacity or will to retrieve the data sets that were under their control. Meanwhile, the Project GROW national office—through its program coordinators at each school site—collected data that were of such poor quality that they did not fully reflect the work that was being done at each high school. For instance, one coordinator implemented an innovative "e-mentoring program, but [she] didn't know how to log" it in the database. She also confessed that she had documented her work in many different files, which she never sent to the national Project GROW office.

During our interviews, it became clear that the national office had not sufficiently communicated with their own program coordinators, which meant that the staff who were tasked with collecting data for Project GROW had not been trained to use the online system, and that the site coordinators did not understand the importance or purpose of collecting the data. A Project GROW coordinator admitted she "never knew what reports [she] needed to have or what kind of data [she] needed to collect" and stated she "would have liked more information about that." Another coordinator assumed that the data collection was a formality, imposed by the national office to "protect their grant." This was most clearly expressed when a staff member admitted that he would exaggerate his entered data because he knew the national office wanted to see entries for students across a variety of college-going activities. For example, he explained that when he had not recorded communicating with parents in several weeks, he then reported that was how he spent his time (even if this was a simple hello during dismissal and no genuine interaction with parents); this type of after-the-fact service entry was echoed by other Project GROW coordinators. The program coordinators often used their own computers and programs to track their work, apart from what they reported to their national office. Thus, the coordinators were not opposed to collecting data, but the data they collected were not useful for the purposes of evaluating the program according to the design that was agreed upon by the public-private partners. By the time we discovered the severity of the data management issues, Project GROW had neared the end of its three-year funding period.

Challenges with Funding Renewal and Job Security

Communication challenges were compounded by high personnel turnover at multiple levels. One on-site coordinator stated that when she started working for Project GROW, there was tension at the school where she was assigned to work. According to the coordinator, the school officials had a bad experience when grant-funding from a similar project fell through, and several staff members were fired and had to re-apply for other jobs. Thus, concerns about funding and job security compounded the public-private partnership from the beginning of Project GROW's implementation. Additionally, Project GROW lost many of its on-site program coordinators during the three-year partnership period. For example, one coordinator found that she was left "trying to pick up the pieces" after she lost her co-worker in the first year of the program. Similar sentiments were expressed by Project GROW's staff at other sites.

In the first year, Project GROW was still expanding to new high school sites. However, during the second year, the state department of education submitted an incorrect funding request to the state legislature, which resulted in an extensive delay in allocating funds to support Project GROW. With financial uncertainty from its public partners, the Project GROW national office was unable to guarantee program coordinators employment for the third year of the program. Several program coordinators left to find jobs elsewhere, and Project GROW was discontinued at several sites. The remaining program coordinators were burdened by a lack of financial support and increased workloads. Some coordinators told us that they had difficulty providing Project GROW services at their sites because they were unable to hire tutors or that they had to lay off paid tutors.

When we conducted our final on-site interviews toward the end of the third year, Project GROW was in the process of laying off its remaining program coordinators. The coordinators were concerned about their job prospects, yet they continued working hard and were dedicated to helping students through the end of the third year. We found that because many of the program coordinators could not rely on the Project GROW national office for future employment, they built close relationships with the administrators at their local school sites and hoped to be employed by the school districts that were their public partners. Moreover, we found that the remaining coordinators began to prioritize finding new revenues to keep the program in operation. One Project GROW coordinator described that her role was "morphing into" something different from the job description she had originally accepted. Toward the end of the third year of Project GROW, she was spending time writing grant proposals, advocating for legislation to release more funding from the state, and engaging in "corporate begging" to try to get donations from local banks. She lamented that the local Project GROW sites needed full-time grant writers to make the program sustainable so that campus coordinators could focus on improving college access.

The Paradox of Too Much Trust

Kirkpatrick (1999) described the paradox of too much trust by writing that "high trust, while necessary for collaboration, is also a potential liability" (p. 10). In this sense, we identified examples of how the educational policy innovation may have been hampered by too much trust between partners. First, the Project GROW national office provided relatively little oversight and assumed that coordinators were doing what was expected of them in terms of collecting data correctly and providing appropriate college access services—despite little training or direction and few resources. One coordinator was asked whether she talked regularly with the national office, and she said, "No. Only if we have to. . . . To be honest, it complicates things; you forget you work for them." Similarly, another coordinator stated that even with digital communication (e.g., email and text messaging), it was simply easier to make decisions based on local needs than to reach out to the national office and wait for direction.

Second, the public-private partners had an extensive (but perhaps superficial) level of trust when it came to sharing data with the external evaluation team. After the parties developed and agreed to the evaluation design, they each assumed that their partners would be responsible for data management. In practice, most constituents reported to us that no one had informed them that specific academic data were needed, except for tracking the delivery of Project GROW services. One coordinator stated that the codes for entering services into the Project GROW database were "not too helpful." She explained: "We don't see why it even matters? . . . I feel like the database itself, it's nice to see how many times we've touched a student, but that's really all it's good for." The absence of training and communication resulted in a lack of understanding about the need to collect data to determine whether Project GROW services helped improve college access.

Finally, as illustrated by our anecdote at the beginning of the chapter, program coordinators developed close connections and trusting relationships with the public school administrators at their school sites, which often resulted in Project GROW staff doing work that extended beyond their contracted responsibilities. In one sense, it was important for them to have collegial working relationships. One site coordinator described that he was able to work with the existing counseling office after he "won over [the] most crusty guidance counselor." Another Project GROW coordinator stated, "We do morph to what the school needs." For example, the coordinator described focusing on helping the "bubble students" or those students whose scores were just below the cut point for being classified as academically proficient on the annual standardized test. By focusing on the "bubble students," Project GROW coordinators helped the school reach its adequate yearly progress goal for the first time in the history of the No Child Left Behind policy. A third coordinator described why it may have seemed logical for Project GROW coordinators to take on tasks that were only tangentially related to college access; he described that as a Project GROW coordinator, "you just gotta make yourself not the outsider," and his solution to that challenge was to make the school administration look good. The public-private partnership broke down when project coordinators effectively stopped working for the Project GROW national office and functioned as public employees. Instead of providing innovative program services, they were more likely to fill in as school staff and duplicate existing school services.

Discussion

In this chapter, we analyzed a case study of a public-private partnership failure to deliver an innovative educational program that was meant to improve college access for low-income and racial or ethnic underrepresented students. This particular program was implemented according to new public management principles (e.g., Brodkin, 2007). Our case study demonstrates that there are several potential challenges to improving educational equity through public-private partnerships.

One of the clearest challenges to public-private partnerships had to do with the inability (or reluctance) of public schools and the state department of education to share student information data with a private, non-profit organization. Kirkpatrick (1999) called for more hierarchical organizational structures to deal with the types of public-private coordination issues that affected Project GROW. If Project GROW services were delivered directly by the state, then there would likely be less of an issue with sharing data and duplicating data systems because everything could be kept in-house, conceivably using the same software and identification systems. Despite the challenges with private-public partnerships, it is unlikely that policymakers will want to return to traditional hierarchical or "top-down" arrangements because they perceive government employees and organizations to be inefficient. Additionally, many non-governmental groups benefit when they are given the opportunity to receive government funds to provide public services. Thus, it is likely not politically feasible to end public-private partnerships to administer educational policy innovations. Going forward, we offer several recommendations to better structure public-private partnerships.

Recommendations to Structure School Success

We argue that new public management approaches are not enough to structure school success, despite the belief that public-private partnerships are more effective and efficient than traditional approaches to delivering educational services. The federal government, state government, and local high schools came together to offer millions of dollars in resources and campuses spaces to help improve college access for low-income and underrepresented students. However, based on our qualitative interviews, we found that there were lapses in communication that manifested themselves as several different types of challenges (outlined above). Thus, each of the stakeholders initially contributed to the effort, but communication floundered. In the end, Project GROW was largely unsuccessful, and it is not clear that any of the stakeholders achieved their initial goals.

To structure school success, we encourage policy entrepreneurs and practitioners to focus on facilitating communication at all levels: within each partner organization, across partner organizations, among organization leaders, and among the staff who deliver services and—by their actions—implement the program. Communication is essential throughout the lifecycle of the program to ensure that educational programs are being implemented properly and are accountable, especially when there are personnel changes. Partners should clearly articulate and delineate responsibilities in writing to minimize the possibility that one organization will assume that another organization will complete tasks. For example, when groups collaborate to implement and evaluate programs, they should clarify the types of data that are being collected and which parties are responsible for managing and archiving data files. Finally, communication may help draw attention to the perils of too much trust. If the Project GROW national office had been in regular communication with program coordinators, the higher-level staff may have sensed that their employees had moved away from providing college access services and were often duplicating existing school programs.

Program Evaluations Can Help Us Understand Why Educational Policies Fail

Strong program evaluations can demonstrate the efficacy of the program to policymakers, make the case for additional funding, and provide data for research that improves our understanding about closing educational achievement gaps. In this era of accountability, it is imperative that educational initiatives include evaluation and assessment designs that are developed in sync with policy initiatives. Our case study demonstrates that even evaluations of failed programs offer lessons about how to structure school success.

Through site visits and qualitative data, we were able to understand some of the struggles that occurred throughout the duration of the program and understand why the policy innovation was largely unsuccessful. To be sure, the issues we identified with Project GROW did not occur because people wanted the program to fail or because public or private workers lacked commitment. Our qualitative interviews showed that program coordinators and government workers were trying to satisfy multiple demands using their own—albeit incomplete—understanding of the project. By and large, all the actors were well-intentioned and committed to providing services—which is consistent with previous literature on public administration (Brehm & Gates, 1993; Dilulio, 1994; Wise, 2004).

Program evaluations are important for documenting the success or failure of a policy innovation. However, program evaluations cannot be done well without a lead stakeholder to coordinate efforts, promote communication, conduct data quality checks, provide institutional memory for staff turnover, and train staff about the importance and methods for collecting high-quality data. Practitioners and researchers should work together to analyze data and help improve educational programs, seek additional funding, and suggest new educational policies.

Conclusion

This chapter tells the story of how an educational policy innovation was implemented through a public-private partnership and failed to achieve its stated goals—supplementing the work of high school counselors by providing unique services to improve college access for low-income, underrepresented minority high school students. Early in the process there was communication failure between the Project GROW national office, the onsite staff, and the state department of education that affected the implementation of the program. When we entered the picture as external evaluators, we found that the public and private partners invested a lot of money, energy, and time into the project, but communication issues led to inconsistently implementing the program, collecting low-quality data, not sharing data, and performing tasks outside their initial scope of work. By the end of Project GROW, many things were accomplished, yet none of the partners ended up with what they had hoped to achieve. In other words, nobody talked, everybody paid, and no one won.

Public and private organizations are both needed to improve schools and make them more equitable. However, partnerships between public and private organizations should be carefully structured, monitored, and evaluated to prevent policy innovation failures. It bears repeating that the people affiliated with Project GROW did a lot of good, even if the program failed to achieve its goals. By observing and interviewing on-site coordinators, we came to see how outside personnel can go into schools, adapt to local needs, build goodwill, overcome skepticism, and work hard to support students. These observations demonstrate that the problem was not a lack of will or motivation. In fact, many coordinators went beyond their job descriptions. Our findings suggest that the challenge is not to find people who will work harder or who will bring new perspectives from outside the school sites. Instead, moving forward, policymakers need to think about how to structure policy initiatives so they can be more successful for all stakeholders.

Note

1 We use "Project GROW" throughout the chapter as a pseudonym to protect the confidentiality of the program's personnel and participants.

References

Brehm, J., & Gates, S. (1993). Donut shops and speed traps: Evaluating models of supervision on police behavior. *American Journal of Political Science*, 37(2), 555–581.

Brodkin, E. Z. (2007). Bureaucracy redux: Management reformism and the welfare state. *Journal of Public Administration Research and Theory*, 17(1), 1–17.

Dilulio, J. D. (1994). Principled agents: The cultural bases of behavior in a federal government bureaucracy. *Journal of Public Administration Research and Theory*, 4(3), 277–318.

Hodge, G. A. (1999). Competitive tendering and contracting out: Rhetoric or reality? *Public Productivity & Management Review*, 22(4), 455–469.

Kirkpatrick, I. (1999). Markets, bureaucracy and public management: The worst of both worlds? Public services without markets or bureaucracy. *Public Money and Management*, 19(4), 7–14.

Lowery, D. (1998). Consumer sovereignty and quasi-market failure. *Journal of Public Administration Research and Theory*, 8(2), 137–172.

Lowery, D. (1999). Answering the public choice challenge: A neoprogressive research agenda. *Governance*, 12(1), 29–55.

O'Toole, L. J., & Meier, K. J. (2004). Parkinson's Law and the new public management? Contracting determinants and service-quality consequences in public education. *Public Administration Review*, 64(3), 342–352.

Sólorzano, D. G., Villalpando, O., & Oseguera, L. (2005). Educational inequities and Latina/o undergraduate students in the United States: A critical race analysis of their educational progress. *Journal of Hispanic Higher Education*, 4(3), 272–294.

Tolofari, S. (2005). New public management and education. *Policy Futures in Education*, 3(1), 75–89.

Van Thiel, S. (2004). Trends in the public sector why politicians prefer quasi-autonomous organizations. *Journal of Theoretical Politics*, 16(2), 175–201.

Wise, L. R. (2004). Bureaucratic posture: On the need for a composite theory of bureaucratic behavior. *Public Administration Review*, 64(6), 669–680.

Yosso, T. J. (2005). Whose culture has capital? A critical race theory discussion of community cultural wealth. *Race Ethnicity and Education*, 8(1), 69–91.

8 The Failure of Accountability in the Milwaukee Parental Choice Program

Michael R. Ford and William Vélez

In 1990, United States President George Bush came to Milwaukee, WI and declared, "When schools compete to attract students, that can't help but to improve education" (Ahlgren, 1990). Scholars John Chubb and Terry M. Moe (1988) shared Bush's optimism, arguing that the school autonomy created by a voucher program could broadly reform public education systems. Two and a half decades later, the National Assessment for Educational Progress Trial Urban Assessment showed that Milwaukee 8th graders trailed their average big city peers on both math and reading assessments. Just 4% and 16% of Black and Hispanic 8th graders respectively were deemed proficient in math, while 7% and 20% of Black and Hispanic 8th graders respectively were deemed proficient in reading. Plainly, 25 plus years of vouchers have not stopped Milwaukee from being one of the lowest performing cities, especially for ethnoracial pupils, on federal achievement tests.

Why did Milwaukee's voucher policy fail to substantively increase academic outcomes? Who or what is at fault? In this chapter, we argue that the failure of the Milwaukee Parental Choice Program (MPCP) to substantively impact academic achievement for Milwaukee K–12 pupils is a result of the absence of a democratic mechanism by which local voters can hold MPCP schools accountable. Never in the history of the MPCP have Milwaukee voters, who fund a sizable portion of the MPCP through their property tax levy, had the ability to cast meaningful votes on the trajectory of the program. Program regulations and participation requirements for both schools and families are determined by the legislature. Notably, the legislature has empowered the state Department of Public Instruction (DPI) to close MPCP schools for financial improprieties; however, the state has had very little academic control over schools. In addition, almost all of the political support for Milwaukee voucher expansion came from Republicans representing areas outside Milwaukee, while the Milwaukee legislative delegation consistently opposed the MPCP.

In this chapter, we explain the failure of the MPCP through a review of the diverse body of existing MPCP research. Specifically, we summarize the conditions that enabled the creation of the program, explain the governance structure of the MPCP compared to the traditional Milwaukee Public

Schools system, and review 25 years of scholarly research on the MPCP. We then use the review of existing research to present solutions that can help address the failure of Milwaukee's voucher policy to gain legitimacy and improve student outcomes, especially for minority pupils.

MPCP History and Implementation

The Milwaukee Parental Choice Program is the oldest and largest urban private school voucher program in the United States. Its origins can be traced back to Milton Friedman's seminal 1955 work, *The Role of Government in Public Education*, in which he proposed introducing market forces into America's public education system as a means to improve performance. Friedman's idea gained traction in Milwaukee due to a confluence of factors. First was the federal court finding that the Milwaukee Public Schools (MPS) system was intentionally and unconstitutionally segregated (Dougherty, 2004). The ruling resulted in a voluntary bussing program designed to desegregate MPS. However, a series of implementation blunders created a situation in which the burden of desegregation was placed primarily on minority families (Dougherty, 2004). Dissatisfaction with the desegregation process gave birth to a Black-empowerment movement that prioritized minority parent rights and Black-led institutions over desegregated schools.

The second factor was growing public dissatisfaction with the failure of MPS to reform from within. In previous work, one of the authors (Ford, 2015) details the growing critiques of Milwaukee's public education system between the years 1975 and 1990. Most notable was a 1980 article in the *Milwaukee Sentinel* (Staff, 1980) detailing that Milwaukee's reading scores were well below national averages despite ongoing claims to the contrary by the MPS school board and superintendent. These ongoing racial tensions and growing lack of public trust in the school system served to open up the policy window for radical change in Milwaukee's education system. Indeed, one of the assumptions behind school choice is that public schools would improve in the face of market competition from non-public organizations. In that regards choice reform could—at least in theory—serve as a panacea.

The third factor—championed through a unique alliance between Black Democratic elected officials in the City of Milwaukee and outstate Republicans—enabled voucher advocates to take advantage of the newly opened policy window (Kingdon, 1995). State Representative Annette "Polly" Williams, State Senator Gary George, and education reform activist Howard Fuller together brought critical on the ground support to the idea of a private school voucher program targeting low-income ethnoracial pupils. Williams, George, and Fuller all supported voucher reform as a social justice movement, arguing that school choice would empower low-income ethnoracial parents to have a say in the education of their children. Outstate Republican elected officials, as well as Republican Governor Tommy Thompson, embraced voucher reform in part due to their ideological belief in the power of market forces, the lower per-pupil cost necessary to fund a voucher pupil as opposed to an MPS pupil, and a desire to increase academic achievement levels in Wisconsin's largest city (Witte, 2000). This unique coalition was aided by Milwaukee's Bradley Foundation (which has long funded conservative causes such as school vouchers) and the Milwaukee Metropolitan Association of Commerce and its education reform consultant Susan Mitchell.

In 1990 the coalition of choice supporters helped pass, and Governor Thompson signed, legislation creating the MPCP. From the very beginning, the MPCP—though a major change in thinking—was an extremely limited experiment. Under the original MPCP law, no more than 1,000 Milwaukee children from households with incomes at or below 175% of the federal poverty level could receive a voucher worth up to $2,445 to attend the participating private school of their choice. Parents applied directly to the school they wished their child to attend. Schools participating in the MPCP faced numerous restrictions. First, due to constitutional concerns, only non-sectarian schools were permitted to participate. Second, voucher enrollment per school was limited to 49% of students (Pugh, 2015). Third, schools were not permitted to screen pupils for prior academic achievement, behavior, or anything else aside from income and residency in the City of Milwaukee. If a school received more applicants than there was space in any given grade level, a random lottery was required. Fourth, schools were required to accept the voucher as full payment. Last, schools were required to meet one of the following four academic requirements:

- Have 70% or more of program pupils advance on grade level;
- Have at least a 90% average attendance rate;
- Have at least 80% of program pupils demonstrate significant academic progress (as defined by the school); or
- Have at least 70% of program parents meet school-established participation criteria.

Establishing the Foundation for Policy Failure

In the 1990–1991 school year, just seven schools and 341 pupils participated in the MPCP. In comparison, MPS enrolled 92,816 students. The MPCP would remain a minor program until 1998, when the Wisconsin Supreme Court ruled that religious schools could participate in the voucher program. As can be seen in Figures 8.1 and 8.2, program enrollment and school participation numbers jumped considerably following the inclusion of religious schools.

In 1995, the program enrollment cap was lifted to 15% of MPS, and the 51% private-pay requirement was eliminated. As the program grew to be a major provider of publicly funded education in Milwaukee, concerns about the overall quality of MPCP schools grew, and a rash of high profile school

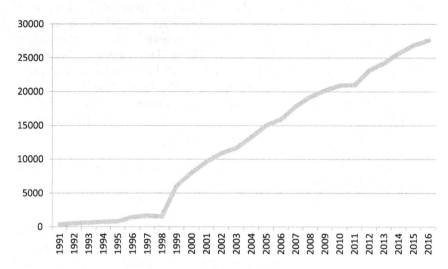

Figure 8.1 MPCP Program Enrollment History

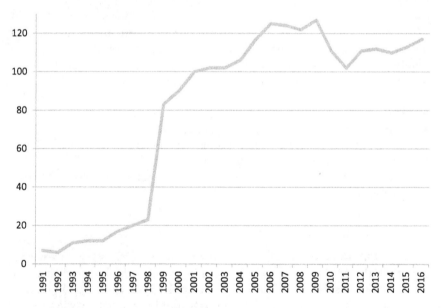

Figure 8.2 Number of MPCP schools by year

failures and incidents of criminal fraud committed by school leaders led to significant regulatory changes in 2003 and 2005.

Wisconsin 2003 Act 155 placed modest fiscal viability requirements on MPCP schools, giving the Wisconsin DPI authority to cut off voucher funding to schools demonstrating an ongoing fiscal concern. Act 155 also required schools to produce a valid City of Milwaukee occupancy permit prior to obtaining voucher revenue. Finally, Act 155 gave the Wisconsin state superintendent the ability to immediately terminate a school deemed to pose an imminent threat to the health or safety of pupils. In 2005 the Wisconsin legislature passed Act 125, a compromise bill that raised the enrollment cap of the MPCP to 22,500 pupils, required private schools to apply for and obtain accreditation from an approved third party, and to administer a nationally normed standardized test to all voucher pupils. However, Act 125 did not require schools to publicly release test score results.

The MPCP evolved further in 2009 with a high profile battle between conservative voucher advocates and Black Milwaukee reformers, arguably ending the longstanding strategic alliance between urban Democrats and outstate Republicans (Fuller, 2014). That same year saw the creation of the New Schools Approval board at Marquette University, a new barrier to entry designed to ensure new school quality, a requirement that MPCP schools administer and release the results of the state standardized tests for all MPCP pupils, and a variety of regulatory changes that required MPCP schools to create policies in key functional areas that mirror public school requirements (Pugh, 2015). More changes came in 2013, when Republican Governor Scott Walker signed legislation eliminating the enrollment cap, raising income eligibility to 300% of the federal poverty level, and allowing suburban schools to enroll voucher pupils.

Further Evidence of Not Meeting Student Needs

Existing research on MPCP impacts, academic and otherwise, have been the topic of significant academic study. We argue the research consensus on the MPCP reveals a general failure of voucher policy to deliver on its original lofty promise to substantively improve the overall quality of Milwaukee's education system. Consider first the city's lackluster performance on the Urban NAEP. Figures 8.3 and 8.4 display Milwaukee's most recent NAEP

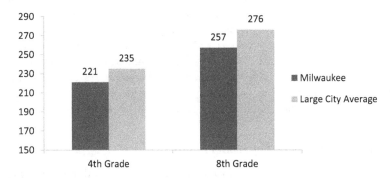

Figure 8.3 2013 Math NAEP Score Comparison

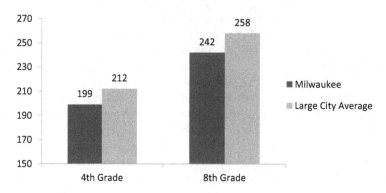

Figure 8.4 2013 Reading NAEP Score Comparison

scores compared with the average performance of the 21 urban districts that participate in the NAEP assessment. In all tested subjects and grades, Milwaukee scores trail large city averages. While the NAEP is just one measure of performance, the results establish that Milwaukee students, in general, trail their other large city peers.

A five-year state-mandated evaluation of the MPCP conducted by the School Choice Demonstration Project at the University of Arkansas also found limited evidence of sizable achievement gains spurred by vouchers. The project, completed in 2012, compared test score growth between a matched sample of MPCP and MPS pupils (Witte et al., 2012). The two groups had similar math and reading growth scores until the final year of the analysis, in which voucher pupils had significantly higher reading test score gains (Witte et al., 2012). The study group cautioned, however, that the gains could be attributable to the introduction of mandatory state testing for all MPCP pupils rather than to the voucher policy itself (Carlson, Cowen, & Fleming, 2014; Witte et al., 2014). The mandated study also found higher graduation and enrollment rates for MPCP pupils; however, that finding is subject to interpretation given the 56% attrition rate for MPCP pupils in the study (Cowen et al., 2013). Lastly, the study showed small test score gains within the public schools occurred when new MPCP schools opened in Milwaukee (Greene & Marsh, 2009). Overall, the recent evaluation conducted by the School Choice Demonstration Project shows, at best, a substantively small academic impact for voucher users, high attrition rates for voucher users, and a lack of clear conclusions as to the utility of vouchers.

Vouchers and the Impact of School Failure

Recent work by one of the authors focuses on the notable externality of school failures spurred by the introduction of market-based education reform in Milwaukee. Between 1991 and 2015, 41% of all schools that participated in the MPCP eventually failed (Ford & Andersson, 2016). A school failure is defined as a school that once enrolled voucher pupils ceasing to exist in any capacity following its exit from the MPCP. These 102 failed schools represent almost 70% of all start-up schools that ever participated in the MPCP. A separate study by Ford (2016a) quantifies the state investment in these failed institutions as $197.6 million between 1991 and 2013, and concludes that an outgrowth of Milwaukee's voucher policy is a significant public investment in impermanent institutions. While school closures are an inherent part of a market-based education system, and potentially desirable in the case of low-performing schools, legislative steps to reduce MPCP school failures, such as the introduction of new barriers to program entry in 2009, (Pugh, 2015) demonstrate a public intolerance for school closures.

Twenty-six years of voucher policy in Milwaukee created an incredibly complex and disjointed dual-education system in Milwaukee. Today, the traditional public schools enroll 75,749 students, while 27,619 attend a private school via a voucher. MPS is a highly centralized system, while the MPCP is a system of decentralized schools. Both systems are funded at different levels via different sources. MPS enrolls substantially higher numbers of special needs pupils than MPCP schools (Wolf, Witte, & Fleming, 2012). The public school system is governed by a democratically elected school board while the MPCP is governed by the state legislature. Voucher schools are not required to adhere to open meetings and records laws. MPS is generally supported by Milwaukee's Democratic legislative delegation while the MPCP is generally supported by non-Milwaukee Republicans. Despite these differences, both systems enroll primarily low-income ethnoracial pupils, and, we argue, face a common challenge of addressing Milwaukee's overall low level of academic performance.

Though Milwaukee's voucher policy has failed to substantively improve academic outcomes for Milwaukee pupils, its significant market-share (nearly 25% of Milwaukee K–12 students attend MPCP schools) has created the damaging consequence of permanence, i.e., despite the failure of voucher policy at this point, it appears highly unlikely the MPCP will be terminated. What happened and what can be done? In the following sections, we seek to explain why the MPCP has failed, who is at fault, and what can be learned from Milwaukee's voucher experience.

Why Did it Fail?

We argue that the failure of the MPCP to substantively improve the state of urban education in Milwaukee resulted from the program's failure to establish itself as a legitimate part of Milwaukee's public education system. Instead of being a partner in a cohesive effort to educate Milwaukee's low-income and largely minority pupils, the MPCP represented the creation of a dual education system that existed outside a traditional accountability structure. As Provan and Milward (2001) detailed, decentralized governance models, such as the MPCP, face an inherent legitimacy challenge tied to accountability. If the provider of a public good cannot be held accountable via the ballot box, how exactly can it be held accountable? The MPCP was and is a creature of the state, and citizens of Milwaukee did not and do not have local control over the MPCP, hence the voucher program lacks the electoral legitimacy and accountability provided by a school board (Lutz & Iannoccone, 2008).

But what is accountability? In education it has shown to be a vague concept that means different things to different audiences. For example, Van Dunk and Dickman (2003) used a case study of the MPCP to suggest that accountability comes in the form of transparency and regulation. Under theories of New Public Management, accountability and legitimacy for MPCP-style programs comes from the ability to be held accountable for performance (Kettl, 2005). Others, most notably Lutz and Iannoccone (2008) and Ravitch (2010), describe accountability as the ability of the electorate to affect the trajectory of local K–12 education through the ballot box. Market theorists such as Friedman (1955) and Chubb and Moe (1988) argue that voucher accountability means parents. Broadly, Milwaukee's voucher policy never clearly addressed the two key questions regarding accountability: who holds schools accountable, and for what?

As mentioned, adherents to market theory argue that voucher programs should be minimally regulated and that parents hold schools accountable via their educational choices (Merrifield, 2008). The early MPCP—despite its small size—reflected this school of thought, as schools were largely held accountable by parents for whatever it is parents desired of their child's schools. However, as the MPCP matured, its regulatory framework evolved in ways that moved away from parental-based accountability. The 2003 empowerment of state regulators to terminate a school for posing a threat to the health and safety of pupils or fiscal stress, for example, marked a change in philosophy in which state regulatory officials became the primary actor holding schools accountable for non-academic measures. The 2005 private accreditation requirement, for the first time, shifted the accountability function to third party agencies. Mandatory state testing, enhanced barriers to entry, and increased reporting requirements implemented between 2009 and to the present further muddled the MPCP accountability framework.

Simply, the answers to the two key accountability questions vary depending on the year of which they are asked and the audience who is being asked. As such, there is no clear understanding of what exactly is expected to result from MPCP policy, i.e., different audiences define success in different ways. From the perspective of MPCP schools, the concept of accountability is equally muddled. Are schools primarily accountable to parents and students, state regulators, or legislators? Are schools held accountability for test scores, fiscal health, program compliance, or parental demands?

A recent survey of voucher school leaders conducted by Ford (2016) finds that school officials are as divergent in their perceptions of their own responsibilities to the public as the public is in their expectations of the MPCP schools. For example, several school administrators defined accountability strictly as progress on standardized tests, while others gave broader answers such as "develop[ing] the whole child, not just academically, but socially, emotionally and creatively to prepare them for a healthy and productive life in society" (Ford, 2016, p. 19).

In 2003 Van Dunk and Dickman offered transparency as the solution to the MPCP accountability question. Their basic argument was that MPCP schools should report the same information as traditional public schools. The logic of Van Dunk and Dickman's (2003) approach strengthened as private schools in Milwaukee became increasingly reliant on voucher revenue. In the 2016 school year, only 21% of MPCP school enrollment was private-pay pupils (Ford & Andersson, 2016). In addition, 71 of the 117 participating MPCP schools enrolled 90% or more of their total student population via the voucher program. So, while technically not public institutions, MPCP schools are primarily publicly funded, which arguably supports Van Dunk and Dickman's (2003) case for transparency. However, the transparency requirements governing MPCP schools vary considerably from MPS. MPCP schools are not required to report student demographics such as race and special needs status, disaggregated test scores by student group, teacher qualifications beyond status as a college degree holder, graduation rates, attendance rates, or a host of other information required of public schools.

Arguably, the decentralized nature of the MPCP as well as the diversity of participating schools makes equal transparency requirements difficult and perhaps impossible to implement. Voucher advocates long warned that equal regulation would constitute excessive entanglement between the state and religious institutions, putting the constitutionality of the MPCP at risk (Bolick, 1998). In addition, MPCP data systems differ considerably from school to school. Wolf, Witte, and Fleming (2012), for example, document the varying ways in which private schools classify special needs students. While MPS has a strong bilingual program in place to serve language minority students since 1976, voucher schools frequently ignore the needs of this growing segment of Milwaukee's student population. A recent study of a voucher Catholic school enrolling mostly Latino students in the city of Milwaukee discovered that the mostly non-Latino staff was very insensitive to the language needs of their students, offering an English-only curriculum while many of the students needed ESL classes. In addition, the staff created an unwelcoming climate for Latino parents, rejecting their efforts to volunteer in school events and activities (Joseph, Velez, & Antrop-Gonzalez, 2016). The practical challenges of applying transparency requirements designed for public school systems to stand-alone non-public schools is a primary reason that recent attempts to incorporate voucher schools into the state of Wisconsin accountability system failed (Richards, 2015).

Given the size and complexity of the MPCP, the only workable answer to the accountability question—we argue—is a system in which Milwaukee voters have a direct say over the program. In such a system, the MPCP is accountable to Milwaukee residents for meeting their needs as expressed in the ballot box. The familiar accountability of local control is synonymous with American education and has, for over 200 years, provided accountably for a public education system in which goals and mechanisms are rarely universally agreed upon (Alsbury, 2008) When Milwaukee residents have expressed themselves at the ballot box, it was overwhelmingly in favor of local officials opposed to the MPCP. Throughout the MPCP's history, a majority of Milwaukee's legislative delegation was opposed to voucher policy (Ford, 2015). It is possible to argue that the MPCP was supported by Milwaukee residents, given the program's size. While true, it is also true that voucher users represent only a small percentage of Milwaukee's nearly 600,000 residents who, via their tax dollars, fund a significant share of the MPCP.

Though the funding mechanism has changed several times (see Pugh, 2015), Milwaukee residents in general have funded a large percentage of the cost of vouchers over the program's history. Between 2002 and 2013, 55% of the MPCP was funded directly through the state's general purpose revenue fund, while 45% of the cost of vouchers was funded through an aid reduction to MPS. MPS was empowered, and did offset the aid reduction via the local tax levy, meaning for all intents and purposes Milwaukee taxpayers funded 45% of the voucher program. The MPCP funding mechanism created numerous issues that at various times have been referred to as the choice program "funding flaw." First, the local share of voucher funding was larger than the average share of local funding for public education in the state, meaning, on average Milwaukee taxpayers funded a higher percentage of the cost of MPCP pupils than MPS pupils (Pugh, 2015). For several years the actual local cost of a voucher pupil was higher than that of an MPS pupil, so despite the lower level of state and local per-funding for vouchers, Milwaukee taxpayers actually suffered when a student transferred from MPS to the MPCP (Costrell, 2009). To make matters worse, the inability of MPS to count voucher pupils for state aid purposes, a key step in determining the share of state support given to all Wisconsin school districts, punished Milwaukee taxpayers by driving up the per-pupil tax rate for MPS pupils (Costrell, 2009). The bottom line is that the MPCP, for much of its history, resulted in overall saving for non-Milwaukee districts, while simultaneously increasing the tax level for Milwaukee residents. The MPCP funding situation caused many local Milwaukee leaders, including mayor Tom Barrett, to be tepid in their support for the MPCP (Barrett, 2011). We share the example of the "funding flaw" because it is indicative of the inability of Milwaukee residents and leaders to influence MPCP policy, and the tendency for political battles over school vouchers to be totally unrelated to the academic impacts of the program.

Overall, the absence of direct local electoral accountability for Milwaukee's voucher program has created an incredibly fragmented and inefficient approach to public education in Milwaukee. Students move back and forth between school systems with different approaches to funding, transparency, and administrative record keeping. Parents make choices between and within systems with no common mechanism for reporting student outcomes. Schools themselves fight for market-share while elected officials throughout the state fight a partisan battle over the trajectory of Milwaukee's voucher policy. While a local democratically elected body overseeing the MPCP may not have led to academic success, it would have provided the built-in electoral legitimacy provided by school boards, and given a mechanism by which those affected by voucher policy could direct its fate.

Who is at Fault?

Multiple actors share the blame for the failure of the MPCP to become a legitimate part of Milwaukee's public education infrastructure. Voucher advocates for years resisted the use of state standardized tests on the grounds that MPCP schools were fully private institutions despite their overwhelming reliance on government revenues (Ford, 2015). The resistance to embracing their role as a core element in Milwaukee's public education scene branded the MPCP schools and advocates as threats to the public education system rather than partners. The MPS school board is also culpable. Aside from a short period in the late 1990s and early 2000s, there is little evidence of MPS working constructively with MPCP leaders and advocates (Chandler, 2002). However, the failures of MPCP policy can be placed primarily at the feet of state policymakers who failed to define the purpose of the voucher policy at the MPCP's inception, failed to address the program's deficiencies in a timely manner, and most importantly failed to create a system for local electoral accountability.

The original MPCP, by design, ignored the accountability question (Witte, 2000; Van Dunk & Dickman, 2003). It was taken for granted that private schools were a superior alternative to MPS, and hence no mechanism for holding MPCP schools accountable to the public was included in the legislation. Though schools were required to meet one of the four mentioned performance requirements, never in the history of the MPCP were schools punished for failing to adhere to this regulation (Ford, 2015). Simply, without cohesion around the concept of accountability, it was impossible for the MPCP to be an accountable public policy. State policymakers also grossly underestimated the difficulty of the task of educating low-income pupils, and failed to consider the externality of school failure inherent in a market-based education system (Ford & Andersson, 2016). If the original MPCP law included reasonable barriers to entry and testing requirements, it is possible that the program's performance challenges and high rate of school failure could have both been identified and mitigated.

State policymakers also failed to take advantage of several critical moments in the MPCP's history when a course correction could have legitimatized Milwaukee's voucher policy. The 1998 religious expansion, which transformed the MPCP from a minor experiment to a significant educator of Milwaukee pupils, could have been accompanied by structural changes to the program's accountability policies or softer efforts to engage the Milwaukee legislative delegation as a constructive partner in MPCP governance. The high-profile accounts of troubled schools in 2003—most notably the state's inability to close a voucher school run by a convicted rapist—was another missed opportunity to normalize Milwaukee's voucher policy (Ford, 2015). While the 2003 crisis did spur new legislation empowering the state to shut down a school posing an imminent threat to safety, it did not include any new academic accountability mechanisms (Pugh, 2015). The first-time release of standardized test scores in 2010, which showed that MPCP students scored similar to MPS pupils, was yet another chance for policymakers to recognize the similar challenges faced by MPCP and MPS pupils.

All of these potential decision points offered opportunities for a constructive pause, and discussion about how to make the MPCP a more effective and credible public policy. Yet, any attempt to create a local accountability mechanism for the MPCP took a backseat to the drive for program expansion at the behest of non-Milwaukee legislators. The program expanded to include religious schools in 1998, the enrollment cap was lifted in 2006 and finally eliminated in 2011, and income eligibility requirements were raised significantly to ensure a large majority of Milwaukee pupils are now eligible for vouchers (Pugh, 2015). The actions of pro-voucher policymakers, whatever the stated intent, demonstrated a preference for a dual education system lacking local electoral accountability rather than a unified effort to improve outcomes for Milwaukee pupils.

Conclusion and Moving Forward

In this chapter, we argue that the lack of local electoral accountability for Milwaukee's voucher system prevented the MPCP from being a legitimate part of the city's education infrastructure, resulting in an inevitable policy failure. We summarized the conditions that led to the creation of the Milwaukee voucher program, explained its governance structure compared to MPS, synthesized the academic research on the MPCP, and placed responsibility for the policy failure on the pro-MPCP policymakers who placed the goal of MPCP expansion ahead of the goals of local accountability and improved academic outcomes. The presented analysis yields several lessons for Milwaukee, and other areas considering the implementation of voucher policy.

First, demonstrated local support and a mechanism for the local electorate to influence voucher policies is a necessary component of a successful voucher policy. Throughout the MPCP's history, Milwaukee voters were unable to influence the direction of voucher policy via the ballot box. Hence, Milwaukee taxpayers funded a significant portion of a local program which they had no means to hold accountable. The structure, we argued, delegitimized the program throughout its history. Second, transparency and funding coherence are necessary if voucher programs are to be legitimized as a provider of public education. The lack of MPCP transparency, as well as the separate funding mechanism for MPCP and MPS, created a dual education system between which constructive comparisons and cooperation were impossible. Third, the goals of a voucher program should be clearly defined by policymakers in order to create a baseline from which to measure success. Was the MPCP about improving test scores for voucher users, public school users, increasing graduation rates, saving money, empowering parents, advancing an ideology, or something else? Without public agreement on the goals of an education policy—and a forum by which the goals can be legitimately articulated—a policy is destined to fail.

What would a local mechanism for accountability look like? We envision an elected body, similar to a school board (if not an actual existing school board), empowered to regulate the schools participating in a school choice program. Such a board would be legitimized by local voters, bound by state reporting requirements applicable to traditional public school districts, and capable of making course corrections in a timely manner. While such a body is inconsistent with the pure-market ideology behind private school vouchers, it is consistent with the democratic values of local control that have long granted legitimacy to public goods and services. This is, we believe, the most transparent approach to genuine policy reform.

References

Ahlgren, P. (1990, June 10). School choice program transcends local roots, *Milwaukee Journal*.

Alsbury, T. L. (Ed.). (2008). *The future of school board governance.* Lanham, MD: Rowman & Littlefield Education.

Barrett, T. (2011, April 24). In calculating school aid, count all the kids. *The Capital Times*. Retrieved from http://host.madison.com/ct/news/opinion/column/tom-barrett-in-calculating-school-aid-count-all-the-kids/article_e940a1a3-7dc8–5f38-bf1b-e001ddd75b7e.html

Bolick, C. (1998). How we won the choice case. *Wisconsin Interest, Fall/Winter*, 43–52.

Carlson, D. E., Cowen, J. M., & Fleming, D. J. (2014). Third-party governance and performance measurement: A case study of publicly funded private school vouchers. *Journal of public administration research and theory, 24*(4), 897–922.

Chandler, K. (2002, November 1). Us vs. them. *Milwaukee Magazine, 27*(11).

Chubb, J. E., & Moe, T. M. (1988). Politics, markets, and the organization of schools. *The American Political Science Review, 82*(4), 1066–1087.

Costrell, R. (2009). Who gains? Who loses? The fiscal impact of the Milwaukee Parental Choice Program. *Education Next, 9*(1), 63–69.

Cowen, J. M., Fleming, D. J., Witte, J. F., & Wolf, P. J. (2012). Going public: Who leaves a large, longstanding, and widely available Urban Voucher Program? *American Educational Research Journal, 49*(2), 231–256.

Cowen, J. M., Fleming, D. J., Witte, J. F., Wolf, P. J., & Kisida, B. (2013). School vouchers and student attainment: Evidence from a State-mandated study of Milwaukee's Parental Choice Program. *Policy Studies Journal, 41*(1), 147–168.

Dougherty, J. (2004). *More than one struggle: The evolution of Black School Reform in Milwaukee.* Chapel Hill, NC: The University of North Carolina Press.

Ford, M. (2015). Nailing shut the policy window: The policy evolution of America's first Urban School Voucher Program. *Journal of Public and Nonprofit Affairs, 1*(2), 87–99.

Ford, M. R. (2016). Milwaukee voucher-school leaders' views on accountability: What are they, and why do they matter?. *Leadership and Policy in Schools, 15*(4), 481–499.

Ford, M. R. (2016a). Funding impermanence: Quantifying the public funds sent to closed schools in the nation's first Urban School Voucher Program. *Public Administration Quarterly, 40*(4), 882–912.

Ford, M. R., & Andersson, F. O. (2016). Determinants of organizational failure in the Milwaukee School Voucher Program. *Policy Studies Journal.* doi: 10.1111/psj.12164.

Friedman, M. (1955). The role of government in public education. In Solow, R. A. (Ed.), *Economics and the public interest* (pp. 123–144). New Brunswick, NY: Rutgers Press.

Fuller, H. (2014). *No struggle no progress.* Milwaukee, WI: Marquette University Press.

Greene, J. P., & Marsh, R. H. (2009). *The effect of Milwaukee's Parental Choice Program on student achievement in Milwaukee Public Schools.* Fayetteville, AR: School Choice Demonstration Project, University of Arkansas.

Joseph, T., Veléz, W., & Gonzalez., R. A. (2016). The experiences of low income Latino families in an Urban Voucher, Parochial School. *Journal of Latinos and Education, 16*(2) 143–155.

Kettl, D. F. (2005). *The global public management revolution* (2nd ed.). Washington D.C.: Brookings Institution Press.

Kingdon, J. (1995). *Agendas, alternatives, and public policies.* New York: Harper Collins College Publishers.

Lutz, F. W., & Iannoccone, L. (2008). The dissatisfaction theory of American democracy. In Asbury, T. L. (Ed.), *The future of school board governance* (pp. 3–24). Lanham, MD: Roman & Littlefield.

Merrifield, J. D. (2008). The school choice evidence and its significance. *Journal of School Choice, 2*(3), 223–259.

Provan, K. G., & Milward, H. B. (2001). Do networks really work? A framework for evaluating public-sector organizational networks. *Public Administration Review, 61*(4), 414–423.

Pugh, C. (2015). *Private school choice programs.* Madison, WI: Wisconsin Legislative Fiscal Bureau.

Ravitch, D. (2010). Why public schools need democratic governance. *Phi Delta Kappan, 91*(6), 24–27.

Richards, E. (2015, April 15). New Senate school accountability bill drops controversial elements. *Milwaukee Journal Sentinel.* Retrieved from www.jsonline.com/

news/education/new-senate-accountability-bill-drops-controversial-elements-b99482298z1-299965451.html

Van Dunk, E., & Dickman, A. (2003). *School choice and the question of accountability: The Milwaukee experience.* New Haven: Yale University Press.

Witte, J. F. (2000). *The market approach to education: An analysis of America's first voucher program.* Princeton, NJ: Princeton University Press.

Witte, J. F., Carlson, D., Cowen, J. M., Fleming, D. J., & Wolf, P. J. (2012). *MPCP longitudinal educational growth study: Fifth Year Report.* Fayetteville, AR: School Choice Demonstration Project at the University of Arkansas.

Witte, J. F., Wolf, P. J., Cowen, J. M., Carlson, D. E., & Fleming, D. J. (2014). High-stakes choice: Achievement and accountability in the nation's oldest Urban Voucher Program. *Education Evaluation and Policy Analysis, 36*(4), 437–456.

Wolf, P. J., Witte, J. F., & Fleming, D. J. (2012). *Special education and the Milwaukee Parental Choice Program.* Fayetteville, AR: School Choice Demonstration Project at the University of Arkansas.

9 How Centralized Implementation Policies Failed the Austrian New Middle School Process

Corinna Geppert

The Austrian Government's aim was to implement a comprehensive school type in secondary I, but it also had a formidable opponent in three factors: time, parental power, and reforms that did not target the needs of specific schools. Our study showed that traditions cannot be changed in just a couple of years and that there prevails strong pressure from parents preferring to retain a school type for the "privileged," similar to the situation reigning in school systems with comprehensive schools such as in the United States. As long as they can choose schools freely, educationally active parents will send their children to "better" comprehensive schools, or they will "go private." Furthermore, schools can ultimately resist, regardless of whether the State has the power to sanction or the local community interferes.

How Centralized Implementation Policies Failed the Austrian New Middle School

The Policy and its Beneficiaries

In the 1980s, Larry Cuban asked himself: "How could teaching over a forty-year period seem almost unchanged?" and with "institutions so apparently vulnerable to change as schools why do so few instructional reforms get past the classroom door?" (Cuban, 1984, p. 14). One answer to these questions might lie in the debates on the decentralization and centralization of school reforms. In the United States, for example, many people and stages, from state to community level, are involved in school reform processes, and it could well be that "too many cooks spoil the broth," which leads to nothing changing because in the end the intended reforms do not reach a single school—they simply fail.

But can the answer be centralization? What if only one authority decided what happens in school? This chapter presents a school reform process in Austria, a small country in the heart of Europe. We have a centralized system where the State decides—through edicts and administrative orders—and schools have to implement the reforms. All other players in the hierarchy are there just to make sure that the reforms are implemented in the schools in the way the State intended. But does it make any difference?

The reform I draw on is the implementation of a new school type in secondary I. It is important to understand that in Austria secondary education is differentiated. Students attend four years of comprehensive primary school and then they have to decide which school type they want to attend in secondary education. Traditionally, Austria has two main secondary school types: the academic secondary school (leading to university education), and the lower secondary school (leading to vocational training or higher vocational education). The academic secondary school is traditionally the school that is attended by students from higher socioeconomic strands; it has entry exams for all students, who are graded with a C in their primary school certificate, and is seen as the school for the "educated middle class." The lower secondary school has a tracking system in the core subjects (German, English, and Math), has no entry exams, the only requirement being the successful completion of primary school.

Since 2009–10, the secondary I stage has become even more differentiated, with the Austrian Government deciding to implement a new school type, the New Middle School (NMS), by means of a school trial. This was more or less a reaction to the calls for reform after the PISA 2000 results indicated that Austrian students were not doing as well in the assessments as Austria would have expected. At first glance this was not so important because Austria was still better than Germany, which has a similar education system. But the correction of a sample weight error then placed Austria behind Germany. So Austria had to find an excuse for the bad PISA results, and found it in Finland. Since Finland had been the winner of this game and had a comprehensive schooling system, the decades-old debate about implementing a comprehensive school at the stage of secondary I came up again and led to the implementation of the New Middle School (NMS), intended to be a "school for all."

The aims of the NMS reform, in short, are the following (www.neuemittelschule.at):

1. **Develop a school type where all students, not only those who would have attended a lower secondary school but also those who would have attended an academic secondary school, are taught in an inclusive school setting.** In contrast to the "old" lower secondary school with its differentiation through tracking in the core subjects, the NMS aims to provide an inclusive school setting with individualized learning support. The curriculum, however, is the same in the NMS as in the academic secondary school. NMSs are meant to attract more highly educated middle-class students, as well as students who do not come from a milieu in which education plays an important role. The aim is to have a social mix where students can learn from each other.

2. **Improve transitions: help students develop high aspirations and guide them to higher secondary vocational education.** This aim refers to the overarching goal of keeping students within the system and reducing

drop-out rates. At best, students go on to higher secondary vocational education, which can lead to certification for university entrance. This is meant to offer career guidance and educational counseling by helping students increase their knowledge of their own strengths and talents, to help them develop aspirations for moving to higher (secondary) vocational education.

3. **Implement innovative forms of teaching to support both high and low achievers at the same time.** One core element of the NMS reform is "individualization and differentiation" to be attained through "new," cooperative, and open forms of teaching (teaching in small groups, team-teaching), practice-oriented, research-based, and topic-centered teaching, interdisciplinary projects, as well as remedial courses and individual programs. Here again, the aim is to have students learning from and supporting each other, which is also expected to create a school setting in which students feel comfortable and can develop their talents.

4. **Limit marginalization processes, i.e., to be a school where especially students from immigrant backgrounds find a supportive setting.** At the NMS students of different abilities and social, cultural, and linguistic backgrounds are taught all together. The NMS sees diversity in society as a challenge and so aims to improve the education of students of immigrant backgrounds. So, intercultural dialogue has to be enhanced.

The aims of the reform were laudable, but calling the tune without paying the piper was bound to fail. Without waiting for any official evaluation results and only three years after its implementation as a school trial, this school type was integrated into the regular school system in the school year 2012–13. By 2015–16 it replaced the lower secondary school, but not the academic secondary school, because the lobby for the latter school type is too strong in Austria. The resulting compromise between the Austrian Social Democrats, who wanted to implement a comprehensive school in secondary I, and the conservative People's Party, fighting for a differentiated system, weakened the very aims of the proposed reform.

The following sections will give an overview on the research methods used to evaluate the proposed aims and the results, explaining if and why the reform failed.

Method

Austria is a very centralized country, which means that this new school type was implemented in all nine Federal States. An official evaluation was administered by the Austrian Federal Institute BIFIE and focused almost exclusively on the achievement levels of NMS students throughout all nine Federal States. Our study, NOESIS, took place in Lower Austria, the largest Federal State that also surrounds the Austrian capital, Vienna.

Research Design

We created a multiple-methods multilevel design, including qualitative case studies (group discussions, peer evaluation, interviews, and classroom observations) and a longitudinal panel study. The four NOESIS sub-studies—Transitions, School Settings, Capacity Building, Instructional Patterns—form a whole with interfacing parts. Each of the parts adds another perspective and so leads to a broader picture and better understanding of the processes underlying the reform.

Transitions: To gain more knowledge of the student environment, a longitudinal study was created in which students were followed from the last years of primary school (4th grade) through to the end of compulsory school (9th grade). To observe the transitions over several waves, we followed three cohorts of students, with 2,000 students per cohort, their parents, and teachers. Every year from 4th to 9th grade, students were periodically asked to fill in questionnaires concerning their school lives, the class climate, their educational aspirations, and how they perceive the instruction they receive. This data was collected from students as well as from parents and teachers to gain views from the most important actors in the education system both inside and outside school (e.g., Geppert, Katschnig, & Kilian, 2012).

School Settings: Different schools (both NMS and lower secondary schools) were selected in Lower Austria by location and social profile to participate in the multi-stage survey process. The process involves school management, teachers, parents, and students, as well as representatives of the school community (social, political, and business associations, etc.), and systematically connects them. This not only allows comparisons between the participating schools, and ones between NMSs and academic secondary schools, but also enables schools to develop further in consultation with the immediate school environment (school community) (e.g., Retzl, 2013).

Capacity Building (Networks and Peers): For this capacity-enhancing sub-study and also to make active use of the results from the other areas, we developed a peer review process in which schools could participate voluntarily, based on a Norwegian model including all school partners and the local environment. The aim was to develop sustainable networks that can strengthen the educational and social potential of the school locations. Both teachers and students had to visit a partner school, teachers authored peer reviews and submitted them independently to the partner school, and the researchers wrote reviews for the students, thus acting as their voices and keeping the student workload down (e.g., Feichter, 2015).

Instructional Patterns: At selected locations, individual classes or cohorts were investigated qualitatively (and to a limited extent quantitatively) with respect to the (reform) measures implemented in the classroom and the effects observed. This was done in focus groups with teachers and students on different case studies (e.g., Hörmann, 2012).

So much for the methods, but what about the outcomes of the reform process?

Outcomes and Their Consequences

The following section draws on results from all four parts of the NOESIS study to ascertain whether or not its four main aims failed.

Aim 1: Develop a School Type Where all Students are Taught in an Inclusive School Setting

To understand why this aim failed, one has to acknowledge that the implementation of the NMS did not result in a comprehensive schooling system, but that the academic secondary school still exists. Therefore, school choice is still a big issue—but did the NMS manage to attract students who would have attended an academic secondary school?

It did not. At the macro level of school choice, various analyses let us conclude that the NMS was not yet a "school for all" and cannot take pressure off the academic secondary school. Educationally active parents still choose the academic track, while parents not wishing their children to travel long distances and fearing their children will be over-challenged in the academic track choose the NMS. Motives hardly differ from those for choosing the former lower secondary schools, which might be attributed to the motivation for attending lower secondary schools (schools transformed into NMSs) being transferred to the new school type (Geppert, Knapp, Kilian, & Katschnig, 2015). The NMS seems to be a good option for parents not wanting their children to travel long distances, whose children need after-school care, and who fear that they might be over-challenged in the academic secondary school. The recommendation of primary school teachers can also influence the choice of NMS, as shown in the literature (e.g., Ditton & Krüsken, 2009; McElvany, 2010). Our results show that the first aim failed because of free school choice and the big lobby to keep the academic secondary school. What about the second aim?

Aim 2: Improve Transitions

When we look at the transition to higher (vocational) education after 8th grade, results from the NOESIS study, and from Statistik Austria (www.statistik.at), reveal that only a few more students follow higher educational paths after the NMS compared to the former lower secondary schools. Although the study showed that students develop high aspirations in the NMS, and maintained high learning motivation and a good class climate (e.g., Geppert, Knapp, Bauer-Hofmann, & Werkl, 2015), the goal of having more students proceed to higher vocational education failed. Data from Statistik Austria on the transition rates in the school year 2013–14 show that about 92% of academic secondary school students proceed to a higher secondary school, with 89% successful at this next stage. Ninety-three percent of students from former lower secondary schools engaged in higher secondary (vocational) education, but only 77% successfully completed the first year of higher secondary education. Data from NMSs show that, compared to lower secondary schools, more students moved to higher secondary education (46%), but 32% did not successfully complete their first school year there (Statistik Austria, 2016). We can conclude that although more students move to higher secondary education, many of them do not proceed. So aim two also failed, perhaps due to the fact that this is a change that will take much longer. What about changes within the school?

Aim 3: Implement Innovative Forms of Teaching

Drawing on the concept of the "daily grind" (Jackson, 1968), schools are characterized by a high degree of standardization and structuring with few situations that are memorable for students. Strict structuring can offer students orientation, but they will have internalized such daily routines so much that they often do not consciously perceive and consider them anymore. For example, the school bell that rings at the start and end of lessons is an integral part of the everyday lives of students and teachers and their temporally structured daily schedule.

Unexpected events and provocative familiar ones can make existing routines consciously perceivable again (e.g., the absence of the school bell). In the case of the NMS, working with new forms of teaching can enhance the activity of students, create variety and interest in teaching, as well as reduce the sensation of overly strict routines, and thus allay boredom. The introduction in the NMS of new forms of teaching, such as independent or individualized working, and project-based work, is intended to make lessons more varied and interesting; findings, however, showed that NMS students only partially perceived new forms of learning (Geppert et al., 2015). If perceptions are not strong enough to make a difference, then this aim, too, can be seen to have failed.

In the longitudinal study, we asked students about group work and independent work, and the results indicated that working in groups was especially noticed by a large majority of students (80%) in 5th grade, the stage right after the transition to secondary school, whereas in 6th and 7th grade, only about 10% of students totally agreed with the item: "We do group work."

Below are two interview passages from group discussions with students talking about their experiences on returning from a peer evaluation visit to the partner school:

Student 2:   *Or that they have more group work than we have, because we have to do our worksheets by ourselves and they just have more group work.*

Interviewer: *And they don't have worksheets, but have to work with their books by themselves?*

Student 1:   *No they have worksheets, but, what was it like?*
Student 4:   *They have a book for Biology.*
Student 1:   *They studied the ecosystem, about CO_2 growth, and they study everything in groups, boys have a group and girls have a group.*
       (Group discussion 11) (Feichter & Krainz, 2014, p. 100)

Student 2:   *Well, we like that. Students come together, five people cooperate with each other for the open learning and solve it together, and we like that, because in our classroom, we have rows of tables where six people are sitting together, and that would be quite good for us.*
Student 4:   *And they do tasks in the corridor, when they have to work together.*
       (Group discussion 12) (Feichter & Krainz, 2014, p. 101)

The discussions seem to show that the students did not really see group work as part of teaching *per se*. Furthermore, an interesting fact about learning with worksheets is that students characterize it by working alone, even if that is not the intention of the teachers (Feichter & Krainz, 2014). The students seem to see working alone to be more effective than working in groups because learning success means working through a list of worksheets that one can get through more quickly alone. Group work can be a disadvantage for high-achieving students because it can slow down their learning progress (Knapp & Geppert, 2014).

Despite the fact that the school facilities (classroom size, rows of tables, corridor) would allow the students to cooperate and work independently of the teacher, the narrations also indicate that the learning tasks/worksheets are not developed in a way that makes sense for being elaborated and experienced in a group. It is more like individualized learning, or better described as a strict execution of learning steps that seem very monotonous. In contrast, the results of our surveys indicate that group work may be a way to make lessons for students varied and stimulating and is also associated with a more positive teacher-student relationship. The sooner students feel they are able to contribute with their own ideas in the classroom and feel they are respected by their teachers, the more positively they also perceive the classroom (Geppert et al., 2015).

Looking at other "new" teaching practices, team-teaching is probably the one innovation that is most visible, but it is also controversial since it means a structural change to the school day. This can affect the daily routines of a school and thus can irritate all involved in organizing and teaching practices, not only students and teachers, but also principals and administrators, who need to handle the exchange of teachers from different school sites. This measure then relates both to a school as an organizational unit, as well as to the lessons in the classroom.

There have been high hopes and expectations for the idea of team-teaching ever since it popped up in the 50s. One of the positive aspects teachers see in team-teaching is the transfer of knowledge within the team. This team-teaching ideal emphasizes the process of "learning from each other" and the exchange between the two-team partners, as mentioned in group discussions. Here aspects of professional development through team-teaching, the impetus for increased reflection on events in the classroom and the teachers' own practices are addressed, and are reflected in the following statement:

> And I think it's really interesting to look at my colleague. And though I have so many years of service, I'm still learning and I like it when someone else brings in new ideas. I benefit myself. If you are alone in the class, you'll never know that.
> *(Group discussion 1)* (Brisch & Geppert, 2013, p. 99).

The group discussions showed clearly that teachers wanted the ideal of a "team as a unit" where there was balanced cooperation to enable a lively transfer of knowledge. As a large proportion of students in a total sample of 2,000 of the NOESIS transition cohorts 1 to 3 confirmed, team-teaching can be introduced as an additional resource in the classroom and can be supportive for students' learning processes. Cooperation between the teachers enables students to receive additional explanations and special support. Students become bored and irritated when they no longer see the second teacher as a meaningful resource, but have the feeling that he or she does not contribute to school life (Brisch & Geppert, 2013). For the question of how well new forms of teaching are implemented in classroom practice, we can conclude that some schools have already integrated these practices into their own "grammar of teaching," but others refuse to change their practices. The failure of this aim can therefore be attributed to both sides: students do not fully perceive new learning forms and the efforts of their teachers, and teachers simply refuse to put effort into new practices because they do not feel the need to do so. This now leads to the fourth aim—what about the immigrant population?

Aim 4: Limit Marginalization Processes

The team-teaching results indicate that this could have been a good option for limiting marginalization processes, but evidence shows that this goal has simply failed. Results from a series of project studies over the four-year period in the NMS indicate a decline in immigrant students' self-concepts and their career aspirations, as well as a strong recourse to private tutoring to compensate for what students fail to learn at school and in order to pass exams (e.g., Geppert et al., 2015; Hörmann, 2012).

In a sub-study (Forghani-Arani, Geppert, & Katschnig, 2014), we examined the correlation between teachers' *implicit* (as opposed to *explicit*) attitudes and their verbalized expectations, and students' achievements, academic aspirations, and self-concepts; this was done using the Implicit Association Test (IAT) response latency (Greenwald et al., 1998), a teacher evaluations scale, student scores in three main subjects (German, English, and Math), and a student-targeted questionnaire collected in the Transition Study.

The analyses based on the IAT revealed that only four out of 60 of the surveyed teachers could be classified as "unbiased," since they had no implicit negative attitudes toward students with an immigrant background. A further 39% of teachers were considered "moderately biased" because they had a tendency to make negative associations with names that could be clearly attributed to an immigrant background. The majority of teachers (55%) clearly had implicit negative associations with respect to such a background of their students.

In contrast, however, the analysis of the survey data showed that teachers had no *explicit* prejudices in relation to the immigrant background of their students. Thus the approval of individual items such as "student is intelligent" or "student is performing well" tended to be even more pronounced for students with an immigrant background. While a majority of teachers exhibited negative implicit attitudes toward students with an immigrant background, the assessments of teachers about intelligence, current school performance, and expected academic success of students with and without an immigrant background did not indicate any discrepancy (Forghani-Arani, Geppert, & Katschnig, 2014). The results concerning the possible limiting of marginalization in NMSs indicate that there is still a high potential for marginalization processes—the fourth aim simply failed as well.

Reasons for Failure and Future Action

What can we learn from the evidence pointing toward policy failure? Our study shows that traditions cannot be changed in just a few years—they need time to allow all involved actors to adapt the administrative orders. The Austrian Government's aim to implement a comprehensive school type in secondary I was thwarted by pressure from parents to retain a school type for the "privileged," similar to the situation in school systems with comprehensive schools such as in the United States. If they can choose freely, educationally active parents will send their children to "better" comprehensive schools, or to private ones. So, expecting a rapid change in student flows is fanciful. The results of our study concur with findings from international studies in that efforts to homogenize educational paths lead to more pressure on out of school resources that ultimately lead to failure (e.g., Baker, 2006). So, we can say that the first reason for failure is: parental power, which simply has to be taken into account when implementing education reforms.

Cuban (1984) writes that "schools are a form of control and sorting" (p. 22), which means that schools have the function of qualification and socialization and that some teaching practices (subjectively) seem better than others: doing group work enables students to learn from each other, but takes much longer than "traditional" forms of teaching where students might do individual worksheets, which can be judged easily. Team-teaching in our case was very cost intensive and often unable to be implemented since a teacher from an academic secondary school and one from an NMS were meant to teach their lessons in the core subjects, German, Math, and English, together. This meant paying for extra lessons for the second teacher. Logistical problems, especially in rural areas, where the next academic secondary school was far away, made cooperation between NMSs and academic secondary schools very difficult, if not impossible. Reasons for failure concerning inner-school activities are therefore: a lack of money to provide teachers a setting to change their teaching practices, which goes hand in hand with refusal to do so.

However, where team-teaching did work, it was very fruitful for students in need of more teacher support, as it was for teachers dealing with student heterogeneity in an inclusive school setting. Yet this heterogeneity was often "treated" as homogeneity, with teacher interviews revealing that they failed to understand what immigrant students (we explicitly speak of "immigration," which is associated with a different mother tongue and culture, rather than "race") understood—indicating that the "grammar of teaching" and the daily routines of teachers needed new forms of teaching, and that new ways of approaching heterogeneity were required for developing the potential of students from different strands. This makes sense not only for personal development, but also for investment in human capital.

Another citation by Cuban (1984): "The organizational structure of the school and classroom drove teachers into adopting instructional practices that changes little over time" (p. 22), in our terms means that eventually teachers can find ways of dealing with many students at one time in an effective way, but where "effective" can mean that students were to be quiet and work alone on a specific topic. The so-called student-centered techniques, on the other hand, "generate a noisier, messier classroom. Far more energy is required from the teacher in managing varied tasks" (p. 23). And the energy that has to be invested is important for teachers. There are too many reform efforts. Many teachers told us in informal talks that they did not even react to new reforms by changing the way they worked because another reform was expected in a few years where they would again need to change. This is true especially for teachers with a track record of more than 10 years. Yet, they knew their schools, and they knew their clients, and how things happened in their town, and had developed strategies for their particular situations. As long as things worked for them, they felt no pressure to change. Besides, when the NMS was implemented in 2009–10 as a school trial, schools were allowed to apply to become NMSs and received extra money. Those schools and their agents were very motivated and they obtained more funds to find out how to implement the new regulations in a proper way.

When the NMS was integrated into the regular school system, all the lower secondary schools had to change, even those that felt no pressure to do so because, for example, they were not in competition with any academic secondary schools. Furthermore, there was no money left for them to change the school structure, and so these schools were neither motivated nor willing to work with the new regulations. This was true for parents, teachers, principals, and students. This leads to the conclusion that the reforms failed because of a lack of money to implement the new strategies, and if failure is to be avoided, education reforms must be implemented cost effectively.

The situatedness of implementation strategies is surely another aspect. In Austria, reform processes start in Vienna, our capital city, and are linked to the situation of Vienna. But as the advertising slogan says, "Vienna is different," and what may fit perfectly well for our capital city is not necessarily a good idea in more rural areas of Austria where often the school type is irrelevant because everybody moves from primary school to the same middle school in their hometown. Context matters, so education reforms must take the specific situatedness of schools into account in order to avoid failure.

Finally, referring again to Cuban (1984, 1990), it makes no difference whether education policies are administered in a centralized or a decentralized way. Schools can ultimately resist, regardless of whether the State has the power to sanction or the local community interferes. Again, context matters! In many schools, things worked not because of reforms, but in spite of them. In others, of course, this was not the case. Moreover, every school is under pressure to deliver; they have to deliver students who fulfill the needs of society.

References

Baker, D. (2006). Institutional change in education: Evidence from cross-national comparisons. In Meyer, H. D., & Rowan, B. (Eds.), *The new institutionalism in education* (pp. 163–186). Albany: SUNY Press.

Brisch, N. M., & Geppert, C. (2013). Teamteaching zwischen Irritation und Kooperation. In Projektteam NOESIS (Eds.), *Zwischen Alltag und Aufbruch: Zur Evaluation der Niederösterreichischen Mittelschule* (pp. 145–168). Graz: Leykam.

Cuban, L. (1984). *How teachers taught: Constancy and change in American classrooms, 1890–1980*. Research on Teaching Monograph Series. New York and London: Longman.

Cuban, L. (1990). Reforming again, again, and again. *Educational Researcher*, *19*(1), 3–13.

Ditton, H., & Krüsken, J. (2009). Denn wer hat, dem wird gegeben werden? Eine Längsschnittstudie zur Entwicklung schulischer Leistungen und den Effekten der sozialen Herkunft in der Grundschulzeit. *Journal for Educational Research Online*, *1*(1), 33–61.

Feichter, H. (2015). *Schülerinnen und Schüler erforschen Schule: Möglichkeiten und Grenzen*. Wiesbaden: Springer VS Verlag für Sozialwissenschaften.

Feichter, H. J., & Krainz, U. (2014). Anpassung versus Innovation: SchülerInnenrückmeldungen zum Umgang mit Arbeitsblättern. In Projektteam NOESIS (Eds.),

Zwischen Routine und Irritation: Zur Evaluation der Niederösterreichischen Mittelschule (pp. 87–108). Graz: Leykam.

Forghani-Arani, N., Geppert, C., & Katschnig, T. (2014). Wenn der Pygmalioneffekt nicht greift . . . *Zeitschrift für Bildungsforschung, 1,* 21–36. doi: 10.1007/s35834-014-0104-x.

Geppert, C., Katschnig, T., & Kilian, M. (2012). NOESIS Arbeitsbericht 11: Übergänge: Neueste Analysen von der 4: zur 6. *Schulstufe im Längsschnitt.* Retrieved from www.noesis-projekt.at/uploads/Arbeitsbericht-Nr.11-September-2012.pdf.

Geppert, C., Knapp, M., Bauer-Hofmann, S., & Werkl, T. (2015). „Das Rad muss sich drehen . . .“—Zusammenfassende Ergebnisse der bisherigen Erhebungen im Rahmen der NOESIS-Evaluation. In Projektteam NOESIS (Eds.), *Gute Schule bleibt verändert: Zur Evaluation der Niederösterreichischen Mittelschule* (pp. 31–59). Graz: Leykam.

Geppert, C., Knapp, M., Kilian, M., & Katschnig, T. (2015). School choice under the pressure of reform efforts. *Studia Paedagogica, 20*(1), 9–28.

Greenwald, A. G., McGhee, D. E., & Schwartz, J. L. K. (1998). Measuring individual differences in implicit cognition: The Implicit Association Test. *Journal of Personality and Social Psychology, 74,* 1464–1480.

Hörmann, B. (2012). „Ja. Also, das war nämlich so . . .“. Erzählungen von Schülerinnen über ihren schulischen Alltag als Mittel zur Evaluierung von Unterricht. In Projektteam NOESIS (Eds.), *Eine Schule für alle? Zur Evaluation der Niederösterreichischen Mittelschule* (pp. 119–151). Graz: Leykam.

Jackson, P. W. (1968). *Life in classrooms.* New York: Teachers College Press.

Knapp, M., & Geppert, C. (2014). Der Kampf mit dem täglichen Trott—Neue Unterrichtsformen aus Sicht der SchülerInnen. In Projektteam NOESIS (Eds.), *Zwischen Alltag und Aufbruch: Zur Evaluation der Niederösterreichischen Mittelschule* (pp. 75–94). Graz: Leykam.

McElvany, N. (2010). Die Übergangsempfehlung von der Grundschule auf die weiterführende Schule im Erleben der Lehrkräfte. In Maaz, K., Baumert, J., Gresch, C., & McElvany, N. (Eds.), *Der Übergang von der Grundschule in die weiterführende Schule: Leistungsgerechtigkeit und regionale, soziale und ethnisch-kulturelle Disparitäten* (pp. 295–312). Berlin: Bundesministerium für Bildung und Forschung (BMBF) Referat Bildungsforschung.

Retzl, M. (2013). *Demokratie entwickelt Schule: Schulentwicklung auf der Basis des Denkens von John Dewey.* Wiesbaden: Springer Fachmedien.

Statistik Austria. (2016). *Bildung in Zahlen 2014/15: Struktur des österreichischen Bildungswesens.* Wien: MDH-Media GmbH.

10 The Unintended Consequences of School Vouchers

Rise, Rout, and Rebirth

Aaron Saiger

On December 12, 2000, the United States Supreme Court decided *Bush v. Gore*. The Court's deliberations had been so tumultuous, its decision so contentious, its dissents so furious, and public attention so blistering, that everyone was ready for a period of calm when the Court's next term began. The 2001 Term would see relatively few cases of the kind that make the front page of the papers and fuel talk at water coolers.

If anything, however, this magnified the interest in the handful of the Court's cases that did have blockbuster potential. And one of those cases was a schools case. The Court, in *Zelman v. Simmons-Harris*, would determine the constitutionality of an Ohio school voucher program that funded private, religious schools along with public ones. The case would mark the first occasion the Court squarely would consider the legality of school choice.

The parties before the Court agreed about little. But they shared the view that the case was portentous for American education. Were the Court to permit state treasuries to fund vouchers for private and religious schools, it would trigger a voucher juggernaut. Newly subsidized private and religious schools would flood the marketplace. The concomitant exodus of students, especially in areas where public schools were distressed or inadequate, would lead public schools, deprived of their better students and of popular support, either to spiral ever downward or to clean up their acts. A judicial rejection of the voucher system, on the other hand, would suffocate the reform movement and offer the strongest possible moral and financial support to the *status quo* state monopoly over free, public education. Private schooling would retreat to its traditional niche. Public schools would not just be protected, but entrenched.

Ultimately, the Court, in the same five-to-four split that it saw in *Bush v. Gore*, blessed Ohio's voucher system. But no paroxysm resulted. The Ohio voucher program, which had always been limited to poor students in a single Ohio city (Cleveland), continued, but did not expand. Neither did sister programs in other states; today, two decades later, only a handful of voucher programs exist. The religious schooling sector saw little growth and less transformation. Nor did the voucher decision transform traditional public schools by competitive pressure, or replace a system based upon local political sovereignty with one based upon the sovereignty of the consumer. As policy reform, vouchers failed to take off. Today, vouchers are more prominent as ideological markers in partisan party platforms than as policy on the ground.

The conventional wisdom to account for this result is that school choice never really enjoyed substantial political support. Most parents are happy with their public schools and disinclined to change them. School choice therefore is a niche reform, confined to distressed urban school districts. At best, vouchers are a policy Hail Mary, justified if at all only by the acuity of local need for sweeping intervention. More cynically, they are pure policy theater, advocated by officials and policymakers who want to appear to be gamechangers without spending money. Either way, they have no traction in most of America.

With the election of Donald J. Trump, this may change. In the first month of his new administration, President Trump named a Secretary of Education, Elisabeth DeVos, who has long been associated with philanthropy and advocacy for school vouchers, along with other forms of school choice. Vice President Michael Pence, moreover, pushed one of the nation's largest state voucher programs when he served as Governor of Indiana. But neither the new administration's policy preferences nor its effectiveness can be assumed. Still, one possible way the *Zelman* story might turn out is that its major surprise was one of timing. The educational revolution by *Zelman* was perhaps simply delayed, rather than stymied, by popular opinion. The eventual political realignment it needed did emerge, but only after the two terms of George W. Bush and the two terms of Barack Obama.

But it is always a mistake to imagine that new presidents will do what they say that want to do. Presidents, and cabinet secretaries, change their priorities. They also sometimes fail. And school policy, ultimately, resides with the states rather than in Washington, whose influence over schools is limited.

This chapter argues that, contrary to the perception in *Zelman*'s immediate aftermath, and regardless of the immediate future, both the case and the broader voucher movement were *not* policy failures. Rather, their successes took forms neither expected nor intended by their proponents. *Zelman* established principles that, today, undergird the still-accelerating charter school movement, a choice-based approach that is now clearly a permanent aspect of American educational organization. In 2016, choice is a quotidian aspect of American educational reality in a way unimaginable when *Zelman* was decided. And the openness of *Zelman* to the participation of religious institutions in choice-based public education is very likely soon to have enormous implications, as charters mature and options for internet-based and virtual education begin to take off.

School Policy in Legislatures and Courts

The term "educational policy" generally calls to mind administrative, bureaucratic, or executive decisions about how schools should run. Educational "policy" is the domain of teachers, principals, superintendents, and boards and departments of education at local, state, and federal levels. But legislators of course make educational policy too. Indeed, in the American educational system they are the *ur*-policymakers. State legislatures bear the duty, under state constitutions, to guarantee that students are educated. It is legislatures that set up school districts and assign them their powers. State law determines which administrative decisions are made at the state level, which by districts, and which by schools. By passing statutes, legislatures can trump or preempt nearly any policy decision made by school officials. And state legislatures, crucially, give out the money. In the United States, it is fair to say nearly all crucial policy decisions about schooling are in the hands of state legislatures. If they delegate those responsibilities to bureaucrats, for reasons of expertise, practicality, or politics, they do so at their pleasure.

To be sure, legislative policymaking is different from that of executive agencies, local districts, or individual schools. Legislatures are generalist bodies that trade money, time, and attention among policy domains. Political pressures are more explicit and bubble closer to the surface; expertise and analysis sometimes take a back seat. But none of this makes the Ohio Legislature's decision that Cleveland should have a school voucher program any less a policy decision. And it was the Legislature, directly, that determined many of the policy details of that program. Lawmakers decided how big the vouchers should be, what kinds of families could receive them, what sorts of schools could redeem them, and what rules would apply to both.

It is perhaps less obvious, but no less true, that courts also make educational policy. Just as legislatures determine the scope of discretion available to agencies, to district superintendents, to principals, and to teachers, so do the courts determine whether that scope has been exceeded. And, critically, courts determine the scope of discretion available to the legislature itself. That these decisions are policy choices is often obscured by judicial insistence, often explicit, that courts are disinterested when it comes to policy: they care, they insist, only about the "law" and not about policy. But a court deciding which educational ends can legitimately be (or must be) embraced, and deciding further what means can (or must) be used to pursue those ends, is surely making policy—even if it does not characterize itself as such.

As is true for legislatures, judicial policymaking has its peculiar institutional constraints. Courts will not act without a dispute of some kind, and moreover will not act without "jurisdiction"—a legal justification for taking the case. In the federal courts, courts will not hear a case on school policy unless it raises an issue of federal law. Educational effectiveness and school funding are, as a matter of doctrinal taxonomy, state-law issues. The challenge to the Ohio voucher program, therefore, found its way into the federal courts and ultimately to the United States Supreme Court only because it had a federal "hook." That hook was the First Amendment. The *Zelman* plaintiffs got into federal court by alleging that allowing religious schools to redeem state-funded vouchers was an impermissible establishment of religion. This was the question that, formally, the Supreme Court agreed to decide.

But that was not the only reason the case was a big one. For many, issues of religion were secondary. *Zelman* would either open or close the door to school choice, and it was choice, not church and state, that concerned them. And the Supreme Court, which only agrees to hear cases it views as momentous or pressing, fully expected that its conclusions about religion would also shape the future of choice.

Intertwined Narratives

Two policy disputes, then, animated the *Zelman* case. One was the question on the surface of the case: did allowing religious schools along with secular ones to redeem vouchers impermissibly entangle church with state? The other was whether school choice, as a concept, was educationally desirable—for Cleveland's schoolchildren, for its public schools, or more generally. The dispute about religion and the one about choice were conceptually distinct but doctrinally and empirically intertwined.

Religion. A voucher program could have been designed that excluded religious schools; instead, the Ohio Legislature baked religious participation into the Cleveland program. Most directly, lawmakers declined to require voucher-accepting schools to function as religious providers of secular services, a model familiar from the health care and welfare sectors. A church-sponsored drug-treatment program or soup kitchen, when it accepts federal funds, generally agrees to scrub its programming of religious content. But religious schools that accepted vouchers would be allowed to behave as they always had: sponsoring prayer, teaching doctrine, and asserting the truth of matters of faith. Religious schools did have to commit to nondiscrimination in admissions and to minor restrictions on curriculum—they were forbidden, for example, to teach doctrines of racial superiority. But they remained fully religious schools.

The legislature also encouraged religious participation in the voucher program by allowing only private schools within city limits to accept vouchers. Developing a new private school is expensive, complicated, and time-consuming, so the first voucher schools were likely to be private schools already in operation. The vast bulk of the private schools in Cleveland were religious.

For the *Zelman* plaintiffs, allowing religious schools to accept vouchers was a frontal assault upon a bedrock principle: government-funded schools should be secular. When a religious school cashed a voucher, it could use the money for any purpose, including religious ones. The voucher program therefore allowed public funds to support explicitly religious activities. State funding for religious activity is just about as close to the core of what the First Amendment forbids as one can get.

Not so, said the State of Ohio. Its argument was also straightforward: school vouchers were issued not to religious schools but to parents. A private school cannot cash a voucher unless a parent chooses that school for her child. Otherwise the school gets nothing. The private parent, not the state, is the one directing public money to the religious school.

And that, argued Ohio, is surely constitutional. Consider a Jewish food-stamp recipient who cashes his stamps at a kosher grocery, a Muslim at a halal butcher, or a Catholic on a Friday trip to the fishmonger. The recipient's food choice is undoubtedly motivated by religion. Moreover, as in the cases of the grocery and the butcher, the receiving organization can be an explicitly religious one. It uses revenue it derives from redeeming publicly funded food stamps for sectarian purposes. Nevertheless, a food-stamp program does not impermissibly establish religion. That's because the state in no way requires or urges people to use their food stamps in religious ways. The state is disinterested whether recipients choose their groceries using secular or religious criteria; all the state cares about is its own secular motivation, which is that recipients be well-fed. So too in the case of schools: the state cares that children get educated. It doesn't care whether parents allow their religious preferences to inflect (or even dominate) their choice of educational institution, or whether that institution is secular or religious—as long as education happens.

In support of this way of looking at the case, the State cited several earlier Supreme Court decisions. The Court had authorized a state tax deduction for private school tuition, which parents could take regardless whether the payee was a religious or nonreligious school. That deduction, said the Court, applied "only as a result of numerous, private choices of individual parents of school-age children"; therefore "no 'imprimatur of state approval' can be deemed to have been conferred on any particular religion, or on religion generally" (Mueller v. Allen, 1983). The Court had decided that states that provided general scholarships for vocational training could extend those scholarships to students training for the pastorate at theological schools; again, it was the student's choice, not the state's, that directed state money to religious institutions (Witters v. Washington Dept. of Servs. for Blind, 1986). And the Court had held that a school district that made sign-language interpreters available to deaf students would not violate the constitution by allowing that interpreter, though on the public payroll, to interpret lessons in a Catholic school, because the student, not the state, had chosen the school (Zobrest v. Catalina Foothills School Dist., 1993).

This, then, was the dispute over religion. Were school vouchers essentially similar to the tax deduction, the vocational scholarship, and the sign-language interpreter: permissible public aid to private persons in furtherance of a secular educational objective, where the private person—not the state—had chosen a religious rather than a secular provider? Or were they public aid to religious institutions in support of religious activity, and therefore forbidden?

This dispute clearly turns on the viability of the argument that private families participating in the program, not public authorities, *freely choose* whether to direct their voucher to a secular or a religious institution. Independent private choice was the fact that would determine the constitutionality of religious schools' participation in the voucher program. For those whose primary desideratum was that religious schools be able to receive state money on the same basis as secular ones, independent private choice was a means to an end, a legal requirement necessary to achieve their goal.

Choice. In a second policy debate—one over school choice—the same issues were in play but with their relationship reversed. In that debate, free choice among schools, in a relatively free marketplace, was the policy outcome that people sought—or sought to prevent. The participation of religious schools, in this frame, was a means toward the end of free choice. Strikingly, the arguments that religious-establishment doctrine essentially forced the State of Ohio to make—that its voucher program offered parents free choice—were precisely the arguments that market reformers cared about.

A central strand of school choice advocacy is rooted in libertarian sentiment. A pure libertarian, of course, maintains generalized opposition to the state providing goods, like schooling, that the private sector can provide, along with a strong preference for allowing people to choose what they want, rather than having the government give it to them. Such persons would advocate for the elimination of both public provision of schooling and compulsory schooling requirements. Although such persons can be found among school choice advocates, this sort of position is a bridge too far for most Americans, where free public schooling has been a central political and cultural fact for over a century. Most choice advocates accept the idea of public subsidy for all and public provision of schools open to all. But they argue that families should be able to choose how state funds are used to educate their children. If a family likes its public school, well and good; but if it finds a different option it prefers, it should send its children to that school, and the public funds allocated to that student should follow her there.

Two major arguments support this approach, one based upon fairness and the other upon quality. The fairness claim is that the state's decision to *subsidize* schools is distinct from its decision to *operate* them. Since the Progressive era, American public schooling has been founded upon a system of discrete local monopolies, in which each school district directly provides public schooling to those resident within its boundaries. Those who avail themselves of schools use them free of charge; they are supported through taxation (usually of local property) that is independent of whether or how intensively a taxpayer uses the schools. Those who wish not to use the local public school system may opt out, but by doing so they forfeit public subsidy and must, under compulsory schooling laws, pay for alternate arrangements. Thus the famous observation that those who opt out of public schooling in the United States pay twice, although, as some have noted, it is more accurate to say that they pay three times (Sugarman, 1991, p. 181). They pay taxes to support the public schools, like every other taxpayer; they do not send their children to the public schools, relieving the public fisc of the duty to expend resources to educate those children; and then, under compulsory schooling laws, they must utilize their own resources to provide that education. It would be fairer, the argument runs, to allow families opting out to carry taxpayer support with them to their chosen school.

This argument can also be framed as a claim about the privilege of wealth. The rich can afford to pay three times. The poor cannot. But the American catechism insists that all children, regardless of means or of any other difference, should have equal educational opportunity. Indeed, the decision that the state should pay for public education demonstrates the conviction that the poor should have access to schooling on the same terms as the rich. Why, then, should the ability to exit to the private market carry such high costs that it is effectively confined to the wealthy?

In the contemporary American scene, both before *Zelman* and since, these arguments have been supplemented by an argument about school *quality*. Publicly provided schools are local monopolists; if you want a free public education, you have to use the school assigned to you by the district in which you live. Both basic economics and simple intuition tell us that monopolists care much less about quality than participants in competitive markets: the latter have to compete for their customers, while the former have customers regardless. In 1990, political scientists John E. Chubb and Terry M. Moe published a book, *Politics, Markets, and America's Schools*, that applied this claim to school districts. Districts, they argued, are governments in the political sense and monopolies in the economic sense. They therefore respond to political pressure but not to consumer preferences. And so they are easily captured by groups whose interests diverge from that of schoolchildren, who are the consumers: teachers' unions most especially, but also contractors, staff, and pressure groups of various sorts. The low quality of public schooling, Chubb and Moe concluded, was a *result* of its organization as a publicly provided monopolist. This will be true, moreover, regardless of any politically based reform that might be introduced.

Inject market pressure into that system by allowing parents to choose schools, however, and quality would improve. Markets need not imply the end of public schools; rather, actual and potential competition would force schools to respond to the consumer preferences for quality rather than to political pressure for patronage and handouts. Allowing parents to choose public schools, the argument runs, not only improves education for those who choose to exit but also for those who remain. As in any standard microeconomic market, inframarginal consumers benefit from the choices of those closer to the margin.

The signal effect of the Chubb and Moe volume, which galvanized the choice movement of the 1990s in the run-up to *Zelman*, was thus to recast choice as a matter of social justice as well as libertarian principle. Already available was the argument that rich individuals who faced public schools that they did not like had the ability to exit—why not extend that prerogative to the poor? To this account, Chubb and Moe added the claim that school districts in rich constituencies did not suffer very much from the political organization of their public schools, because the rich can organize political pressure for quality. But poor people, in poor districts, were politically outmatched by labor and by monied interests. Choice was therefore an organizational reform that favored the poor, by allowing some to exit and improving public school incentives for those who stayed. Indeed, pro-choice coalitions in the 1990s included some organizations that represented poor and minority communities, although most recoiled from the right-wing, market-based ideology and cast their lots with the teachers' unions and against choice policies.

Where does religion fit into this account? That depends on whom one asks. Some observers viewed the entire enterprise of choice advocacy as a false flag designed to distract policymakers, including the courts, from the actual goal of achieving state funding for religious schools. But this was unfair. Rather, choice proponents tended to welcome the participation of religious schools in choice programs for two reasons. At the level of principle, they recognized that many Americans genuinely prefer religious schooling. The goal of robust free choice is to offer families educational options that they want. Anything that extends the range of choice is good. A libertarian, classical economic (some might say "neoliberal") set of mind will see no reason to exclude religious feeling from the set of concerns and issues that might lead parents to prefer one kind of school or another.

At the level of practicality, moreover, religious schools comprised about 85% of the private schools sector. In order to get a voucher-funded marketplace off the ground, it needed a base of existing private schools to jump-start it, so that supply could meet demand relatively quickly. In Cleveland certainly, and likely elsewhere, only religious schools had the numbers and institutional capacity to fit that bill. Without them, choice was going to be much harder.

From the point of judicial policymaking, however, the key feature of the vouchers argument turned out to be that both policy debates were focused on the same phenomenon: free choice by parents among competing schools. The pro-choice camp favored choice because choice was its goal; religious schools and their allies favored it because it was the doctrinal key to state subsidy for their operations.

Decision

In the end, the Supreme Court upheld the Cleveland voucher program, with the issue of parents' free, independent choice front and center. Remarkably, the Court did not pretend that *Zelman* was only about religion. Its opinions made clear that the case was also about politics, markets, and America's schools.

The Justices did say a great deal about the establishment of religion. Chief Justice Rehnquist, writing for the five-Justice majority, wrote a clean, crisp opinion that treated vouchers as a straight-line extension of the Court's earlier decisions regarding tax credits, theological scholarships, and sign language interpreters. Those practices were constitutional because no public money arrived at a religious institution without a freely taken, intervening decision by a private person who had the option to direct the funds in either a religious or a secular direction. That is exactly what the Cleveland vouchers do, argued the Court: they allowed each eligible family to decide whether to send their child to the traditional public school, to various secular charter schools, to secular privates, or to religious privates. Money only arrived at religious schools if families selected the final option.

The four dissenting Justices objected vociferously to this approach. Intervening private choices should not matter, they argued, when the state permits funds in such substantial amounts to flow to religious schools. Justice John Paul Stevens went so far as to predict that the opinion would generate renewed "religious strife," citing religious mistrust at the root of conflicts in "the Balkans, Northern Ireland, and the Middle East" (*Zelman v. Simmons-Harris*, 2002, p. 686). In this prediction he was joined by Justices Breyer and Souter.

But the Justices also undertook to determine whether the choices that the voucher program allowed were sufficiently free and independent of the government that it could be said that private persons, not the state, were directing state funds to religious recipients. Although no material facts were in dispute, the implications of each were strenuously debated. It was clear, for example, that 90% of vouchers were used, ultimately, at religious schools. To the Court's majority, this empirical observation was immaterial. What was required was that that parents *could* direct vouchers to secular schools; that they did not do so was indicative only of their private, and therefore irrelevant, preferences. To the dissenters, this datum was damning: it showed that the program was directing or influencing people to use vouchers at religious schools, especially by allowing their secular alternatives—including above all the public schools run and managed by the Cleveland City School District—to become so deplorably bad. This kind of disagreement is common when one considers the availability of "choice" to poor people. To the classical economist, everyone, poor and rich alike, chooses subject to their budget constraint. To the contemporary left in American politics, choosing between a dysfunctional public school and a religious one, like choosing between bread and medicine, is not "free, genuine choice."

Likewise, the Justices, especially Justices O'Connor and Souter, joined the question of what parents were choosing among. O'Connor greatly elaborated an argument offered in the Court's opinion that parents enjoyed a range of secular schooling options because, outside the voucher program, they could opt into magnet or "community" schools, the latter category being Ohio's term for charter schools. Souter responded that non-voucher options were irrelevant. Moreover, most of the charters posted academic results no better than, and sometimes worse than, the traditional public schools, so they could hardly be thought of as alternatives. To this, O'Connor offered a rejoinder self-evident to a classical economist: such schools must be preferable alternatives for some parents, because parents were choosing them.

The result of all this was that the *Zelman* opinions read as if they are as much about choice as they are about religion. The debate over what constitutes "free and independent choice" forced the justices to describe Cleveland's quasi-market for education, of which the voucher program was a major part.

This allowed many in the educational policy community to read *Zelman* as a referendum on choice. For example, Caroline Hoxby, one of the nation's most prominent educational economists, wrote:

> For a long time, I have thought that the church-state issue in school choice debates was a red herring. . . . The tendency of current voucher recipients to attend religiously affiliated schools is an artifact of the tiny scale and uncertain prospects of the voucher experiments we have observed so far in cities like Cleveland. . . . This is why I did not expect the Supreme Court's opinion in *Zelman v. Simmons-Harris* to be exciting. But it was.
>
> One reason the *Zelman* decision was exciting is that it opened the way for a wide variety of new school choice programs. . . . The second reason I found the *Zelman* decision exciting is more subtle, but very important. When I read the Court's opinions, both majority and minority, I was struck by the degree to which the justices cared about the *details* of the Cleveland school program and the *environment* in which it operated. The justices might have focused narrowly on the church-state question, but they did not. They considered the *amount* of the vouchers; they considered the *other school choice programs* operating in Cleveland. . . . The justices described the record of failure of the Cleveland Public Schools, in spite of previous reform efforts and infusions of cash from the state. Simply put, the justices, after devoting serious thought and energy to the problem of school choice, started to think a lot like researchers who have devoted serious thought and energy to the problem of school choice.
>
> (Hoxby, 2003, pp. xi–xiii)

In her view that the church-state issue was a red herring, Hoxby was joined by Justice Clarence Thomas, who insisted in concurrence that the focus on religious establishment was no more than a tactic by those who wished to deprive poor children in inner cities of the chance to go to decent schools. Thomas wrote:

> Today, however, the promise of public school education has failed poor inner-city blacks. While in theory providing education to everyone, the quality of public schools varies significantly across districts. Just as blacks supported public education during Reconstruction, many blacks and other minorities now support school choice programs because they provide the greatest educational opportunities for their children in struggling communities. Opponents of the program raise formalistic concerns about the Establishment Clause but ignore the core purposes of the Fourteenth Amendment.
>
> While the romanticized ideal of universal public education resonates with the cognoscenti who oppose vouchers, poor urban families just want the best education for their children, who will certainly need it. . . .
> (*Zelman*, 2002, pp. 682–683)

Others, of course, did not see in *Zelman* a dismissal of the church-state issue, but simply an endorsement of the set of educational choices that Ohio had created for poor Cleveland families. The Court, of course, forbore from any claim that these choices were *wise* (except for Thomas, who wrote only for himself). But it said these choices were *proper*, and that, coupled with the detailed analysis of choice, was good enough.

Aftermath

So: the Supreme Court blesses the Cleveland voucher program. It makes clear that a state may offer parents the opportunity to direct, in the exercise of their own free and independent choice, state dollars to religious schools. Moreover, the Court not only removed a major constitutional barrier to choice but discussed choice itself in a lengthy, thorough, and approving way. Its decision therefore portends, even more than advocates had hoped, a new flowering of voucher programs. Hoxby, writing in the immediate aftermath of the case, reports that "many states' school choice proposals have already been revivified" (Hoxby, 2003, p. xii).

But, in fact, voucher programs failed to multiply. The Cleveland one continued but did not expand, not even to the city suburbs; a few others persisted; a handful more began. But most jurisdictions, state and local, seem flatly uninterested. James Forman, in 2007, wrote that

> *Zelman* was thought to be important because many assumed that once the Court held vouchers to be constitutional, states would rush

to implement such plans. For many, the uncertain legality of school vouchers had been a reason not to institute voucher programs. . . . Yet, in the years since *Zelman*, school vouchers have made little political headway. They have been proposed in a variety of cities and states, but have overwhelmingly been rejected. This is just as true in states run by Republicans as in those led by Democrats.

(Forman, 2007, pp. 549–550)

This description remains roughly apt today (Minow, 2011, pp. 832–833). Republicans in particular do continue to propose voucher programs, and a few pass; but mostly vouchers have been a sideline. By 2014, only five states and the District of Columbia made school vouchers (rather than just tax credits) available to nondisabled students living in poverty or whose local public schools were deemed inadequate. Several of these states restricted the scope of their programs severely. Private schools continue to provide about 15% of all K–12 desks, with 85% of these schools religious.

As noted, the new President Trump might upend this status quo. But since *Zelman*, many other republican administrations, at both federal and state levels, have lauded vouchers in theory only to neglect them in practice.

The dearth of vouchers on the ground can be understood as a fairly dramatic failure of judicial policymaking. Formally, of course, the Court in *Zelman* purports neither to encourage nor discourage vouchers, but only to permit them. But the Court is embedded in a larger policy environment of advocates, state legislatures, and interest groups. Voucher proponents made heroic efforts to develop the *Zelman* case, to litigate it, and then to win. This was not supposed to lead to a static policy environment. Constitutional doubt resolved, states were supposed to plunge headlong into a new, market-based world, authorizing private schools to receive funds and transforming public schools in the process. None of that happened.

This can be traced in part to provisions in state constitutions, stricter than the federal document, that explicitly forbid any transfer of public funds in support of religious activity. These so-called "Blaine amendments" were not addressed by *Zelman*, a federal case. There are strong arguments that they forbid as a matter of state law the sort of programs that the U.S. Supreme Court had found that the First Amendment permits. But Blaine Amendments don't exist in most states, and it seems clear that the reason for the voucher fizzle went deeper.

The conventional account is that, in the end, people just didn't want school choice very much. Public schools were fairly good in most places, and parents in those places liked their schools well enough to see no reason to change. As Martha Minow, later to become Dean of Harvard Law School, put it: "Despite enormous political efforts and dramatic legal success, the movement for vouchers halted in 2008—right at the feet of suburban parents who liked their public schools. Disillusionment with privatization after the Iraq War, Hurricane Katrina, and the stock market collapse may have contributed to declining interest in school vouchers as private market-based solutions lost cachet" (Minow, 2011, pp. 832–833).

Moreover, in places where public schools were indeed terrible (like Cleveland), local politics was more interested in direct improvements than the possibility of adopting new forms of institutional design. For distressed jurisdictions, the impetus for vouchers tended to come from higher-level institutions like statehouses, national political parties, and, in the case of schools in Washington, D.C., the Congress. But, ultimately, voucher problems for distressed areas share the basic political feature of most welfarist programs that target the poor: it is difficult to make them politically salient, much less popular, among a majority of voters.

Zelman, then, is a story of elite opinion outpacing politics. Thought leaders believed that the time for vouchers had come, and induced the courts to agree; but the body politic did not want them. In a variation on the famous argument that courts follow the ballot box, courts in this instance could not expect the ballot box to follow them. Without political support, whatever promise vouchers offered poor schoolchildren—those who exited public schools and those who remained—would remain unrealized.

Going Forward

Except, maybe not. Consider the charter school, undoubtedly the decisive educational reform of the past 10 years. In 2012–13, 2.3 million children were enrolled in over 6,000 charter schools. By comparison, 450,000 children were enrolled in 1,993 charters in 2000–01, and there were no charter schools in 1990 (U.S. Department of Education, National Center for Education Statistics, 2015, tbl. 216.20). All government-funded schools in New Orleans are now charter schools; other large districts, including Los Angeles, Chicago, Houston, Philadelphia, and Miami-Dade, enroll more than 10% of their students in charters (Saiger, 2013). Chartering, a fairly new arrangement when *Zelman* was decided, is now ubiquitous.

Charters are not vouchers. More accurately, they are not *called* vouchers. Charter proponents have been extremely careful to insist that charter schools are a species of the genus "public school," not the antithesis of public schooling. Every state that permits chartering includes in its charter law the claim that charter schools are public schools. This permits charter advocates to deny that they seek to compete with or empty public schools; how could they, when they are themselves public schools? Minow, explaining *Zelman*'s failure to galvanize change, offers a fine example of such framing: "By 2008, public vouchers to support private schooling receded from the public stage, leaving entrepreneurial school reformers engaged with charter, magnet, and pilot schools, as well as other forms of school choice, within public school systems" (Minow, 2011, pp. 832–833).

But on close inspection, it is hard to see many differences between contemporary charter schools and the voucher schools supported by advocates like Chubb, Moe, and Hoxby. Charters can be established by any group of people or institution that can meet the regulatory requirements and attract students. This group might be made up of teachers, parents, not-for-profit, or for-profit actors. Charters are thus private, incorporated entities; in some ways the government-issued charter is more like the corporate "charter" issued to all private companies than the organizational documents of a public school or school district. And families choose charters; no child is forced to attend. State funding only arrives at a charter school when a family freely decides to enroll a child there. Charters, like private schools, therefore face market discipline. Within whatever regulatory strictures are imposed, charters compete for students with other charters and with other types of schools. If students enroll, a charter thrives. Otherwise it disappears (Vergari, 2003, p. 500).

To be sure, charter schools are subject to regulation. Unlike voucher schools, they do not admit privately paying students and may not charge tuition (Mead, 2003, p. 367). But the Cleveland voucher program also severely capped tuition charges. Likewise, charters are also prohibited from discriminating among students in admission, and oversubscribed charters must admit students by lottery—but these rules applied to the Cleveland voucher schools too. And the jury is still out over the key question of whether either charters or privates generate improved academic achievement more than traditional publics, all else equal.

In short, charters do most of the things that vouchers were supposed to do. They permit and satisfy parental choice, they diversify the system, and they expose traditional public schools to competitive pressure—an exposure evident from the consistent opposition to chartering and its expansion that comes from traditional public schools, teachers' unions, and their allies.

Zelman said nothing about charters, beyond the conclusion that their nascent presence in Cleveland at the time the case was decided was relevant to the genuineness of parents' choice in its educational marketplace. *Zelman* surely did not authorize charters, which were clearly already permissible under federal law. But *Zelman*'s focus on parental choice among schools nevertheless legitimized the idea. And the civil rights frame that Chubb and Moe developed and that Justice Thomas echoed in his separate opinion is carried on today by charter advocates who insist that their enterprise seeks to empower inner-city kids badly served by public school monopolists.

The big difference between charters and vouchers is, of course, religion. Charters cannot be religious, while voucher schools can. That might lead one to say that if charters have displaced vouchers, then *Zelman*, as a religion case, really is a bust. Again, however, *Zelman* may not have drawn its last breath. The mantra of the charter movement has been that a thousand flowers should bloom—that traditional schools are not for everyone, indeed that no single school is for everyone. Students benefit when charters vary by learning style, by approach, and by theme. Some charters are progressive and some regimented; some charters focus on algebra and others on the arts.

Especially as schooling shifts to blended and online forums, it will become harder and harder to say that schools can focus on any area that generates student demand—any area, that is, except for religion. Charters, in their proliferating diversity, already include schools that push the boundaries of church-state separation. As such schools proliferate and intensify, we are likely to hear renewed arguments that in a non-monopolistic, market-based, and partly online systems of schools, the exclusion of religious institutions is illiberal, unconstitutional, and detrimental to children's welfare. When those arguments are finally made, *Zelman* will be the case to cite. Then nobody will call it a fizzle.

References

Chubb, J. E., & Moe, T. M. (1990). *Politics, markets, and America's schools*. Washington: Brookings Institution Press.

Forman, J., Jr. (2007). The rise and fall of school vouchers: A story of religion, race, and politics. *UCLA Law Review, 54*, 547.

Hoxby, C. M. (Ed.). (2003). *The economics of school choice*. Chicago: University of Chicago Press.

Mead, J. F. (2003). Devilish details: Exploring features of charter school statutes that blur the public/private distinction. *Harvard Journal on Legislation, 40*, 349.

Minow, M. (2011). Confronting the seduction of choice: Law, education, and American pluralism. *Yale Law Journal, 120*, 814.

Mueller v. Allen, 463 U. S. 388 (1983).

Saiger, A. J. (2013). Charter schools, the establishment clause, and the neoliberal turn in public education. *Cardozo Law Review, 34*, 1163.

Sugarman, S. D. (1991). Using private schools to promote public values. *University of Chicago Legal Forum, 1991*, 171.

U.S. Department of Education. National Center for Education Statistics. (2015). *The condition of education 2015* (Report No. NCES 2015–144) (supporting tables). Retrieved from https://nces.ed.gov/programs/digest/d14/tables/dt14_216.20.asp

Vergari, S. (2003). Charter schools: A significant precedent in public education. *NYU Annual Survey of American Law, 59*, 495.

Witters v. Washington Dept. of Servs. for Blind, 474 U. S. 481 (1986).

Zobrest v. Catalina Foothills School Dist., 509 U. S. 1 (1993).

Zelman v. Simmons-Harris, 536 U.S. 639 (2002).

11 Challenges and Unintended Consequences of Student-Centered Learning

Lea Hubbard and Amanda Datnow

Historically, teacher-centered approaches to teaching and learning have been the norm, but research has shown that they have not worked for all students (Darling Hammond, 2010; Oakes, 2005). Consequently, students in many schools across the U.S. find themselves disengaged, immersed in classrooms with curriculum that is ill suited to challenges they will face and the occupations they will fill. More recently, student-centered learning has gained considerable interest among educators, though its roots are longstanding in the field of education (Rallis, 1995). The idea of putting students' needs, motivations, and interests at the center is applauded by some districts, principals, and teachers. Proponents of student-centered learning argue that it offers the opportunity to personalize instruction, target student learning styles, preferences, goals, and needs, and may be more appropriately responsive to the well-being and experiential aspects of being a student (Friedlaender, Burns, Lewis-Charp, Cook-Harvey, Darling- Hammond, 2014; Levin, Datnow, & Carrier, 2012). In some cases, however, this promising innovative educational strategy has been merely programmatic and peripheral to students' learning and has not fulfilled its intended goals (Levin et al., 2012). In general, the successes and challenges of implementing student-centered learning, particularly as a school-wide reform, are not well understood.

As educators, researchers, and policymakers engage in efforts to fundamentally reform American education, they are consistently met with significant challenges. Some research suggests it is because there is a "grammar of schooling" (Tyack & Cuban, 1995) that keeps certain traditional pedagogies and expectations for schools in place. Similarly, Hargreaves and Goodson (2006) suggest that the success and sustainability of reforms is challenged because administrators have "neglect[ed] the political, historical, and longitudinal aspects of change," reaffirming "traditional identities and practices . . . and pull[ing] innovative ones back toward the traditional norm" (p. 3). In other words, the leaders of educational change often underestimate how strong the forces against change may be and do not fully understand the complexity of the processes that are involved in change (Fullan, 2012). There are limits on the impact of educational reform, argues

Labaree (2007), because reform remains at the rhetorical level and often fails to penetrate the core.

Other research points to practices inside the educational system, such as tracking, that are so embedded in the fabric of American education (Oakes, 2005). Educators and parents are sometimes reluctant to move away from tracking or do not know how to restructure schools to make them more equitable. Teacher beliefs also frequently challenge educational reform. Mehan, Hubbard, and Datnow (2010) explain how teachers tend to resist reforms when they believe they are "top-down," especially when the changes are inconsistent with their prior experiences and dispositions. The research on educational change emphasizes the constructivist nature of reform and provides a perspective that calls for a closer examination of reform within a school context—one that takes into account school structural arrangements, cultural beliefs, and the actions and capacities of teachers, parents, school leaders, and district administrators (Mehan et al., 2010).

This chapter examines findings from an investigation of a new California public elementary school that places student-centered learning at the core of its efforts to improve teaching and learning. As we will explain, efforts to create student-centered learning exist along a continuum where traditional methods of teaching and "doing school," on the one hand, conflict with personalized learning and student-centered practices, on the other hand. Educators find that they are not completely free to implement a teaching philosophy that holds creativity, innovation, and design thinking at the core. Instead, structural arrangements, such as high-stakes testing demands, as well as entrenched cultural beliefs about teaching and learning—both inside and outside the school—interact to shape teachers' actions, in profound ways. As this case study will show, reform is challenged by factors that adhere to more traditional approaches to teaching and learning, resulting in significant unintended consequences in efforts to place students at the center of instruction.

Theoretical Framework in Sociocultural Context

In an educational context, a "theory of action" encompasses the beliefs and interconnected explanatory structures that underlie education leaders' approach to instruction, curriculum, and the organization of schools. It articulates the relationship among goals, describes strategies for attaining the goals, and provides justifications or explanations for why those strategies should produce the designated goals. These elements are especially important in attempts to guide educational reform. Previous research has suggested, however, that a school's "espoused theory of action" may not necessarily align with their "theory in practice" (Argyris & Schon, 1978). Actions change in large part because they are embedded in contexts that are messy, complicated, and often unpredictable.

Like other reforms, student-centered learning is layered on top of existing routines and relationships. In order to fully implement student-centered learning, some research suggests that there must be evidence of expanding learning opportunities so that they may occur " 'anytime, anywhere'; reshaping the role of the educator to guide more than drive instruction, and determining individual progression based on mastery" (Levin et al., 2012, p. 20). These principles translate into changes in what is taught and when it is taught, and can interrupt school schedules and confront power relationships between teachers and students.

Teachers' actions, capacities, and beliefs can also influence the implementation of student-centered pedagogy. Previous research has pointed out that teachers' responses to reform are often shaped by their social contexts (Coburn, 2001; Olsen & Sexton, 2009). The importance of context is key to Spillane's (2012) explanation that interpretations are "not just a function of their [educators'] prior knowledge and beliefs, but also a function of their interactions with others in which they negotiate what information is worth noticing and how it should be framed" (p. 14). Thus, the actions and belief systems of teachers are part of a complex dynamic, interwoven with the structural and cultural features of their school.

The school we studied offers a particularly interesting place to examine these dynamics, since the school is at its early stages of development when tensions around change are most evident. This investigation examines the espoused theory that promised to guide student-centered teaching and learning at the school and the actual theory in practice. We asked specifically: how is teachers' theory in practice similar or different from their espoused theory of action? What tensions emerge when shifting from a traditional to a student-centered learning environment, and what are the consequences for teacher practice? This chapter uncovers the unintentional consequences when educators attempted to bring an espoused theory to life in their enacted model of schooling.

Methodology

This research utilized qualitative case study methods, which allowed an examination of the "theory of action" at the school as it unfolded (Yin, 2014). Case-study methodology is an ideal strategy for exploring situations in which the intervention being evaluated (i.e., student-centered learning) has no single set of outcomes (Stake, 2011; Yin, 2014). It is also an ideal method for studying a change effort in the real-life context in which it occurs.

The Learner-Centered Public School (LCPS)—a pseudonym—opened in Fall 2014 as part of a district effort to reinvent schooling. Located in California, the school serves 950 students in kindergarten through 7th grade, and the school will add an 8th grade in 2017–18. The district aimed to organize schooling in a student-centered way and to develop a model for other sites in the district. It is located in a growing suburban area. The student population is predominately White and Asian, with smaller numbers of Latino, African-American, and mixed race students. Approximately 16% of the students are classified English learners.

A variety of data collection techniques, including document review, interviews, and observations were employed over the course of two years. We began with a review of documents that detailed the original plans for the school to understand the school's espoused theory of action (Argyris & Schon, 1978). We conducted 16 teacher interviews representing grades K–7 to learn about the implementation of student-centered learning from the perspective of those involved in the daily life of the school. We also conducted interviews and focus groups with parents and held conversations and interviews with several of the school and district administrators. We conducted 20 observations of classroom practice and 15 teacher collaborative lesson-planning sessions. Transcribed interviews and field notes were coded to ascertain themes (Saldana, 2013; Strauss & Corbin, 1998) to help explain the structural and cultural factors that informed how teachers made decisions, initiated policies, and navigated constraints. Constructivist theory was used to make meaning of the findings from this study. Constructivist theory emphasizes the phenomenon being studied through the gathering and analysis of data and takes into consideration the systemic aspects of social contexts in which data are collected (Charmaz, 2011, 2006).

Student-Centered Learning in Practice

Much planning and documentation of the school's vision preceded the opening of the school, and an espoused theory of action was articulated. As a result, LCPS looks very different from a traditional school in numerous important ways. All students move fluidly across rooms—even kindergarten students change classes—and they work at movable furniture, whiteboard tables, and chairs that rock to accommodate their desire to be active. Students do not have assigned seats. They sit where they choose to and are occasionally asked to find a new seat if the arrangement isn't conducive to their learning. There is no desk at the front of the room, and the teacher is often working among the students. Teachers' theory of practice translates into planned opportunities for students to collaborate and engage in inquiry-based instruction. Teachers work each morning for an hour before school officially starts with their grade level colleagues creating lessons to support hands-on instruction, choice, and exploration. They discuss what it means to learn and how to use different mediums such as art, math, or computer coding to address a variety of learning styles. Students are encouraged to "deep dive" into subjects *they choose* to learn about, and teachers constantly challenge themselves and each other to better support all students.

Design Thinking (DT) is at the core of LCPS's student-centered instructional practices. DT is a process or strategy for problem solving and for stimulating "out of the box" thinking. It is a response against traditional instructional models that require students to work until the "correct" answer is generated to achieve success on standardized tests. In LCPS classrooms, students develop "empathy" and conduct research on a problem they have identified as significant. They brainstorm and ideate to explore potential solutions and then create a prototype or model that displays their solution to the problem. They typically present their model to their classmates who question, test, and evaluate. Students continue the process by publishing or producing their product.

A similar process exists at the school level. Teachers and school leaders engage in DT to improve the school. The process encourages collaboration rather than top-down administrative decision-making. Teachers and the administrators work together as a team to identify system problems and to create solutions. For example, teachers puzzle together over the best ways to assess students' real world learning goals or how to organize them most effectively for math instruction.

According to research on student-centered learning (Jobs for the Future, 2013; Wolf, Steinberg, & Hoffman, 2013; Friedlaender et al., 2014; Corley, 2012; Ito et al., 2013; Pane et al., 2010), when learning tasks reflect and respond to students' particular needs and interests, when they employ effective learning strategies, when learning is personalized and at the same time, learning is supported as a social process, and when instructional practice encourages students to have a "growth mindset" (Dweck, 2007), deep learning ensues. At LCPS there is substantial evidence that instruction supports these student-centered learning tenets. Practice is grounded in the idea that students are individuals who learn differently, are interested in different topics, have different strengths, and face different challenges (Rallis, 1995). Teachers articulate the importance of a growth mindset and purposefully pair a "growth mindset student with a fixed mindset student to better support each student," as one teacher explained.

Learning is personalized and also competency-based. Academic performance is assessed according to the California Common Core Standards. Student-centered learning at LCPS means giving students choice where they become active decision-makers regarding what to study, what learning strategies work best for them, and how to display learning in their own way. Students choose which piece of technology to use to help solve a particular math problem and how to represent the solution. Some of the choices they are typically given include employing Google drive, Wiki, or pencil and paper. A first-grade teacher, for example, explained student choice in her classroom this way:

> [One student] was thinking he could take a picture of the equation and put it on his Wiki page; [another student] was thinking he could write

the problem on the table and take a picture of it, then put it on his Wiki page. [Another student] had another really cool idea. He is going to try to explain his thinking by recording his voice and putting that on his journal.

Personalized learning leads to "student-owned learning." Students are encouraged to select a social problem that interests them, to "deep dive" into that problem, construct a solution, and then choose a way to represent that solution to their classmates. Students are engaged because the content and the problem solving is theirs. One teacher explained the change she made in her own teaching to personalize learning:

Open-ended time has just been really powerful for kids—here's this concept of geoscience or how the earth is constantly changing—and I can say, how can you show what this means to you at a sixth-grade level? For myself—to step away from, 'here's these little check marks [assessment] I have to do,' to saying, I care more about the bigger picture and kids understanding—that's been really cool.

Teachers identify student strengths so that grouping arrangements can be supportive of each student. As explained by one teacher, "it's more of, you know, how can we organize kids, how can we maybe group kids to more personalize the learning experience. And we do tend to look at the students' *super powers* as often as possible." In one of the focus groups a teacher explained that grouping is "not based on grade level, but here's where you are. It's more fluid, it's more expansive, it's what you might be doing if you're this age or this grade." Another teacher explained:

Grouping fits with personalization because, you know, if I'm really excited about [studying oceans], I could be a fourth grader, and why can't I join the ocean group and study what I want to study, I just need a teacher to be there supporting me. I don't need a teacher standing on stage teaching me about the ocean.

Also indicating the fluidity across grade levels, one teacher explained that, "Older kids mentor younger kids—I mean, we could have, you know, a first grader and a fifth grader, both really interested in coral reefs and they could both be studying together just at their own level, whatever that might look like."

Learning is inquiry-based where critical thinking is encouraged, as indicated in the observation of this teacher-student interaction. Instead of providing an answer, a teacher prompted her student to research and problem solve on his own. When the student asked the teacher to explain a 3D printer, the teacher instructed him to research it on Google, learn more, and then come back to her. The student did so, and then the teacher asked what he had learned. After the student had conducted his own investigation, he and the teacher worked through the information together.

Learning is also "anywhere." Students choose where to work, often taking their work outside, on the playground, on the floor, in the "Makery Room" (a space where they are free to build prototypes of solutions to their problems), and in collaborative spaces. Student-centered learning at LCPS involves collaboration, teamwork, critical thinking, and a push for innovation and creativity. Student engagement is notable. When one student was asked, "What's the best thing about school?" he replied, "Walking in the door and thinking, 'What am I going to create today?'"

Giving students considerable autonomy, "using what [the student] already knows to figure out the next piece or the next day" (teacher), pacing teaching and learning to differentiate instruction, suggests much to be applauded. With these successes, however, it is clear that LCPS educators also confront many of the same challenges faced by other public schools. Meeting the Common Core State Standards and addressing parent and district community pressures, as well as teachers' own conflicted dispositions regarding teaching and learning, call student-centered learning practices into question. By the end of the second year of implementation, teachers were reflecting and rethinking their practice. The ways in which their espoused theory of action has been modified indicate the power of traditional ideologies and practices and the influence of structural and cultural factors in shaping a theory in practice. In the next sections, we describe some of the challenges that have occurred at the instructional level that undermine student-centered reform efforts at LCPS.

Internal Challenges around Student-Centered Learning that Create Unintended Consequences

Teachers choose to come to LCPS because they want to teach using a new innovative model—a model that rejects textbook teaching and direct instruction—a model that was formerly in place in the schools where they previously taught and a model that teachers feel did not work for all students. Most of the teachers had the opportunity to work together to co-construct what LCPS would look like in practice and were strongly wedded to the ideals of the school when it opened.

Despite general support for student-centered teaching and learning, the pushback on student-centered learning came in part from the teachers themselves, many of whom are somewhat confused about what it should look like in practice—often turning to direct instruction (DI) strategies. According to one LCPS administrator who conducted routine walkthroughs of all classrooms, approximately 70% of the teachers were engaging in a considerable amount of direct instruction every day. Some teachers estimated that the number of teachers using DI was closer to 50%. Most agree that there is variation across teachers.

To make the distinction clear, one teacher described the difference between student-centered learning and traditional direct instruction this way:

> *Student-centered*: "[Teachers] don't model. We model behavior, we model expectations, we model how to problem solve but I'm not going to show you how to do an addition problem. No, that is your struggle, you think about how you want to solve it, you show us your strategies, we talk about all the different strategies then, maybe, I will show you a trick that maybe a different teacher would have done on day one."
>
> *Traditional, DI instruction*: "These [teachers] have more of a standard lesson ready to go. They are more skill based; they streamline the process, a right answer, a final product. Like now, we figured it out, now we have the answer. It's cleaner; decisions are made."

Teachers vary in which pedagogical approach they take. How do we account for this instructional variation and change when initial commitments to student-centered learning seemed so tenable in year one?

While it might be expected that teachers who joined LCPS in year two and were not part of the original envisioning process for the school would be the teachers who were more traditional, this was not the case. One of the upper grade original LCPS teachers clarified by equating "out of the box thinkers" as student-centered supporters. She said, "We have veteran . . . teachers who are really outside the box thinkers."

Some of the original teachers challenged the student-centered learning model because they felt that the model initially envisioned simply did not work in practice. A veteran teacher explained it this way,

> I think that some people, myself definitely one of them, were questioning the vision when we saw it in the hands of real seven-year-old kids. You're like, is this the best thing to give a seven-year-old kid? Nine options? Probably not. Let's give him two, let's give him three, and that doesn't mean that's a bad thing. That's one of the wrestling matches on this campus, how true are we to this original vision, or are we realizing that the original vision can be tweaked.

Others accounted for the move to more direct instruction by complaining that student-centered teaching is just too hard to do. Another teacher elaborated:

> My perception, because design thinking is messy and it takes a lot of time; it is not easy and it is not clean and it is not structured; it moves all over the place and there have been people who have voiced frustration about those processes and want decisions made and want structures for decision-making. So they like the quickness, they like the action [that traditional teaching provides].

The pushback from some teachers caused this educator to wonder: "Do we need to do one or the other [student-centered or traditional] or, are there times when one version is more appropriate than another version? Is there a happy medium?"

Philosophical differences regarding fidelity to the model created "camps" of loyalty, however, and there was a growing sentiment that if you were not faithful, you would be stigmatized. This teacher explained,

> There's a real stigma on campus that you can't change that vision, if you change that vision well, you are part of this team or you are betraying what we stood for, but that original vision was great, but it was on paper. It's not a living breathing seven-year-old. So, we keep going back to this. It's hard to adhere to the vision and especially when you see that it may not be the best thing for kids.

Teachers varied in their beliefs about the extent to which student-centered learning should remain the sacred cow. One of the original teachers explained her experience trying to work out these ideological differences with her colleagues. She said it's about, "talking it out, you know, trying things out, . . . I would try to convince them this way, and they'd try to convince me this way. . . ." While most classrooms could best be described at the end of year two as a combination of direct instruction and student-centered pedagogy, teachers were decidedly more traditional than initially predicted.

Another important challenge emerging within the school that threatened student-centered instruction was the pushback from the students themselves, who teachers described as simply not ready or not used to the new freedoms and new demands placed upon them. Moving from class to class for example did not work for all students. Teachers explained they had to "slow it down a little bit." Asking students to analyze their own knowledge and progress also proved too difficult for some students, especially those in the early elementary grades.

These internal challenges to student-centered instruction—challenges coming from inside the school walls—are playing out alongside challenges stemming from forces outside the school. We discuss those next.

External Forces that Create Unintended Consequences

Standardized Tests and Regulatory Policies

The pressure of teaching to the Common Core State Standards and the accompanying assessments also exerted tensions on student-centered learning. These comments from a teacher emerge from concerns regarding whether LCPS educators were adequately teaching to the standards.

> When I look at students' content knowledge there's just some standards gaps, there's just some knowledge that they don't yet have.

We're focusing at this place a lot on soft skills, there's a lot of soft skills development— communication, collaboration—you know, you can't measure that stuff and if you could measure that stuff, we'd be off the charts, however, I think we emphasize soft skills at the expense of some hard skills. So, that pendulum needs to swing and we need to just make sure we're doing some good teaching. And, let's not forget that *we know how to teach.*

The push to teach more content created pressure on the teachers, but "good teaching" came to mean the need for more direct instruction. Another teacher explained it this way:

So I think that they [the teachers] struggle personally to figure out what does it mean to do design thinking and still meet all of our content because they still feel the pressure of the content. And I know that from being a part of [the upper grades] that we do struggle with that quite a bit. We struggle with okay, I have this stuff that is not of interest to kids and yet it is really important because it is the only time in their life they are going to learn about ancient Egypt.

This teacher posed the following question: "And so then this is our struggle—how do you bridge content with design thinking and still provide choice for kids?" Another teacher explained the struggle: "the goal is that the child is at the center of all of our decisions. Now that's bringing around some of my biggest challenges, like, how do I personalize for that child? How do I make sure that one's being pushed, while this one's being dragged back up to grade level?"

For some LCPS educators, this struggle meant "using what they have learned about *how* students learn, incorporating it into their instructional practice and connecting their teaching to the standards. . . ." But as this teacher points out, that's "hard to do."

We need to integrate art, extension courses, deep dive, whatever you want to call them, [they] need to be connected to the core curriculum and that's incredibly hard to do. The amount of work that it takes is enormous and we've been scared away from it for a while because it's just a hard thing.

The initial plan for instruction was to get rid of lesson guides and daily create "just in time" lessons. This left teachers saying that, "it's killing us to be that responsive," despite the collaborative time built into their schedule each day.

Observations of this collaborative time indicate that at least some of the teachers have come to acknowledge that everyone doesn't have to teach the same way. While general topics can be mutually agreed upon, how a teacher takes up that content, how they choose to design instruction, varied considerably—with evidence suggesting the trend among teachers is toward more traditional teaching.

Assessment Practices Face Pushback from Parents

Another externally driven tension that threatened the innovative practices of student-centered learning became evident as teachers worried about collecting, assessing, and reporting student achievement to parents. With project-based learning and other student-centered practices, educators did not rely on standardized test driven assessment tools. Instead, they frequently asked students to write answers to math problems on whiteboard tables that then get erased, leaving teachers to ask, "where's the evidence?" and "how do I assess students' progress and report it to parents?" The philosophy of anytime and anywhere teaching and learning presented challenges for assessment. A primary grades teacher explained that a student very nicely counted by twos on the playground, a task that the student had not yet demonstrated in the classroom but, outside the classroom walls, teachers wrestled with how to capture and record student accomplishments.

LCPS educators were committed to "doing things differently," which meant replacing traditional assessment reports and methods of communicating with parents. Instead of traditional report cards, they relied on "Growth Guides," that were tied to the Common Core State Standards. These arguably more complex and nuanced reports coupled with alternative assessments, no nightly homework, and no obligatory back-to-school nights, pushed up against parents' traditional notions of assessment and opportunities that they viewed as strategies that supported parent-teacher communication. Parents complained that they could not tell how their child was performing, what they were learning, and how they were achieving compared to other children in the school/district. One parent explained her confusion:

> There is a bunch of digital things [reporting mechanisms] that are optional, and one is just incredibly terrible and the other one is okay [to keep us informed]. It seems to help but I don't know if that is connected to what is going on in the classroom or if that is just what the program provides.

Without traditional formally arranged opportunities to meet with teachers, this parent did not find out her child was below average until after she got the results of a district-administered benchmark assessment which revealed that her child was performing one year below grade level. She explained: "I had no conversation with the teacher prior to that and that is concerning. So with my kindergartner [communication], it's okay, and with my third grader, I have no idea and I don't know how to help her." In general, the teachers did not see the benchmark assessments as a valid measure. However, the district required it for all of their schools, and the parents were accustomed to receiving the results.

Teachers varied in their perspectives as to the legitimacy of parent complaints, with some claiming that they sent frequent emails and did their best to keep parents informed. Others, however, agreed with parents, saying that the information they provided was far less than what was provided by traditional report cards. Still others expressed anger that their assessment model didn't get more support from the principal.

LCPS's attempt to move away from traditional assessment practices in favor of Growth Guides and emails left parents unhappy, and teachers and the administrative team generally agreed that they needed to take some action. According to an administrator, using the design thinking process, we "set sail not knowing where [we] were going to end up." Parents were called in, assessment problems were identified, brainstorming ensued, and plans were made to move toward a new model. Consistent with their mission, they focused their attention on how to empower *students* to prove that they were learning, because at LCPS it's all about *"the Chair"*—the metaphor for "it's all about the *student*." In attempting to solve the problem, they decided that teachers would be the facilitators and thus, the students would be at the heart of the solution; "the student would show the parents that they're learning" (teacher). One administrator explained that they wanted to move away from the paradigm of teachers proving to the parent that their child was learning. Instead, it was the student who needed to prove to the parent that they were learning.

In the second year after the school opened, "Workstreams"—a group of teachers comprised of a representative from each grade span—came together to work on this school-wide problem. They organized to determine how to empower students to monitor their knowledge, assess what they know or don't know, work with their teacher to improve learning and importantly, provide "proof of learning" to their parents.

Although parents were actively involved in discussions about this new assessment policy and the focus was decidedly student-centered, it was too early to predict whether this new response would meet parents' needs and expectations or whether LCPS will face similar pushback from parents advocating in favor of more traditional methods of assessment and communication.

Challenges Implementing Student-Centered Learning for Special Education Students

Providing student-centered learning for special education students also presented challenges for LCPS, given their 80/20 model. Eighty percent of students in the class are general education, and 20% of the students are special education. This allows for special education students in the general education classroom and provides all the benefits of a more inclusive education. Dual credentialed teachers receive help from a resource teacher who pushes in to provide support for the students. This model was challenged by the district, who pointed out they were not meeting special education legal requirements, which specify the amount and kind of intervention. Each of the special education students had an Individualized Education Plan (IEP) that details a scheduled time when the student should receive individual attention and specifies goals that are to be met. For example, a student might be scheduled for four days a week for 60 minutes, or four times a week for 60 minutes. The resource teacher explains, however, with the LCPS schedule, responding to those requirements is problematic—special education compliance and school schedules conflict.

> They have their math block, and then they have a 'deep dive,' so pulling them out four times a week for 60 minutes to work on whatever their goals are, or pushing in to that class; I can't get to all the kids and all the different ways their IEP are written.

The traditional model of pull-out instruction was recently adopted because it is easier to meet legal demands. The dilemma was readily apparent to the teachers, who explained that while traditional pull-out programs work in addressing IEP goals they comprised class goals. As one teacher explained:

> I also know that kids miss out on so much that's going on in their class when they're pulled out. They're just getting farther and farther behind when the class is still going, and then, finding those times that aren't as important to pull them out, but then they're missing out on the fun stuff.

According to some LCPS educators, this new pull-out model was not meeting their notions of student-centered learning. One teacher stated that this year there were a lot of special education students in the upper grades and meeting their needs, well, "it's a train wreck."

Conclusions and Implications

While making significant strides in attending to the needs of each student, educators at LCPS are bumping up against traditional notions of school culture and structure, leading them to re-conceptualize what student-centered learning means in practice and resulting in unintended consequences for teachers and students. Internally, teachers who were arguably committed to student-centered learning feel the model is not working and is simply too hard to implement and turn to more direct instruction. Those concerned over standardized tests and that students are not receiving enough subject content or the right content to meet the Common Core State Standards and other high-stakes accountability measures also revert to a greater amount of direct instruction. This move has resulted in the unintended consequence of teacher-centered rather than personalized or individualized instruction. External policies and requirements regarding special education students also cause educators to turn to traditional pull-out models in lieu of more inclusive and innovative pedagogies. Expecting traditional reporting and assessment practices, some parents push back and resist innovative practices. In general, LCPS's espoused theory of action faces challenges that are resulting in a theory of practice that is somewhat more traditional than predicted and where the focus on the individual needs of each student is once again challenged in favor of expedience, policy, and tradition.

The successes and challenges experienced in the school's early development provide evidence of the complexity of implementing student-centered learning and other innovative teaching practices. Accountability demands and policies at the state and district levels, as well as entrenched cultural beliefs about teaching and learning both internal and external to the school, shape educators' actions and decisions. And, although many of the teachers and the administrators at LCPS remain committed to their initial vision of schooling, as they continue with implementation, this study raises questions as to how policy and practice will be negotiated.

Given the many possibilities of reform, it seems crucial to engage in research that informs educators as well as the broader community how to navigate the pull of traditional models of education while moving forward with an array of pedagogical strategies that deepen student-centered learning. This case study provides evidence specifically on the complexity of implementing student-centered teaching, but contributes to our understanding of the unintended consequences of educational reform more generally. When policymakers and educators introduce student-centered practices and other progressive educational reforms that offer greater opportunity to improve the academic lives of *all* students, traditional models of education or the "grammar of schooling" must be challenged (Tyack & Cuban, 1995). This study offers insight into some of the reasons behind the powerful pull for traditional schooling and the unintended consequences of this pull for educators and students.

We find that the most diligent attempts to create an educational equity agenda and reform schooling are likely compromised by the influence of cultural beliefs, structural arrangements, and other contextual issues that are embedded in and support traditional schooling models. Stakeholders, including teachers, school leadership, parents, district and community members, as well as accountability mandates, such as standardized tests and state curriculum standards, shape stakeholders' beliefs and practices in ways that retain traditionally held notions of how best to "do school." This study shows that it is imperative that we understand the interrelatedness of these dynamics so that inequitable educational outcomes can be replaced by innovative practice designed to better support the needs and enhance opportunities for all students.

References

Argyris, C., & Schön, D. (1978). *Organizational learning: A theory of action perspective*. Reading, MA: Addison Wesley.

Charmaz, K. (2006). *Constructing grounded theory: A practical guide through qualitative analysis*. Los Angeles, CA: Sage.

Charmaz, K. (2011). Grounded theory methods in social justice research. In Denzin, N. K., & Lincoln, Y. S. (Eds.), *The Sage handbook of qualitative research*, 4th ed. (pp. 359–380). Thousand Oaks, CA: Sage.

Coburn, C. (2001). Collective sensemaking about reading: How teachers mediate reading policy in their professional communities. *Educational Evaluation and Policy Analysis*, 23(2), 145–170.

Corley, M. A. (2012). *TEAL center fact sheet No. 6: Student-centered learning*. Retrieved from https://teal.ed.gov/tealGuide/studentcentered

Darling-Hammond, L. (2010). *The flat world and education*. New York, NY: Teachers College Press.

Dweck, C. (2007). *Mindset: The new psychology of success*. New York: Random House.

Friedlaender, D., Burns, D., Lewis-Charp, H., Cook-Harvey, C. M., & Darling-Hammond, L. (2014). Student-centered schools: Closing the opportunity gap. Research brief. Palo Alto: Stanford Center for Opportunity Policy in Education. Retrieved from: https://edpolicy.stanford.edu/sites/default/files/scope-pub-student-centered-research-brief.pdf

Fullan, M. (2012). *Change forces: Probing the depths of educational reform*. New York: Routledge.

Hargreaves, A., & Goodson, I. (2006). Educational change over time? The sustainability and nonsustainability of three decades of secondary school change and continuity. *Educational Administration Quarterly*, 42, 3–41.

Ito, M., Gutierrez, K., Livingstone, S., Penuel, B., Rhodes, J., Salen, K., Schor, J., Sefton-Green, J., & Watkinds, C. (2013). *Connected learning: An agenda for research and design*. Irvine, CA: Digital Media and Learning Research Hub.

Jobs for the Future. (2013). *Putting students at the center: Reference guide*. Quincy, MA: Nellie Mae Education Foundation.

Labaree, D. F. (2007, September). *Limits on the impact of educational reform: The case of Progressivism and U.S. Schools, 1900–1950*. Paper presented at The Century of the School: Continuity and Innovation During the First Half of the 20th Century, Monte Verità, Ascona.

Levin, B., Datnow, A., & Carrier, N. (2012). *Students at the center: Teaching and learning in the era of common core standards: Jobs for the future*. Washington, DC. Retrieved at http: www.studentsatthecenter.org/papers/changing-school-district-practices.

Mehan, H., Hubbard, L., & Datnow, A. (2010). A co-construction perspective on organizational change and educational reform. In Penuel, B., & O'Connor, K. (Eds.), *Learning research as human science, Vol. 109 of the National Society for the Study of Education* (pp. 98–112). New York: Columbia University.

Oakes, J. (2005). *Keeping track: How schools structure inequality* (2nd ed.). New Haven, CT: Yale University Press.

Olsen, B., & Sexton, D. (2009). Threat rigidity, school reform, and how teachers' view their work inside current education policy contexts. *American Educational Research Journal, 46*(1), 9–44.

Pane, J. F., McCaffrey, D. F., Slaughter, M. E., Steele, J. L., & Ikemoto, G. S. (2010). An experiment to evaluate the efficacy of Cognitive Tutor Geometry. *Journal of Research on Educational Effectiveness, 3*(3), 254–281.

Rallis, S. (1995). Creating learner centered schools: Dreams and practices. *Theory into Practice, 34*(4), 224–229.

Saldana, J. (2013). *The coding manual for qualitative researchers*. Thousand Oaks, CA: Sage Publications.

Spillane, J. (2012). Data in practice: Conceptualizing the data-based decision-making phenomena. *American Journal of Education, 118*, 113–141.

Stake, R. E. (2011). Qualitative case studies. In Denzin, N. K., & Lincoln, Y. S. (Eds.), *The Sage handbook of qualitative research*, 4th ed. (pp. 443–446). Thousand Oaks, CA: Sage Publications.

Strauss, A., & Corbin, J. (1998). *Basics of qualitative research: Techniques and procedures for developing grounded theory* (2nd ed.). London: Sage Publications.

Tyack, D., & Cuban, L. (1995). *Tinkering toward utopia*. Cambridge: Harvard University Press.

Wolfe, R. E., Steinberg, A., & Hoffman, N. (Eds.). (2013). *Anytime, anywhere student-centered learning for schools and teachers*. Cambridge, MA: Harvard Education Press.

Yin, R. K. (2014). *Case study research: Design and methods* (5th ed.). Thousand Oaks, CA: Sage.

12 School Discipline Policies That Result in Unintended Consequences for Latino Male Students' College Aspirations

Adrian H. Huerta, Shannon M. Calderone, and Patricia M. McDonough

Since policy has gone to school in major ways since Brown v. the Board of Education, Sputnik, and the Civil Rights and Great Society legislation, it has generated research evidence on how policy intention translates into school practice. Repeatedly, in small- and large-school analyses and evaluations, two research findings show up again and again: 1) educational policies and school practices are at best only loosely connected, and 2) effective policy implementation rests with the "end of the line" implementers, mostly teachers (McLaughlin, 1987). But let's talk about school discipline policy at the federal, state, and local levels.

Aggressive school disciplinary policies have been a key factor in the educational derailment of young men of color (Brown, 2007; NCES, 2012; Losen, 2015). Each school day, thousands of students—largely men of African-American and Latino descent—are forcibly removed from the classroom for punitive reasons. The culture of aggressive discipline within schools evolved as a response to a rise in juvenile crime experienced in the mid-1990s. Political scientist John Dilulio's now infamous claim of an emerging adolescent "superpredator" in 1996 and the Columbine High School massacre in 1999 shepherded in a wave of zero-tolerance policies within school districts nationwide and normalized the presence of security apparatuses like law enforcement and metal detectors on school campuses (Miller, 1998; Kang-Brown et al., 2013). A zero-tolerance school culture maintained as its goal the elimination of all potential threats to school order (Castillo, 2015; Kennedy-Lewis & Murphy, 2016; Noguera, 2003). By mandatorily removing disruptive students from the classroom, schools ensured that non-disruptive peers were guaranteed a safe and productive learning environment (Hirschfield, 2008). No attention was paid to the learning environments of the removed students.

At face value, a safe and productive learning environment seems an admirable goal. Yet, the competing goals of equity, elimination of institutionalized racism, responding to federal mandates, and the economic necessity of having 60% of our high school graduates prepared for, enrolling in, and graduating from college are also concurrently mandated or legally required policy goals. What has resulted from this aggressive stance, however, is marked disproportionality in *who* is disciplined. Recent statistics indicate that students of color are three to four times more likely to be suspended or expelled as compared to White students (Kang-Brown et al., 2013; Office of Civil Rights, 2014). Moreover, one out of five Latinos are likely to receive some form of school discipline suspension by the 9th grade (NCES, 2012). Latino boys and other young men of color are treated poorly in schools and their communities (Conchas & Vigil, 2012). Disproportionality in school discipline has resulted in the diminishment of educational opportunity and proportional increases in alienation from school. These effects have a long lasting impact on educational attainment given that less than 5% of suspended Latino male students go on to earn a Bachelor's degree by the age of 26 (Shollenberger, 2015). Why might this be the case? How do these punitive responses serve to undermine the college aspirations of those students with a history of school discipline?

Understanding Unintended Consequences

In this chapter, we examine the ways in which suspensions and expulsions dampen the college-going aspirations of Latino males, a largely under-researched intersection of disciplinary policy and a college-educated work-force policy. Culling from a larger, multi-school qualitative study (Yin, 2011) on school discipline and college-going (Huerta, 2016), we introduce you to Mateo, a composite Latino high school student (based on semi-structured interviews with 26 suspended or expelled males from this district) who has been classified as a "habitual disciplinary problem." Mateo has been involuntarily transferred from a comprehensive high school to Viejo Continuation School (VCS) located within the Rock County School District (RCSD). Through this personal narrative, we consider how aggressive disciplinary policy implementation overlooks the pressures and challenging contours that make up the lives of low-income students of color by forcibly locating them at the educational margins for the sake of other students' school safety. We also consider how disciplinary labels attenuate the relationship between school and student: frustration, alienation, and diminishing hope follow such labels and lead to a form of self-actualization that undermines students' hopes and dreams for the future (Kim, 2011). Mateo's personal narrative and journey serve as powerful context for a broader discussion about the unintended consequences of school disciplinary policy for college-aspiring Latino males.

Mateo's Story

Mateo, a first-generation Mexican-American, is a bright, soft-spoken 16-year-old sophomore who has been attending VCS for the last year. His dark skin and thin-build stand out amongst his light-skinned athletic Latino peers as most of them play basketball during P.E. while Mateo prefers to walk around the court and process his family problems with a male peer. The oldest of four, Mateo lives with his mom, his mom's boyfriend, and his three younger siblings in a rented two-bedroom apartment within five miles of VCS. Mateo's father has been largely absent from his life since Mateo was six. Throughout his young life, Mateo has watched his mother struggle financially as she worked a succession of restaurant jobs. Mateo's family's economic and social conditions have improved since his mom's boyfriend of eight years, Jesse, arrived on the scene. Jesse works as a part-time truck mechanic for the city's public utility company. While still not enough to make bill paying comfortable, the additional income does help. In her ongoing search for better work, Mateo's mom has moved the family three times in the seven years since his half-brother Ronnie was born.

Mateo wants to make life easier for his mom and dreams of getting a job someday and helping out his family. He knows he's smart, capable, and when he sets his mind to it, school comes easily to him. He can get A's and B's, but he doesn't always find himself in class long enough to demonstrate his capabilities. He understands that college is the next step—but he wonders if it is the next step for him? Now he simply does what he can by caring for his younger siblings while his mom and Jesse are at work. On some level, he feels bad that his problems at school require his mom to get involved because he knows she doesn't have the time or patience to deal with it, but there's not much he can do about that these days. Let us walk you through Mateo's journey.

Classified as a Habitual Disciplinary Problem

Mateo joined VCS following his expulsion from Sunnyside High School in the spring of 2015. Viejo has been a behavioral rehabilitation site for the district since it was first established in the 1940s. Its motto of "Safety! Climate! Academics!" speaks to its espoused commitment to "encouraging social growth in order for all students to become productive members of society" (Huerta, 2016). Viejo boasts of having one of the lowest teacher to student ratios (8:1) in the state, and its enrollment of 188 students is largely comprised of students of color (86%), with a high percentage qualifying for free and reduced lunch (68%). The vast majority of students identify as Latino (> 65%), with a far smaller representation of African-American (< 20%), and the rest are White students.

VCS is one of two senior high continuation schools located within the district, which serves over 300,000 students, a majority of whom are Latino, Asian-American Pacific Islander, and African-American (Huerta, 2016). The district's over 350 schools are divided into multiple geographic regions, placing it solidly among the top five largest districts in the western U.S., if not the country (Huerta, 2016). RCSD (2014) mirrors national patterns in use of school discipline and truancy rates for students of color, low-income students, and students with disabilities. Among Latinos attending RCSD, disciplinary numbers decreased from over 40% of students in 2012–2013 to less than 35% of students in 2015–2016.

RCSD disciplinary policy is determined in accordance with state statutes, which prioritize the stability and order of schools. The first item of the policy regulations states that ". . . every teacher and principal [is charged] with maintaining order and discipline among students and [will ensure] that students who do not comply with [these] reasonable rules may be recommended for disciplinary action" (Huerta, 2016). District regulations go on to outline a cumulative disciplinary system premised upon the goal of "controlling and correcting undesirable student behavior" (Huerta, 2016). Disruptive behavior that is deemed "antisocial" or "dangerous" represents "just cause" for discipline within the district, whether it occurs on a school campus, at a district-owned facility, or even off-campus if it is within close proximity of a school. While efforts are made to define antisocial or dangerous behavior through specific behavioral guidelines outlined by the state, the latitude by which principals (the primary arbiters of disciplinary decision-making) must adhere to them is ultimately subject to individual interpretation. In testament to RCSD's pervasive disciplinary culture, if teachers and principals don't act, they themselves will be subject to "disciplinary action."

For students like Mateo, who have received two or more incidents of prior violent or disruptive behavior, principals have the authority to classify them as a habitual disciplinary problem and suspend the student for no more than one school semester or expel the student outright. Consistent with RCSD's cumulative disciplinary policy, Mateo's disciplinary path has led to his removal from regular high school and placement in VCS. How he wound up there, we'll speak to next.

Mateo's Disciplinary Pathway as a So-Called "Troublemaker"

Since middle school, Mateo would routinely find himself in the wrong place at the wrong time. Teased mercilessly by his classmates, Mateo often fought back against his tormentors, and in the process, would often end up in the principal's office. "I used to get bullied a lot. Like I was very short, I had the glasses, the big backpack. . . . People would try to do stuff to me and one day I was like, 'You know what, I am not doing this anymore!'" As Mateo protected himself from his middle school bullies, he also began to be suspended for his troubles. This pattern of disciplinary action carried over from middle school into his short time at RCSD's Rosemead and then Sunnyside High Schools.

Mateo finished out his freshman year at Sunnyside High School suspension free. However, the fighting resumed with the new school year, but unlike middle school, the stakes were higher in high school: fighting was defined in regulation as more severe, and the consequences far more dire. States Mateo: "I started [fighting with] whoever would mess with me. In middle school you just get RPC [required parent conferences], [then] you are suspended. In high school you get arrested or sent to continuation school. So I would fight almost every day and I got suspended, suspended . . . and then you know after certain amount of suspensions they can't [deal with you]." When he received his fifth suspension in a little over a semester in sophomore year and acquired his designation as a habitual disciplinary problem, Mateo was summarily expelled under "extraordinary circumstances" as a threat to the school and his fellow pupils. His bullies escaped notice for their provocation and were not disciplined.

Being "At-Risk" in the Classroom

The label of troublemaker was a particularly powerful form of school disincentive for Mateo (McNulty & Roseboro, 2009), and he reflected that his alienation from school resulted from being "messed with" by his classmates, but also spoke poignantly of the resentment he felt for the way in which his teachers often treated him. He states, "Most of the teachers that I had would get loud. They were constantly yelling at you. . . . I tell teachers, 'How would you want kids to respect you if you are not showing them the same type respect?' " Although he acknowledged his disciplinary history, he expressed a strong need to feel respected by his teachers as he recalled repeated inappropriate teacher behavior. For him, respect received would result in reciprocated respect by him. After being told by a teacher to be respectful, Mateo spoke out, "How can you say to treat others how you would want to be treated? If you're yelling at me then obviously you want me to yell at you." School was no productive learning environment for Mateo, rather it was a space in which he was constantly required to do battle—be it with his classmates or his teachers who challenged him in front of his peers and would often say disparaging comments about Mateo, his family, and his community. This situation was an impossible context for Mateo to thrive academically and certainly not a "safe and productive learning environment."

The strained relations he had with his teachers inevitably resulted in further alienation from the classroom: ". . . [s]o that's why my grades were so bad—because I would be constantly arguing [with my teachers] and constantly would get sent out of class." Mateo spoke about how his grades were negatively impacted by ongoing removal from school. "Yeah, I get A's and B's when I go to school, I get good grades. It's just stuff happens and then I get kicked out and locked up, but I get good grades. I'm smart."

Mateo's academic struggles were not a result of his intellectual abilities, but rather were a product of student bullying and teacher and staff provocation. The pressure to navigate those who sought to dominate or "punk" him into following their demands was all too much for Mateo (Huerta & Rios-Aguilar, 2016), and the need to maintain a defensive posture at all times began to wear him down. Any trust he had in the school was lost. Even in those instances where he received in-school suspensions at Sunnyside, the instruction offered was minimal and betrayed a disregard by the school and teachers for his learning. Mateo recalls a time in which he was placed in study hall while at Sunnyside as punishment for speaking out in class. When asked if he actually learned in the In-School Suspension Classroom, Mateo said, "No, I didn't even go because it was just [handout] paperwork that they were giving us and that was it." If an academically talented student like Mateo can't succeed, who will?

For Mateo, being removed from the classroom did not help him learn necessary course content. When students are removed, it diminishes the opportunities for students to build trust with teachers and other school personnel, including college counselors (Holland, 2015; Stanton-Salazar, 2001). Obligation and trust are critical between individuals and social organizations because if there is not an investment between individuals, the expectation of ongoing mutual obligations fails (Coleman, 1990; Stanton-Salazar, 2011). If students are unable to forge trusting relationships with teachers and counselors, the students will be less likely to learn the nuances of college admissions, how to prepare through high school coursework and entrance exams, or how to secure financial aid information (Calderone, 2017; Perna, 2000). For example, the social bonds between Latino students, families, and school personnel will influence how messages about financial aid are interpreted and used in deciding postsecondary education opportunities (McDonough & Calderone, 2006; McDonough, Calderone, & Venegas, 2015).

As a society, we often forget that in reality the composite Mateo and all the other Mateos of the U.S. are *vulnerable Latino males*, and not just as an archetype of a "problematic" student. This not uncommon image from the U.S. collective consciousness of a problematic student makes these students no less deserving of their right to a quality education. The students who are labeled school discipline problems are disproportionately not only Latino and African-American males, but males with disabilities, and sometimes gifted students who are bored and rarely educationally challenged.

However, let's take a look at the research evidence about another composite, *the schools* where the vast majority of the Mateos attend. Although Sunnyside and VCS are real schools, they easily can be stand-ins for another U.S. archetype: *broken down, last chance schools* (Kelly, 1993; Muñoz, 2005). Typically, students who run afoul of school discipline policies the most come from public schools that most frequently are in urban areas, serving low socioeconomic status (poor) neighborhoods, have appallingly low achievement scores, frequently have burned-out or underprepared teachers, have inadequate and unsafe physical plants, prototypically are in neighborhoods that are riddled with gangs and high crime rates, and have been labeled "schools that shock the conscience" (Oakes & Lipton, 2004, p. 1). Also according to research evidence, these schools have high rates of institutionalized racism, high turnover of teachers and principals, and low teacher expectations of students, even though those same students and parents have high rates of college expectations (Hirschfield, 2008; Kennedy-Lewis & Murphy, 2106; Klugman, 2012; Obidah, Christie, & McDonough, 2004).

Given the head-on collision of the Mateos and the schools that serve them, the probabilities of successful student outcomes are miniscule. Bourdieuian theory reminds scholars that social actors make decisions that "make sense" to them based on their specific culture and field of action, even if those decisions don't make sense judged in a larger societal context or judged against other goals (Bourdieu, 1973). Our Mateo, forthrightly and in a soft-spoken natural style, fully admits his fighting problems. However, his neighborhood and school are teeming with gangs that use schools as recruiting grounds. Gang members constantly challenge students, mostly males, to join them with an initiation test of fighting (Estrada, Huerta, Hernandez, Hernandez, & Kim, in press). If the recruited student rejects the "admissions offer," that student needs to defend himself at that moment and in perpetuity from being "punked," that is, being disrespected or worse. The neighborhood cultural laws are that you never allow someone to punk you without challenging the affront and perpetrator, otherwise the incidents will escalate. Also, if the individual joins the gang, they have to pass the fighting test. Either way, in this cultural field fighting is a pervasive cultural *requirement*, which is precisely why schools have a zero-tolerance policy.

Safe and productive learning environments are ultimately created by school leadership and teachers, who spend the bulk of every day with students in classrooms. Teachers are also the embodiment and role models of school culture, the arbiters of learning expectations, providers of learning opportunities, and the first line of defense in school discipline. Let's take a look at how VCS teachers are perceived by the composite Mateo, who begins by saying, "I think some teachers just want their paychecks, but I think there are some hard-working teachers that want to help you learn." That seems to be a pretty balanced statement from a "teenaged troublemaker."

However, Mateo also voiced frustration and anger at the lack of help he experienced, "I am not getting help from anyone at this school," and the general lack of teacher interest in VCS students' ability to go to college, "Definitely not any chance in hell are they preparing *anybody* for college." Moreover, VCS staff have very low expectations of their students, making comments within earshot of students like "*These kids* don't want to go to college," and "*These kids* are going to big boy jail."

Without any attempt to be discrete, school staff make racist comments toward students, their families, and the community including, "Black people are entitled," "I can't be racist and teach at *this* school," "This generation of Mexicans are lazy compared to their parents . . . they just want free handouts, cellphones, housing, and computers." More perniciously, Mateo described the outright racism of the school principal (not all of his school discipline problems were about fighting):

The Blacks and the Mexicans, we're the main people getting sent to the office. *For what purpose?* . . . I was always getting sent up there because of my shirt. If not my shirt, then my earphones, if it wasn't my earphones it was because my pants were too low. Like there's tons of White kids dressed exactly the same way as I'm dressing . . . but they don't get sent up there and I do? It's just the principal . . . he's racist, and he's the principal so he feels like he has the high power. . . . Ok I understand that you're racist but it doesn't mean you have to take it out on . . . half of the kids at this school . . . it doesn't make sense to me. Like you're a principal—you're supposed to be the mature one.

Taken together, these teacher and principal comments and the perceptions of their students do not substantiate a safe and productive learning environment for Mateo or his fellow students.

A Future Thwarted

Mateo's confidence in his intellectual ability should not be overlooked. While the disruptions in class undermined his relationships with teachers and peers, his hopes for his future were never in doubt. Mateo was quite clear about what he wanted to do once he graduated and his path for getting there. Moreover, he saw these plans as a reason to remain resilient despite his disciplinary troubles. When asked the question, "What keeps you in school," Mateo said:

Well because I still just want to get my diploma because I want to do [auto] mechanics, that's what I've been wanting to do for a while. . . . [I want to attend] a [for-profit] college in Colorado, it was like out of 500 students from the entire United States, but since I got kicked out, like I just told [the recruiter] that I was having problems . . . [and asked] if I could [be considered for the future]. [The recruiter] was like, "Yeah." . . . I just try to get past this, like get the diploma and stick to like doing mechanics.

Despite these aspirations, Mateo expressed that he rarely felt supported at any of his schools and often described himself as following a singular path and keeping his aspirations to himself. Teachers, counselors, and school administration were not trusted. He didn't reach out to anyone for help, didn't utilize the resources that would presumably be available to him at school, and generally determined that any plans he might make for himself were his private business. On the rare occasion he sought out information, he was sorely disappointed. He states, "If you bring [ideas about college] to their attention, you make it known that you want to go to college . . . they don't answer you. I would ask Mr. Berry [social science teacher] if he knew of any colleges that have good sociology programs. He was like, 'Most colleges have a sociology program.' . . . He didn't say, 'Oh! You are going to college, [let's] talk about it.' "

The pattern of disruption continued for Mateo even after Sunnyside formally expelled him. District processing of his paperwork was slow, and Mateo was forced to wait nearly five weeks before his transfer to Viejo was confirmed. He shares, "[I was expelled for a] month and a week . . . I was out of school . . . they [the school administrators] were slacking." Over that span, he spent his time watching television, playing video games, and hanging out with friends until his younger siblings arrived home from school, and then he satisfied his childcare responsibilities.

RCSD placed a high premium on the safety and security of some of their pupils. They did so through aggressive disciplinary policies—aggressive in their implications for the students labeled dangerous or anti-social as well as in the substantial latitude provided to principals as they made determinations over who was so categorized. When a student was labeled as a disciplinary problem, there was little opportunity for a student to move beyond the label or the co-occurring lowered expectations. Resentment, frustration, and quashed hope lead to an impasse, especially for a student who aspired to graduate and go to college. In the eyes of a student like Mateo, aggressive disciplinary policies served to label, alienate, and breed mistrust.

While Mateo may have enjoyed dreams and aspirations that took him far beyond the confines of Viejo, those aspirations were largely undermined by a set of disciplinary policies that (1) favored universal order over local school (and student) contexts; (2) fueled continuing angst with and alienation from the school community for those disciplined; and (3) served to disrupt any possibility for consistent and continuous learning among those disciplined. For low-income Latino males like Mateo, the process of self-actualization is one that is largely undermined by a disciplinary policy environment that is not only overly punitive, but continues to punish long afterwards. The effects of this cumulative disciplinary approach set the stage for a more nuanced conversation about the contradictory effects these policies have on the lives of Latino males like Mateo.

The Structuring of School Disadvantage

Nationally, less than 5% of Latino male students with at least one out of school suspension will go on to earn a Bachelor's degree by the age of 26 (Shollenberger, 2015), and by the 9th grade, one in five Latino males were suspended from school for behavioral issues (NCES, 2012). Virtually 90% of Latino sophomores in high school hold high aspirations to pursue a college education, but gradually this number declines to 28.9% by their senior year of high school (Klasik, 2012). Although the reasons for this steady decline in students' college aspirations is multifaceted and complex (Huerta, 2015; McDonough, 1997; Kiyama, 2010; Klugman, 2012; Perna, 2000), no other demographic group has experienced a 61% decline in aspirations!

To date, there is little evidence-based research that speaks to the ways in which school discipline policies impact Latino male students' college aspirations or the requisite impact of these policies on their readiness for postsecondary studies. What we do know is that these policies come at a substantial cost for students of color: little to no improvement in school safety, behavior, academic learning, or grades. Rather, these policies encourage students to drop out or virtually push them out, and more troubling, stand as a direct pipeline from school to prison (Arcia, 2006; Brown, 2007; Hirschfield, 2008; López-Aguado, 2016; Losen, 2012; Morris & Perry, 2016; Noguera, 2003).

Mateo's story speaks to the contradictory forces at play when it comes to aggressive disciplinary policies. What we see is a student who is actively alienated by schooling. Second, we examine the impact of these disciplinary policies on individual postsecondary aspirations by highlighting the voices of the students themselves. Through these narratives, we arrive at the following six themes: (1) the "othering" effects of the school disciplinary label; (2) perceived disconnects between school behavioral expectations and student intentionality; (3) the deterioration of trust in educational authority and internalized devaluation of perceived life chances; 4) the erasure of provocations and contributing school conditions underlying student behavior; 5) inappropriate and racist behaviors of teachers and principals regarding who gets disciplined; and 6) policy and practice disconnects.

Based upon our findings, we argue that aggressive school disciplinary policies may serve to create safe spaces for learning while simultaneously inhibiting college aspiration formation among suspended Latino male students de facto deemed as incapable of such learning. Moreover, using district disciplinary policy statements, we make the argument that disciplinary discourses operate as a reinforcing mechanism of social reproduction that serves to reify exclusionary patterns of postsecondary participation. Our findings address these points in four important ways: RCSD disciplinary policies instantiate existing perceptions of school order and decorum in a manner that overlooks a history of institutional racism and cultural bias inherent in certain school settings through (1) an over-reliance upon objective assessments as to what constitutes threatening or disruptive behavior; (2) the assumption that threatening or disruptive behavior should be viewed as a "moment in time" and therefore isolated from the challenging life and school circumstances of students; (3) an emphasis on efficiency as an institutional value that operates at the expense of students' perceived due process; and 4) a policy that leaves objective discretion (unfettered by precipitating factors) in the hands of subjective deciders who can themselves be punished for not punishing.

To better understand how Latino males' aspirations are undermined, we rely upon Pierre Bourdieu's theory of social reproduction, and more specifically upon his concept of *habitus*. Habitus refers to the combination of values, dispositions, and expectations that fundamentally shape the universe of possible choices available to an individual actor (Bourdieu, 1977). It is, in effect, an embodiment of class origins that is reflexively or pedagogically based. Children unconsciously incorporate habitus through norms, values, and practices handed down by their parents.

The enactment of these norms, values, and practices is rewarded or disregarded within a "cultural field" (Bourdieu, 1977). A cultural field represents a social arena of struggle, whereby resources are competitively distributed based upon one's ability to comply with the rules that regulate it. Within a cultural field, our decisions will lead us to maximize our tastes, our budgets, or our opportunities available in our neighborhoods. What differentiate actors with different decisions from others are the individual preferences of the actors. Bourdieu argues that individuals enter a particular cultural sphere of activity with their talents and skills (cultural capital). What differentiates their use of those skills and talents is their ability to know how best to maximize different goals in order to acquire the benefits of the field. This capacity to know, to even have an appreciation for the probabilities of success, is derived from one's habitus. Cultural field, therefore, represents the space in which advantages and disadvantages are disseminated in accordance with class habitus.

Bourdieu's less-frequently applied ideas on cultural fields provide an explanatory lens for determining how the application of school disciplinary policy has led to significant disproportionality in who is disciplined and how. In our standards and accountability-heavy policy environment, the aggressive disciplinary approach of RCSD speaks to the ways in which the *cultural field of schools* rewards order over disruption, rules compliance over non-compliance, and in the case of misbehavior, assumptions about student intent over more nuanced understanding of motivation. Through Mateo, we learn that students who fall outside the behavioral expectation are quickly "othered"—banished from the local school community through out-of-school suspension or expulsion or placed in continuation schools. The consequence of this banishment, of course, is a lack of trust by the student in the school community. The deterioration of trust in educational authority perpetuates the "othering." As we saw with Mateo, the sense of alienation was felt from his teachers to his classmates. This "othering" also resulted in his needing to protect himself—and his aspirations—from the school and those who appeared to devalue his life chances.

The RCSD's disciplinary policies also instantiate a cultural field of disciplinary policy that favors school order and decorum in a manner that overlooks the substantial history and current presence of structural racism and cultural bias inherent in school settings, a centralized district-driven disciplinary policy that over-relies upon building-level assessments as to how, and in what contexts, the policy should be applied. The damning label of habitual disciplinary problem, while an artifact of district-level policy, was applied to Mateo by his Sunnyside principal, where he maximized stability and order, while Mateo maximized life and death. The cumulative nature of the policy also ensures that repeated infractions escalates the punishment, leaving no room for assessments of cultural bias, the complexities of student home life, or the historical impasse between schools and families of color. The cultural field of disciplinary behavior relies upon a standardized institutional response to a far more complex and historically problematic tension between school expectations, on the one hand, and the skepticism of students of color on the other. In this way, the cultural field of disciplinary policy also assumes that a student's threatening or disruptive behavior should be viewed as a "moment in time" and therefore isolated from the challenging life circumstances of that student.

Finally, the cultural field of school discipline policy is structured to reflect values of efficiency that often confound the disciplinary process. As we saw in the case of RCSD, aggressive disciplinary policy is cumulative and operates at the expense of students' perceived due process. Policy efficiency is dependent upon objective application to ensure a properly functioning, minimally disrupted school system. Consider, for example, another school policy: the use of grades. The grade issued at the end of a course is intended to reflect a level of competency for the course content offered. It summarizes how well a student did relative to a series of criteria as outlined by the instructor of record. We assume that the grade, issued fairly and judiciously, reflects a student's individual level performance and that such performance was objectively assessed. The sustainability of this efficiency is only as effective as the objective measures used to reach the determination of that grade. School disciplinary policy operates in much the same way. The efficiency of a centrally outlined framework for discipline operates as an efficient tool for adjudicating behavior. However, as we discussed earlier, the inherent "efficiency" of the disciplinary system is at odds with the historical relational patterns between schools and students of color. The overreliance upon efficient, cumulative disciplinary policy is the disproportional discipline of students of color within the RCSD and at countless districts nationwide.

To look at Mateo's situation from a policy perspective, implementation and effectiveness is always a problem of the smallest unit; in education, therefore, it is a problem of the individual actors—teachers and principals—in their local context. How these actors interpret and act upon the policy will be greatly influenced by their understanding (or lack thereof) of the intentions behind the policy's formation, their motivations to use the policy and toward what ends, and the competing or conflicting policy, resource, or personal demands that shape their daily practice.

Generally speaking, last chance schools are not only the last chance of students but are more often than not the last chance of the educators working there. Those educators often are burned out and unhappy teaching in schools where they feel trapped. In addition, principals' jobs are not only tied to safety, but also learning as measured by test scores, etc. Under these conditions, an aggressive school discipline policy can be a welcome and effective tool in the toolkit of educators who want less demanding teaching and learning conditions.

Exclusionary policies are built into the DNA of American education, and we are not condoning the racist or callous disregard of underrepresented students' futures. What we are saying is that policymakers at the national, state, and local levels rush to make their mark on high-profile electoral issues like school safety without any forethought to implementation fidelity and unintended consequences or conflicts. Moreover, many policymakers do not have an understanding of the conflicts and conditions of the end of the educational implementation line and don't think about how the implementers will handle conflicting policies, missions, and mandates. Expediency is a fact of organizational life and complacency helps to maintain it. Schools that "shock the conscience" (Oakes and Lipton, 2004) are a relatively recent American educational phenomenon that most policymakers and educational administrators either do not acknowledge or do not plan for when making policy.

Our take-away message of this chapter is that policies with consequences for implementers, like testing accountability or discipline for those who don't discipline, become first-order policies to be fulfilled in the daily life of school personnel. Also, policies that match the implementers' own needs, not the policy's original intent, are also likely to be implemented but often create new problems (McLaughlin, 1987). Regardless, discipline policies that are differentially implemented (intentional or otherwise) for underrepresented minorities are illegal and unacceptable.

Conclusion

Based upon our findings, we argue that aggressive disciplinary policies of schools serve to create safe spaces for learning while simultaneously labeling suspended students as incapable of such learning. Moreover, using RCSD's district-wide disciplinary policy statements, we make the argument that disciplinary discourses operate as a reinforcing mechanism of social reproduction that serves to reify exclusionary patterns of postsecondary participation and by extension, college aspiration formation among Latino males.

We argue that schools are critical areas for interventions that may serve as the building blocks for improved Latino male student success, and ultimately, school success. Districts should consider restorative justice programs led by male teachers, counselors, or school leaders to create safe environments for young men to process their infractions and experiences in schools. Coupled with these efforts, districts should be intentional in building relationships with local non-profits that focus on counseling or mental health needs for communities of color. Mateo and other boys of color may be processing problems that are beyond the professional capacity of school counselors and teachers (e.g., dealing with absent parents). These non-profits can connect Mateo and his family to other social support services they may need. Lastly, school districts should hire male alumni who have been suspended or expelled to co-facilitate professional development sessions to understand the individual impact the school discipline policies had on their educational goals and aspirations.

References

Arcia, E. (2006). Achievement and enrollment status of suspended students: Outcomes in a large, multicultural school district. *Education & Urban Society, 38,* 359–369.

Bourdieu, P. (1973). Cultural reproduction and social reproduction. In Brown, R. (Ed.), *Knowledge, education, and cultural change: Papers in sociology of education* (pp. 56–68). Alameda, CA: Tavistock.

Bourdieu, P. (1977). *Outline of a theory of practice.* Cambridge, MA: Harvard University Press.

Brown, T. M. (2007). Lost and turned out: Academic, social, and emotional experiences of students excluded from school. *Urban Education, 42*(5), 432–455.

Calderone, S. M. (2017). Deadlines and differentiation: The financial aid advising strategies of college counselors. *Manuscript submitted for publication.*

Castillo, J. (2015). Tolerance in schools for Latino students: Dismantling the school to prison pipeline. *Harvard Journal of Hispanic Policy, 26,* 43–58.

Coleman, J. S. (1990). *Foundations of social theory.* Cambridge, MA: Harvard University Press.

Conchas, G. Q., & Vigil, J. D. (2012). Streetsmart schoolsmart: Urban poverty and the education of adolescent boys. New York: Teachers College Press.

Estrada, J. N., Huerta, A. H., Hernandez, E., Hernandez, R., & Kim, S. (in press). Socio-ecological risk and protective factors for youth gang involvement. In H. Shapiro and associates (Eds.), *The handbook of violence in education: Forms, factors, and preventions.* Hoboken, NJ: Wiley-Blackwell.

Hirschfield, P. J. (2008). Preparing for prison? The criminalization of school discipline in the USA. *Theoretical Criminology, 12*(1), 79–101.

Holland, M. M. (2015). Trusting each other: Student-counselor relationships in diverse high schools. *Sociology of Education, 88*(3), 244–262.

Huerta, A. H. (2016). Gangs and college knowledge: An examination of Latino male students attending an urban alternative school (Unpublished doctoral dissertation). University of California, Los Angeles, CA.

Huerta, A. H. (2015). 'I didn't want my life to be like that': Gangs, college, or the military for Latino male high school students. *Journal of Latino/Latin American Studies, 7*(2), 156–167.

Huerta, A. H., & Rios-Aguilar, C. (2017). "Treat a cop like they are God": Exploring the relevance and utility of funds of gang knowledge among Latino male students. Manuscript submitted for publication.

Kang-Brown, J., Trone, J., Fratello, J., & Daftary-Kapur, T. (2013). *A generation later: What we've learned about zero tolerance in schools.* Vera Institute of Justice: New York, NY.

Kelly, D.M. (1993). Last chance high: How girls and boys drop in and out of alternative schools. New Haven, CT: Yale University Press.

Kennedy-Lewis, B. L., & Murphy, A. (2016). Listening to "frequent flyers": What persistently disciplined students have to say about being labeled as "bad". *Teachers College Record, 118*(1), 1–40.

Kim, J. H. (2011). Narrative inquiry into (re)imaging alternative schools: A case study of Kevin Gonzales. *International Journal of Qualitative Studies in Education, 24*(1), 77–96.

Kiyama, J. M. (2010). College aspirations and limitations: The role of educational ideologies and funds of knowledge in Mexican American families. *American Educational Research Journal, 47*(2), 330–356.

Klasik, D. (2012). The college application gauntlet: A systematic analysis of the steps to four-year college enrollment. *Research in Higher Education, 53*, 506–549.

Klugman, J. (2012). How resources inequalities among high schools reproduce class advantages in college destination. *Research in Higher Education, 53*, 803–830.

Losen, D. J. (2012). Sound discipline policy for successful schools: How redressing racial disparities can make a positive impact for all. In Bahena, S., Cooc, N., Currie-Rubin, R., Kuttner, P., & Ng, M. (Eds.), *Disrupting the school-to-prison pipeline* (pp. 45–72). Cambridge, MA: Harvard Education Press.

Losen, D. J. (Ed). (2015). Closing the school discipline gap: Equitable remedies for excessive exclusion. New York: Teachers College Press.

McDonough, P. M. (1997). *Choosing colleges: How social class and school structure opportunity*. Albany, NY: State University of New York Press.

McDonough, P. M., & Calderone, S. (2006). The meaning of money: Perceptual differences between college counselors and low-income families about college costs and financial aid. *American Behavioral Scientist, 49*(12), 1703–1718.

McDonough, P. M., Calderone, S., and Venegas, K. M. (2015). The role of social trust in low-income Latino college financing decisions. *Journal of Latin/Latino American Studies, 7*(2), 133–148.

McLaughlin, M. W. (1987, Summer). Learning from experience: Lessons from policy implementation. *Educational Evaluation and Policy Analysis, 9*(2), 171–178.

McNulty, C. P., & Roseboro, D. L. (2009). "I'm not really that bad": Alternative school students, stigma, and identity politics. *Equity & Excellence in Education, 42*(4), 412–427.

Miller, J. (1998). Riding the crime wave: Why words we use matter so much. *Nieman Reports, 52*(4), 47.

Morris, E. W., & Perry, B. L. (2016). The punishment gap: School suspension and racial disparities in achievement. *Social Forces, 63*(1), 68–96.

Muñoz, J. S. (2005). The social construction of alternative education: Re-examining the margins of public education for at-risk Chicano/a students. *High School Journal, 88*(2), 3–22.

National Center for Education Statistics. (2012). *Higher education: Gaps in the access and persistence study*. Retrieved from http://nces.ed.gov/pubs2012/2012046.pdf

Noguera, P. A. (2003). Schools, prisons, and social implications of punishment: Rethinking disciplinary policies. *Theory into Practice, 42*(4), 341–350.

Oakes, J., and Lipton, M. (2004). Schools that shock the conscience: Williams v. California and the struggle for education on equal terms fifty years after Brown. *Berkeley Journal of African American Law and Policy, 6*(2), 152–179.

Obidah, J., Christie, T., & McDonough, P. (2004). Less tests, more redress: Improving minority and low-income students' educational access in the post-Brown era. *Penn GSE Perspectives on Urban Education, 3*(1), 1–17.

Office of Civil Rights (2014, March 21). *Civil Rights data collection data snapshot: School discipline.* Washington, D.C.: U.S. Department of Education Office for Civil Rights.

Perna, L. W. (2000). Differences in the decision to attend college among African Americans, Hispanics, and whites. *Journal of Higher Education, 71*(2), 117–141.

Rock County School District. (2014). *Suspension data by race and ethnicity.* Retrieved from school district website. URL withheld.

Shollenberger, T. L. (2015). Racial disparities in school suspension and subsequent outcomes: Evidence from the National Longitudinal Survey of Youth. In Losen, D. L. (Ed.), *Closing the school discipline gap: Equitable remedies for excessive exclusion* (pp. 31–43). New York: Teachers College Press.

Stanton-Salazar, R. D. (2001). Manufacturing hope and despair: The school and kin support networks of U.S.-Mexican youth. New York: Teachers College Press.

Stanton-Salazar, R. D. (2011). A social capital framework for the study of institutional agents and their role in the empowerment of low-status students and youth. *Youth & Society, 43*(3), 1066–1109.

Yin, R. K. (2011). *Applications of case study research* (3rd ed.). Thousand Oaks, CA: Sage Publishers.

13 When Special Education Policy in Ontario Creates Unintended Consequences

Lauren Jervis and Sue Winton

A recent headline in an Ontario, Canada newspaper exclaimed, "Parents fuming after 2.5 year wait for learning disability test" (Carter, 2015). The news story's subject was Julian, a grade 5 student in the public education system who, according to his teachers, doctor, and other experts, needed special programming at school to address his learning disability. He couldn't access these services until his diagnosis was confirmed by a psycho-educational assessment, and Julian had been waiting to take this test for over two years. If his family could have paid for the testing to be done privately rather than by the school board, he could have by-passed the waiting list and accessed the special education supports more quickly. This was not an option Julian's parents could afford. Consequently, Julian waited while others jumped the queue.

In 1980, Ontario adopted legislation that guaranteed students with special needs—such as Julian—would receive the supports and services they need for success in the province's public schools. Since then, school boards have been required to provide resources to their students with identified exceptionalities. Importantly, to be officially recognized as an exceptional student and be legally entitled to special education supports, a board committee must formally identify a student. Regulations specify that the identification process will normally include the committee's consideration of various kinds of assessments (Ontario Ministry of Education, 2007).[1] Access to these assessments, as Julian's case illustrates, is a much more complex issue than the policy text suggests.

The issue of special education assessment wait times is one that has affected Ontario's education system for decades. Since its earliest days, People for Education (P4E), a non-governmental organization in Ontario, Canada, has drawn attention to these waiting lists and their detrimental impact on some students, and the group has advocated for the provincial government to address the issue. Twenty years after P4E's formation, the waiting lists still exist.

In this chapter we examine the unintended consequences of Ontario's policy requirement that students be formally assessed before they are entitled to access special needs identification and services. These consequences are analyzed in conjunction with an important aspect of the policy's context: the advocacy efforts of P4E. We show that the assessment policy has unintentionally created inequities between children, based on income and geography. Furthermore, P4E's advocacy efforts have been influenced and constrained by broad cultural discourses and the policy's particular socio-historical context, including funding shortfalls, increasing privatization in education, and neoliberal conceptions of good parenting. Let us walk you through this complex web of contexts that contributes to the unintended inequalities in Ontario's special education system.

Ontario's Special Education Policy

In Canada, K–12 public education is the responsibility of individual provinces and territories. The *Education Act* is the legal framework for Ontario. The province has 72 school districts in four publicly funded systems: English Catholic, English public (i.e., not Catholic), French Catholic, and French public. The vast majority of school age children attend schools in one of these systems, and school boards are legally obligated to provide resources to students with special needs. This requirement became law in December 1980 after the passage of Bill 82, *Education Amendment Act, 1980*. The principles of Bill 82 were straightforward: "all exceptional pupils were to have, by right, access to appropriate education programs without additional fees" (Gidney, 1999, p. 155). Before the passage of Bill 82, boards were permitted to offer special education programming, and many did, but they were not obligated to do so for all students who needed it. After Bill 82, many children who had attended private institutions or had not previously attended school at all joined the public system (Morgan, 2003).

Bill 82 included the requirement that a board committee formally identify students as exceptional, and once a student is formally identified, the committee also determines the student's program placement and reviews that placement regularly. These committees are commonly known as Identification, Placement, and Review Committees (IPRCs). Ontario's regulation 181/98, s. 15 explains that IPRCs "shall obtain and consider an educational assessment of the pupil" and "shall also obtain and consider a psychological assessment of the pupil if the committee determines that the assessment is required to enable it to make a correct identification or placement decision" (Government of Ontario, 2005). IPRCs are also permitted to consult health assessments if they determine it is necessary. Notably, this regulation does not specify who can conduct the assessments and who should be responsible for paying for them, although boards do conduct various assessments at no cost to students.

Ontario's *Education Act* is thus a central policy text in the province. However, our view of Ontario's special education policy is not limited to this text or others created at the provincial, board, or school levels. We adopt Bowe, Ball, and Gold's (1992) conception of policy as a cycle that includes three contexts: the contexts of influence, texts, and practices. The context of influence includes public and private arenas wherein policy discourses are constructed, circulated, and contested. Texts representing various and contested policy meanings and decisions are produced in the context of policy text production (Bowe et al., 1992). The context of practice is the site the other contexts hope to influence and where policy is enacted (Bowe et al., 1992; Ball, Maguire, & Braun, 2012). Thus, we view formal government and board policy decisions as only one aspect of policy. In this chapter we describe P4E's participation in the context of influence in Ontario's special education assessment policy cycle as the group attempted to influence formal policies and change practices surrounding assessment wait times.

P4E, Policy Advocacy, and Rhetorical Strategies

According to the most recent figures available, in 2010–2011 over 191,600 students in Ontario's public schools were identified by an IPRC as exceptional students and were receiving some kinds of special education services and programs (Ontario Ministry of Education, 2016). Thus, many children appear to be benefitting from Bill 82 and the IPRC process. However, the IPRC process has also unintentionally created or perpetuated regional and class-based inequities between students. Some students encounter long waiting lists of up to three years to receive the assessments that would enable them to be identified as exceptional students (Carter, 2015; Rushowy, 2011, June 1). Others move much more quickly through the IPRC process. These variances occur for a number of reasons, including family income, geographic location, and board processes. We discuss each of these issues following a brief introduction to P4E, the group that has long called for policy changes that would reduce assessment wait times and the inequities they (re) produce.

P4E was founded in 1996 by parents who were concerned about changes to education policy taking place in Ontario (Crawford, 1996). From a small grassroots organization, P4E has grown into a well-known advocacy group that conducts research on the state of Ontario's public schools. P4E has tried to persuade Ontario's successive governments to address the special education assessment wait times issue since 1996 using a range of strategies. We identified these strategies through a rhetorical analysis (Winton, 2013) of 54 texts published between 1996 and 2016. Of these texts, 29 were produced by P4E. The other 25 texts include explicit references to P4E, eight of which were produced by teacher unions in Ontario and two of which were produced by the Ontario Human Rights Commission. The remaining 15 texts are media articles that appeared in major Canadian newspapers between 1996 and 2016. Texts produced by People for Education were accessed from the group's website. The media texts were identified through searches of the online database *Canadian Newsstand*, and the other documents were located through internet searches. Rhetorical analysis involves identifying the strategies actors use to persuade others to interpret particular social practices in a particular way (i.e., as a policy problem) and to respond to the issue in ways that reflect that understanding. There are many facets of rhetoric, including: how the problem is constructed; how the audience is positioned; persuasive discourses; and the canons of disposition, style, memory, delivery, and invention (Leach, 2000). The canon of invention includes appeals to the audience's reason (logos), deeply held values and emotions (pathos), and confidence in the speaker (ethos; Selzer, 2004). These appeals are key aspects of rhetoric and are the focus of our discussion below.

Assessment Policy Creates a "Two-Tiered System"

Since its inception in 1996, P4E has defined the issue of assessment wait times as one that perpetuates and exacerbates inequality. A parent involved in one of P4E's earliest protests told a personal story to the *Toronto Star* (one of Canada's major newspapers) that highlighted the concern about assessment wait times; she was told that her child would have to wait months for special education assessments unless she could pay for private assessments herself (Crawford, 1996, April 21). She framed this issue as one of inequality, saying, "That's okay for us because we can afford it, but what about other families? We have to maintain a public system equal to all" (Crawford, 1996, April 21, p. F5).

In 1998, P4E launched the first of what was to become a unique annual survey of Ontario's elementary (and later secondary) schools. The survey, conducted in collaboration with Metro Parent Network, aimed to gather data about how a range of government policy changes were impacting schools. Collecting data, citing and publishing survey findings, and using numbers and statistics are some of P4E's main persuasive strategies, which appeal to logos, or reason. The first survey found that 2,377 students in 642 schools were on waiting lists for special education assessments (Chamberlain, 1998, June 12). In 2000 the group reported: "Waiting lists for Special Education assessment and services remain very long. . . . To avoid these waiting lists, some parents are paying privately for Special Education assessments, which raises further concerns about inequity within the system" (P4E, 2000, p. 12). By 2002 P4E was describing the assessment situation as a "two-tiered system" wherein affluent parents were by-passing waiting lists by paying up to $1700 for private assessments for their children (P4E, 2002). Notably, schools serving higher-income families reported shorter waiting lists in 2011 than schools serving lower-income families (Rushowy, 2011, June 1). In 2014, "25% of elementary school principals report[ed] that 'some,' 'most,' or 'all' parents use private assessments" (Gallagher-Mackay & Kidder, 2014, p. 8). Further, P4E (Gallagher-Mackay & Kidder, 2014) found that the likelihood that parents will utilize private assessments is strongly related to average family income per school.

P4E's annual surveys have also found that the length of waiting lists for assessments varies widely between schools and boards. Some boards place restrictions on how many children can be assessed in a year; in 2015, 57% of elementary principals and 53% of secondary principals reported limits on the number of students that may be placed on waiting lists for assessment (P4E, 2015). In addition, some regions of the province are more easily able to access psychologists who conduct assessments than other regions. In 2012, 37% of elementary schools in Northern Ontario reported they did not have any access to psychologists; this number was 4% for elementary schools in the Greater Toronto Area (P4E, 2012b). P4E's 2016 Annual Report demonstrates that geography and restrictions interact: 72% of elementary schools in small towns/rural areas have restrictions compared to 50% of elementary schools in urban/suburban areas. Family income and geographic location thus both impact the ability of Ontario students to obtain needed special education assessments.

The surveys have also enabled the group to track and report changes in assessment waiting lists over time. For example, in a special 2002 report called "Special Education and the Funding Formula," P4E used data from its annual surveys to show that the number of students on wait lists for services related to special education had risen by 14% since the 1999–2000 school year, and that 65% of the students on those waiting lists in the schools that filled out the survey were waiting for assessments specifically (P4E, 2002, p. 17). Similarly, the surveys demonstrate that the number of schools reporting restrictions on assessments have increased since they first asked about them (P4E, 2015). These survey results—figures that compare access between regions, data regarding the number of students seeking private assessments, and trends that indicate changes in waiting lists over time—help P4E construct assessment wait times as a problem of inequality through rhetorical appeals to logos.

P4E has also tried to persuade its audience to view Ontario's assessment wait times policy as a problem through pathos—that is, by appealing to members' "most deeply and fervently held values" (Selzer, 2004, p. 284). In particular, the group argues that long wait lists for special education assessments combined with the option to pay for private assessments undermines the public education system's commitment to equal opportunity for all students. For example, the group's 2001 Elementary Tracking Report states: "if we are to preserve the most important tenet of public education—that every child deserves an equal chance to succeed—growing inequities in the system must be addressed immediately" (P4E, 2001, p. 3). By failing to do so, P4E explains that Ontario's children and future are at risk. The group reminds audiences of this central purpose of education in its 2012 annual report on schools (P4E, 2012a) when it asserts that "providing every child—rich or poor—with an equitable chance of success is one of the central missions of any publicly funded education system" (p. 8).

P4E shares violations of this commitment to equity in its reports, often quoting survey respondents, as part of its efforts to stir up readers' emotional responses. The responses include sympathy, anger, and feelings of injustice. For example, a 2013 summary of that year's survey findings related to special education shares this perspective from an elementary school principal: "There are, quite simply, never enough resources (human and financial) to support our most needy students. I'm disheartened by the promises made to parents by government that are impossible to fulfill at the local level" (P4E, 2013, p. 1).

An excerpt from P4E's 2014 report on special education also uses the comments of a principal to employ the rhetorical strategy of pathos:

> Families and educators are deeply frustrated when students cannot get timely psycho-educational assessments. As one principal wrote, 'We have students (and families) who have been on a wait list for psycho-educational assessment for 2–3 years due to the limited allowance/ schedule.' Many principals express similar concerns.
>
> (Gallagher-Mackay & Kidder, 2014, p. 7)

In the two preceding excerpts, the use of the emotional words "disheartened," "frustrated," and "concerns" suggests that assessment wait times, a major obstacle to providing exceptional students with necessary supports, causes anger. The reader, it follows, would also be justified in feeling angry about the wait times for special education assessments. Furthermore, P4E's framing of this policy issue as one that exacerbates inequity provides a reason for anger that itself has an emotional appeal: injustice. As previously discussed, the group has described special education assessment provision as a "two-tiered system" (P4E, 2002) and has claimed that students who cannot afford private assessments are being "penalized" by sitting on waiting lists (P4E, 2001, p. 8). These phrases highlight the apparent unfairness of the situation for students with exceptionalities from lower-income families and underserved regions through use of emotionally charged language.

In addition to using rhetorical appeals to reason (logos) and to emotion (pathos), P4E has also employed the rhetorical strategies of ethos, or appeals to its own expertise and authority. This set of rhetorical strategies can draw on the legitimacy a speaker has due to an official role or to his/ her reputation, as well as the credibility a speaker constructs in the text itself (Selzer, 2004). P4E has used appeals to ethos in many different ways. Early in its history, the group emphasized that it was composed of parents who were speaking from firsthand experiences of having their own children in the province's public education system, as in the case cited previously of the parent at the protest whose child needed a special education assessment. Once it launched its annual surveys to determine the effects of policy decisions on Ontario schools, the group was able to cite its survey results, including findings on assessment wait times, to support its advocacy. Since no other organization conducts similar surveys in the province, P4E's survey data is valuable and not easy to challenge, which lends the group credibility in the realm of education policy in Ontario.

P4E's reports gain further authority from their inclusion of comments of principals who fill out the survey. These quotations lend support to P4E's claims by citing the views of people who work in schools and therefore have a situated credibility of their own. Moreover, in many of its reports, P4E recommends that the provincial government take specific actions regarding education policy. The very act of making these recommendations suggests that the group is able to provide policy advice on educational matters. For example, its 2014 report on special education included four policy recommendations directed at the Ontario government, including one that addresses the issue of assessment wait times: P4E urged the government to "standardize processes for assessment, identification and placement to provide adequate, timely and equitable services and access to education for every Ontario child" (Gallagher-Mackay & Kidder, 2014, p. 10).

Other individuals and groups have contributed to the construction of P4E's ethos and helped establish the group's situated credibility. For example, politicians and other prominent policy actors have made appearances at P4E's events, and the organization has partnered with high-profile groups and scholars on research and advocacy projects. Journalists regularly ask the group for comment in news stories on Ontario's education system and report on the latest data from P4E's annual surveys. In turn, P4E has actively worked to engage with the press and to gain media coverage. In its early days, the group organized rallies, often involving theatrical performances, outside the provincial legislature (Winton & Brewer, 2014). While P4E has ceased to hold protests in recent years, the group still puts on media events to mark the release of its annual reports of survey results and puts out press releases to communicate with reporters. The group's consistent presence in the Ontario mainstream media's coverage of issues related to public education has bolstered its credibility as a legitimate and influential actor on the province's education policy scene.

The Influence of Context

Bill 82, *Education Amendment Act, 1980,* was passed into law to ensure all exceptional pupils in Ontario had access to appropriate education programs in the province's public schools. Not only has this access not yet been achieved, but the legislation's requirement that students be identified as exceptional by a committee that would consult psychological and other assessments as part of the identification process has created inequities between children based on income and geography. Factors that have given rise to this unintended outcome and P4E's inability to influence policy change include those that are specific to the special education policy itself (i.e., variations in board restrictions on assessments; consideration of private assessments by IPRCs; the requirement that psycho-educational tests be considered by IPRCs) and those that transcend this particular issue. These broad contextual factors include the increased privatization of public education in Ontario (Robertson, 2005), neoliberal expectations that "good parents" do whatever it takes to enable their children to be successful in a context of scarce opportunities and public resources (Landeros, 2011; Lareau, 2011), and reduced government spending on public education. Both kinds of factors are discussed below.

First, in some regions of the province, school board decisions to limit the number of special education assessments performed each year and parents' decisions to pay for private assessments suggest that there is not enough money available in the public education system to pay for all the recommended assessments. Second, in some cases, access to professionals who can conduct necessary assessments is limited (e.g., P4E, 2012b). This troubling situation suggests that IPRCs that deem it necessary to consult psycho-educational assessments are contributing to the inequities between students in different boards and different regions. A third factor that has given rise to assessment wait times is the loophole that permits parents to pay for a private assessment that will enable their children to by-pass waiting lists and receive special education supports sooner.

The practice of parents paying for assessments is a manifestation of the broader trend toward privatization in Canada's public education systems and the influence of neoliberalism and its constructions of good parenting and education. Neoliberalism has been a dominant political, economic, and social ideology in Ontario since the mid-1990s and throughout P4E's existence (Carpenter, Weber, & Schugurensky, 2012; Winton & Pollock, 2015). According to Brown (2006), neoliberalism is a "political rationality," which "is a specific form of normative political reason organizing the political sphere, governance practices, and citizenship" (p. 693). Neoliberalism values the principles of the free market and promotes individualism and competition (Brown, 2006; Larner, 2000). Under neoliberalism, parents are responsible for making choices that will enable their children to be successful, and children's achievements likewise reflect back on the quality of the parenting they've received (Landeros, 2011).

Neoliberal discourses emphasize parents' roles as consumers, highlighting their personal agency and ignoring institutional and other constraints on their choices (Kimelberg, 2014). After all, a parent's ability to engage in this kind of advocacy for their child is dependent, in part, on their financial resources, access to time off from work, cultural capital, and language skills. When a child is identified as in need of an assessment for special education supports, the parent(s) may feel they should pay for a private assessment out of concern for their child's success, but as P4E points out, only parents who can afford the cost can make that choice.

P4E's advocacy regarding special education assessment wait times policies has also taken place over a period of increasing privatization in the

Ontario school system more generally (Carpenter et al., 2012; Pinto, 2012). Privatization has not affected special education assessment wait times so much through an official, government policy choice, but rather through a de facto state of affairs, specifically the ability of wealthier parents to pay for private assessments and thereby jump the wait list (not to mention the motivation provided by long wait times to do so). This unofficial privatization policy goes hand in hand with general funding shortages that contribute to the existence of the wait times in the first place.

Neoconservative commitments to lower taxes and reduced public spending on social services have also been part of the neoliberal political climate dominant in Ontario. Funding cuts and shortfalls in education have been key parts of the context that has limited the success of P4E's efforts to shorten waiting times for special education assessments. For example, in a 2002 report, "Special Education and the Funding Formula," P4E stated "the funding provided for special education is inadequate" and recommended that the Ontario government increase funding to clear the waiting lists, employ enough assessment professionals, and provide access to these professionals even in school boards with smaller populations (P4E, 2002). In 2006, the provincial government provided $20 million in one-time funding for psychologists to provide student assessments, with a view to reducing wait times (Ontario Ministry of Education, 2006, June 8). P4E's (2007) report the following year found that the number of students waiting for special education services had dropped by 6%. This change suggests the one-time funding helped address the issue. The group's 2009 report identified another reason that could help explain decreases in the length of waiting lists for assessments: more students were informally receiving special education services without first going through the official process of assessment and identification (P4E, 2009). In 2013, P4E (2013) reported that the number of students on waiting lists for assessment was once again on the rise. In the context of scarce public resources and the accompanying incentives that are created for parents to pay for private assessments if they can, P4E's objections to assessment wait times would be easy for Ontario's wealthier parents and school boards to ignore.

Policy Alternatives: How Can We Address the Inequities?

The factors giving rise to the unintended consequences of Ontario's IPRC process for special education provision suggest a number of possible changes that could address the inequities perpetuated by the policy. One option could be that IPRCs find alternatives to psychological assessments when making identification and placement decisions, especially in those boards where access to psychologists is difficult. They might also find alternate ways for the assessments to take place (e.g., people other than psychologists might be trained to conduct the assessments, or if this is not possible due to the specialized nature of the tests, tests could be administered by school staff and then sent elsewhere to be interpreted by psychologists). Another option would see the Ontario government increase the amount of funding for assessments so that all children who need assessments receive them. While more funding does not always solve a problem, the reduction—albeit slight—in waiting lists that followed the one-time cash infusion for psychologists in 2006 suggests that funding levels matter in this case. If increasing funding from the provincial government is not an option, the government or school boards could ensure that access to assessments and placements is at least more equitable (if not more prompt) by banning IPRCs' consideration of private assessments; in that case, all students in publicly funded schools would need to obtain their assessments through their schools. Finally, the government could standardize procedures related to restrictions on assessments across school boards. These final two possibilities reflect P4E's 2014 recommendation that the Ontario government "standardize processes for assessment, identification and placement to provide adequate, timely and equitable services and access to education for every Ontario child" (Gallagher-Mackay & Kidder, 2014, p. 10). Indeed, P4E has primarily advocated for policy changes at the level of the provincial government; however, given that the decision to consult psychological assessments is made by district-level IPRCs, P4E could direct more of its efforts to school boards as well.

Conclusions

The story of P4E's policy advocacy for changes to special education wait times in Ontario demonstrates that advocacy does not take place in a vacuum. The rhetorical strategies employed by P4E—strategies appealing to logos, pathos, and ethos—were both influenced and constrained by the policy's socio-historical context in which they were employed. Cultural discourses of neoliberalism and neoconservatism, especially as they relate to parents, privatization, and funding of social services, influenced the persuasive power of P4E's activities regarding assessment wait times. P4E's framing of the assessment wait times issue as a problem of inequity may not resonate with parents who are operating in a neoliberal context that emphasizes the importance of getting the best for one's own children from the scarce resources available. Furthermore, this case suggests that engaging in advocacy for policy change in a context of multiple levels of government may impact the way that advocacy is received. Arguments regarding assessment wait times directed at the provincial government do not directly address school boards, which administer the provision of assessments under circumstances that vary significantly based on their geographic region and the affluence of the local communities.

Ultimately, P4E's advocacy efforts regarding special education assessment wait times point at the unintended consequences of a policy meant to guarantee provision of specialized education services for all students with exceptionalities. The group's efforts nonetheless failed to effect significant or lasting policy change. Our findings highlight the importance of responding to cultural discourses and a policy's context as part of actors' change efforts. In short, context matters.

Note

1 In 2011, a memorandum from the Ontario Ministry of Education specified that "[a]ll students with demonstrable learning based needs are entitled to appropriate accommodations in the form of special education programs and services," including those students with undiagnosed medical conditions that contributed to such "learning based needs" (Finlay, 2011, p. 1). Nonetheless, as Julian's case shows, Ontario students are still sometimes denied the special education services they need when they have not undergone the formal assessment and identification process that is set out in the regulations.

References

Ball, S. J., Maguire, M., & Braun, A. (2012). *How schools do policy: Policy enactments in secondary schools*. New York: Routledge.

Bowe, R., Ball, S. J., & Gold, A. (1992). *Reforming education and changing schools: Case studies in policy sociology*. London, UK: Routledge.

Brown, W. (2006). American nightmare: Neoliberalism, neoconservatism, and de-democratization. *Political Theory*, 34(6), 690–714.

Carpenter, S., Weber, N., & Schugurensky, D. (2012). Views from the blackboard: Neoliberal education reforms and the practice of teaching in Ontario, Canada. *Globalisation, Societies and Education*, 10(2), 145–161.

Carter, A. (2015, January 21). Parents fuming after 2.5 year wait for learning disability test. *CBC News Hamilton*.

Chamberlain, A. (1998, June 12). Parent survey keeps eye on schools: Groups trying to assess effect of Tory changes. *Toronto Star*. p. A2.

Crawford, T. (1996, April 21). Middle class standing up to be counted. *Toronto Star*. p. F1.

Finlay, B. (2011, December 19). *Categories of exceptionalities [Memorandum]*. Toronto: Ontario Ministry of Education. Retrieved from www.edu.gov.on.ca/eng/general/elemsec/speced/2011CategoryException.pdf

Gallagher-Mackay, K., & Kidder, A. (2014). *Special education: A People for Education report*. Toronto, ON: People for Education.

Gidney, R. D. (1999). *From Hope to Harris: The reshaping of Ontario's schools*. Toronto, ON: University of Toronto Press.

Government of Ontario. (2005). *O. Reg. 181/98: Identification and placement of exceptional pupils [Text]*. Retrieved June 9, 2016, from www.ontario.ca/laws/view

Kimelberg, S. M. (2014). Middle-class parents, risk, and urban public schools. In Lareau, A., & Goyette, K. A. (Eds.), *Choosing homes, choosing schools* (pp. 207–236). New York: Russell Sage Foundation.

Landeros, M. (2011). Defining the "good mother" and the "professional teacher": Parent-teacher relationships in an affluent school district. *Gender and Education*, 23(3), 247–262.

Lareau, A. (2011). *Unequal childhoods: Class, race, and family life* (2nd ed.). Berkeley: University of California Press.

Larner, W. (2000). Neo-liberalism: Policy, ideology, governmentality. *Studies in Political Economy, 63,* 5–25.

Leach, J. (2000). Rhetorical analysis. In Bauer, M. W., & Gaskell, G. (Eds.), *Qualitative researching with text, image and sound* (pp. 207–226). Thousand Oaks, CA: Sage.

Morgan, C. (2003). A brief history of special education. *ETFO Voice.* Retrieved from www.etfo.ca/SiteCollectionDocuments/Publication%20Documents/Voice%20-%20School%20Year%202002-3/Winter%202003/Brief_History_Special_Ed.pdf

Ontario Ministry of Education. (2006, June 8). *McGuinty government invests $50 million in special education reforms.* Toronto: Queen's Printer for Ontario. Retrieved from http://news.ontario.ca/archive/en/2006/06/08/McGuinty-Government-Invests-50-Million-In-Special-Education-Reforms.html

Ontario Ministry of Education. (2007). *Highlights of Regulation 181/98.* Toronto: Queen's Printer for Ontario. Retrieved from www.edu.gov.on.ca/eng/general/elemsec/speced/hilites.html

Ontario Ministry of Education. (2016). *An introduction to special education in Ontario.* Accessed January 29, 2016, from www.edu.gov.on.ca/eng/general/elemsec/speced/ontario.html

People for Education. (2000). *The tracking report 2000: The effects of funding and policy changes in Ontario's elementary schools.* Toronto: People for Education.

People for Education. (2001). *The 2001 tracking report: The effects of funding and policy changes in Ontario's elementary schools.* Toronto: People for Education.

People for Education. (2002). *Special education and the funding formula.* Toronto: People for Education.

People for Education. (2007). *Annual Report on Ontario's School 2007.* Toronto: People for Education.

People for Education. (2009). *Wanted: A renewed vision for public education: People for Education Annual Report on Ontario's public schools 2009.* Toronto: People for Education.

People for Education. (2012a). *Making connections beyond school walls: People for Education Annual Report on Ontario's publicly funded schools 2012.* Toronto: People for Education.

People for Education. (2012b). *Special education.* Toronto: People for Education.

People for Education. (2013). *Special education.* Toronto: People for Education.

People for Education. (2015). *Ontario's schools: The gap between policy and reality (Annual report on Ontario's publicly funded schools 2015).* Toronto: People for Education.

People for Education. (2016). *The geography of opportunity: What's needed for broader student success (Annual report on Ontario's publicly funded schools 2016).* Toronto: People for Education.

Pinto, L. (2012). *Curriculum reform in Ontario: "common sense" policy processes and democratic possibilities.* Toronto, ON: University of Toronto Press.

Robertson, K. (2005, Summer). The many faces of privatization. *Our Schools, Our Selves, 14*(4), 43–59.

Rushowy, K. (2011, June 1). Special-ed wait times troubling. *Toronto Star.* p. GT1.

Selzer, J. (2004). Rhetorical analysis: Understanding how texts persuade readers. In Bazerman, C., & Prior, P. (Eds.), *What writing does and how it does it: An introduction to analyzing texts and textual practices* (pp. 279–307). Mahwah, NJ: Routledge.

Winton, S. (2013). Rhetorical analysis in critical policy research. *Qualitative Studies in Education, 26*(2), 158–177.

Winton, S., & Brewer, C. (2014). People for Education: A critical policy history. *Qualitative Studies in Education, 27*(9), 1091–1109.

Winton, S., & Pollock, K. (2015). Meanings of success and successful leadership in Ontario, Canada in neoliberal times. *Journal of Educational Administration and History, 48*(1), 19–34.

14 Latina/o Farmworker Parent Leadership Retreats as Sites of Agency, Community Cultural Wealth, and Success[1]

Pedro E. Nava and Argelia Lara

Over the past decade in California's San Joaquin Valley, the Educational Leadership Foundation (ELF) and Migrant Education Program (MEP) have collaboratively organized parent leadership retreats with the purpose of raising consciousness around the needs of (im)migrant families and communities and the leadership roles that parents can play in addressing them. ELF is a community benefit organization (CBO) founded on July 3, 2007 in Fresno, California by Raúl Moreno, a university and community leader, and former migrant student himself. The mission of ELF is to "empower communities through educational opportunities, leadership development, and civic engagement." As a community-based organization, ELF has strategically focused on forming partnerships with other key community organizations and businesses to leverage support for students and families.

In addition to resources and mentorship, migrant students and their families throughout the San Joaquin Valley also require professional and leadership development. Toward addressing these needs, ELF develops parent retreats that build on culturally and community responsive methods (Tintiangco-Cubales et al., 2015). This chapter examines the ways that Latina/o parent leadership retreats foster Community Cultural Wealth (Yosso, 2005) in (im)migrant communities as parents develop into leaders through cooperative and community responsive practices (Tintiangco-Cubales et al., 2015).

We examine the unique dimensions of leadership development within (im)migrant farmworker communities, and argue for the need to rethink what is meant by parent engagement and capacity building for leadership and agency in such communities. This chapter is guided by the following research question: how do Latina/o migrant parental retreats help develop the leadership skills and abilities of parent participants? In contextualizing parent engagement and capacity building, we first review the literature on Latina/o parent engagement and examine how these retreats are different from traditional forms of parental involvement. Next, we draw on Community Cultural Wealth and document how it provides a powerful framework for illuminating critical features of leadership to understand and engage Latino migrant communities. Finally, the study's findings are revealed, and we conclude with a set of recommendations that includes the use of *testimonio* as a pedagogy of leadership development as an alternative form of successful educational policy development emanating from the community itself.

The Power of *Testimonio* in Latina/o Migrant Communities

Within the field of education, the use of *testimonios* has attained heightened visibility broadly and, in particular, within the critical work of Chicana/Latina scholars undertaking pedagogical and methodological approaches (Delgado Bernal, Burciaga, & Carmona, 2012; Cruz, 2012). *Testimonios* are powerful narrative accounts with historical roots in Latin American liberation movements (Burgos-Debray, 1984). *Testimonios* can be understood as an account told by a person who "has experienced or witnessed great trauma, oppression, forced migration, or violence, or of a subject who has participated in a political movement for social justice" (Cruz, 2012, p. 461). There is a particular sense of urgency in which the *testimonio* directs attention to a cause or an issue as a way of raising consciousness (González, Plata, García, Torres, & Urrieta, 2003). As pedagogy (Freire, 2000), the use of *testimonios* centers critical reflection of lived experience, connects individuals to collective knowledges, and disrupts the silencing of voices so prevalent in "top-down" approaches commonly used in parent involvement and leadership development—especially in providing alternative policy developments in non-dominant communities. This approach toward leadership development requires a deep faith in the ability of people to critically think, reflect, and engage as active participants in their local communities, schools, and the social worlds of their children.

Why is this Work Important?

Literature has documented that parental involvement is linked to improved student academic achievement (Henderson & Mapp, 2002). Recently, scholars have examined the engagement practices of low-income Latino families (Auerbach, 2002; Ceja, 2006; Olivos, 2006) and have acknowledged the differing notions of involvement that often times exist between working class and immigrant families and school officials. Few studies have yet to examine the engagement practices of farmworking families (Lopez, 2001), an occupation overrepresented in the region examined here. Most research on family engagement still conceptualizes being "involved" in school-centric terms defined by school officials (Olivos, 2006; Pérez Carreon, Drake, & Barton, 2005) and assumes egalitarian power relations in "partnerships" between the school and the home (Auerbach, 2002), ultimately subscribing to assimilatory ideologies.

A small but increasing number of studies are beginning to examine the role that community-based organization can play in developing broader and deeper forms of engagement between families and schools (Warren, Hong, Rubin, & Uy, 2009). Some CBOs are developing the leadership capacity of parents to self-advocate and engage with schools around family and community needs, simultaneously building relationships and political power (Johnson, 2012; Warren et al., 2009). This study makes a contribution to that literature by exploring the ways one CBO utilizes *testimonios* in leadership retreats as a way to center migrant family and community needs in leadership and educational policy development.

Community Cultural Wealth Framework

The concept of cultural capital (Bourdieu, 1986) has been applied extensively in sociology and education to study U.S. inequality. An overemphasis in that literature toward forms of cultural capital that dominant groups possess (Dixon-Román, 2014), has resulted in a failure to examine the cultural capital held by non-dominant groups. Yosso (2005) has proposed a model of Community Cultural Wealth (CCW) to suggest that centering the research lens on the cultures of Communities of Color makes "visible" their "array of knowledge, skills, abilities, and contacts" (p. 77). Yosso (2005) fleshed out empirical examples in the literature that revealed how Communities of Color nurture cultural capital through dynamic and overlapping processes leading to CCW in the following ways:

- Aspirational Capital: a hopefulness rooted in dreaming of possibilities beyond what is present today.
- Linguistic Capital: the intellectual and social skills learned from communication experiences, more so than from language or style.
- Resistant Capital: oppositional dispositions undertaken to challenge inequality and marginalization.
- Navigational Capital: maneuvering through social instructions.
- Social Capital: networks of people and resources, often overlooked.
- Familial Capital: cultural knowledges nurtured among *familia* grounded in community history and memory.

In conceptualizing the different forms of capital in CCW, Yosso (2005) contributes a framework that struggles for social and racial justice through a firm commitment to "conduct research, teach and develop schools" (p. 82). CCW exposes the cultural deficit theorizing privileged in solely "seeing" cultural capital through its dominant forms, while highlighting how societal institutions could potentially transform and be remade by incorporating the experiences and knowledges of Communities of Color.

CCW's anti-deficit framework focuses on ways to open channels that encourage dialogic leadership to emerge from within Latina/o migrant schools, organizations, and spaces. While all six forms of Yosso's capital are present, this chapter focuses on three dimensions of CCW that exemplify ways researchers can redefine leadership in relation to parent engagement in migrant communities. Here, we highlight the role of social, familial, and resistant capitals because they privilege the role of shared experiences, cultural knowledge, and community-based collective action in the service of challenging inequities in schools and communities of these participants.

What Did We Do in the Field?

This qualitative study explored the use of *testimonios* as part of a case study (Yin, 2014) that examined leadership development across two parent leadership retreats led by ELF in partnership with MEP. The three-day retreats took place in April and October of 2007 in a remote location in the California San Joaquin Valley. This study relied on multiple sources of data, including individual and collective *testimonios*, ethnographic field notes (Bogdan & Biklen, 2003), and collective reflections. In addition, leadership styles pre- and post-assessments from participants in both retreats were also examined.

Data collected from the leadership retreats were analyzed and compiled into two separate reports produced on behalf of the Migrant Education Program. *Testimonios* were encouraged and shared across the six days. *Testimonios* were transcribed and manually coded (Saldaña, 2015) to identify ways parents articulated roles of leadership and the ways that community cultural wealth was expressed in relationship to schools, families, and communities.

Raúl's *Testimonio* and the Farmworking Context

Raúl Moreno frequently opens the parent leadership retreats by providing his powerful *testimonio*, or his own lived experience, as a product of the migrant farmworking context. As part of his and the ELF's vision, working with communities necessitates a perspective that privileges a focus on the lived experience of (im)migrant families, yet from an asset-based perspective. Raúl's parents and older siblings migrated to the U.S. from Mexico in 1973, leaving him and his younger siblings behind until the following year, when the family reunited in the community of Planada, in the San Joaquin Valley in California. A few months after settling in, he experienced a life-changing event at 12 years of age that would radically transform his educational and life trajectory. Participants in the educational leadership retreat listened intently as he shared his *testimonio*:

> I was riding like a kid on a brand new bike . . . I remember seeing a beautiful girl that really caught my attention as she was sitting on the rear seat of the station wagon that her father was driving . . . I pedaled faster . . . to show off in front of her. . . . By then I was going full speed, but the station wagon suddenly turned to the left, and I wasn't paying close attention . . . a car coming from the other side hit me throwing me 12 feet up in the air. I landed on my head in the pavement. Six months

later, I remember waking up in a hospital in Santa Clara . . . the first thing that I asked my father when I saw him was. . . "Dad, why don't you bring me a comic?" My father didn't respond and instead he got up and withdrew a little. Then after he came closer, and I asked him "Dad, why don't you bring me a book? Bring me the [comic]" . . . It took him a couple of days but he brought me one. . . . When he took me the comic, I had a big shock when I realized I could no longer read! I had lost 75 percent of my vision. So I asked him, "What happened Dad, why can I no longer read?"

He told me, "Well, the doctor said that maybe down the line."

"So then, I can't read?"

"Well son, what do you want me to do? I would read for you, but I don't know how to read either." Because he didn't know how to read, he only went up to the first grade. . . . Excuse my language but I was very angry at God. I would curse at God. "And why me? Why did he do this to me? Why did I lose my sight?" I was angry at God because I returned to the fields to pick figs and guess what happened to me? I could no longer pick . . . because I could no longer see well.

And so I failed. . . . My dad pulled me aside one day and said to me, "Son, you have no other choice but to [pause] . . . but to go to school." So there I go with a deep pain in my heart off to school. I went with that pain for two reasons . . . because at school I did not know a single person and second, because . . . I deeply admired my father and I yearned to be like him. I would often look at him and say, "One day I want to be like my father. I too want to be a foreman of the picking crew." So then my dreams of becoming a foreman were shattered. I no longer had an option but to go off to school. Go to school without even speaking English, without being able to see the blackboard, and without friends? Forget about it.

Raúl had little time to dwell on what he had lost as a result of the accident. He learned to rely on his hearing, he reached out for reading and writing support, and struggled, but graduated from high school. In college, he drew motivation from courageous students struggling against greater adversity. He leaned on study groups for support, transferred to a four-year university, and graduated with Bachelor's and Master's degrees, and now assists others.

One day a few years ago, when my father visited me at the university he said to me, "Do you remember son when you used to curse at God because you suffered your accident and lost your eyesight? Do you realize now, that it was all a blessing by God—a blessing in disguise?"

Raúl's *testimonio* conveys a response to experiencing a tragic incident that left him no option but to tackle adversity head on.

I tell you my *testimonio* . . . to each of us, our task is not so much to see our weaknesses, but to find the means to overcome them, to focus on the assets and strengths that we do have. I no longer have my eyesight, but God helped me to hear better . . . I invite you, if you have a particular weakness or are struggling with something—move that aside and let's keep going forth as if there is no other option.

He invites participants in the retreat to collectively reflect around their own experiences of oppression and marginalization, and to focus on their areas of strength and think of particular ways to collectivize to overcome adversity.

Migrant Leadership Retreats as Alternative Community Policy Advancement

In this section, examples from the approach employed in education and leadership retreats speak to the particular ways that these less formal, out-of-school spaces are culturally relevant and responsive (Tintiangco-Cubales et al., 2015) to Latina/o communities. We primarily focus on three of the six ways that CCW of these parents was "seen" and legitimated.

Building Social Capital

Social capital includes the networks of people and the embedded resources within their communities (Yosso, 2005). First, teambuilding and icebreaker (*dinámicas*) activities were utilized strategically from the beginning of the retreat as a way to have parents interact in entertaining and engaging ways with each other. The *dinámicas* consisted of playing games where they were encouraged to learn each other's names, birthdays, and ages and line up alphabetically. Other collaborative *dinámicas*/teambuilding activities implemented over the three-day retreat included participating in an assortment of hula-hoop activities, as well as "team skis"—participants utilized listening, communication, positive reinforcement, and cooperation skills. The *dinámicas* served the purpose of helping to forge relationships among parents, move outside of their comfort zones, and engage in activities that were also entertaining.

Second, after developing a stronger sense of community through the assortment of teambuilding activities, they began work—hand-in-hand with other parents from their school districts—on student and community needs efforts. In these groups, parents were asked to engage in dialogue identifying specific and common issues in their communities and schools.

The primary objective of these dialogues was to begin to discuss and raise consciousness in a community context and propose possible roles parents could play in working toward addressing these pertinent issues. After the identification of the community needs and problems, representatives from each group incorporated possible solutions in their Parents Advisory Council (PAC) Operational Plan and then presented them to the larger group. Included in table 14.1 are some of the identified needs and corresponding actions which parents committed to undertake.

Table 14.1 Parent Advisory Council Identified Needs & Actions

Migrant Student & Community Needs	PAC Operational Plan & Actions
1. Increased parent involvement 2. Reliable transportation 3. Cleaner and friendlier schools 4. More bilingual/bi-cultural teachers	1. Share information we learn with others in community 2. Ensure that more parents participate 3. Recruit more families 4. Create a supportive environment in meetings
1. Academic counseling for students and parents 2. Information about universities and financial aid 3. Better student assessments	1. Advocate so that schools provide our children the necessary academic support 2. Know about our rights as parents and community members
1. Improve one's own schools 2. Add more after school programming 3. Improved instruction in Math/English	1. Work closely with schools 2. Organize to generate new ideas 3. Participate in MEP activities
1. Health services (visual and dental) 2. Food and clothing 3. Racial discrimination in schools	1. Participate in direct action in community 2. Help create agency in those around me 3. Provide help to the neediest students

To conclude this session, members from each parent group presented the action steps that they vowed to take as a means toward addressing the needs they had identified.

Third, parents also participated in a networking and business card session where they were introduced to the hidden curriculum (Giroux & Purpel, 1983) around networking and engaging school and community leaders through mock school board presentations. Parents were provided with a protocol on how to "formally" address and engage school board members and power brokers in their respective communities. For most of these parents, entering formal spaces of power to engage "leaders" on a one-to-one basis is not something they have been socialized to do. They were reminded that by introducing themselves as members of an organization like MEP, they are advocating not just for the interests of their own child, but are seen as members of a collective. Mock school board presentations provided a safe space for parents to practice and have a platform to raise issues that emerged in prior dialogues.

Tapping into Familial Capital

Familial capital is the "cultural knowledges nurtured among *familia*," all of which are grounded in community, history, and memory. In this context, familial capital addresses the migratory experience and how it extends the notion of family to include relatives and non-kin networks such as *compadres*. This form of wealth engages a commitment to community well-being and expands the concept of family.

The collaborative approach of the retreats structured opportunities for families to draw on each other's familial capital and engage with one another in ways that surpassed typical leadership work in school spaces. For instance, Raúl Moreno guided parents through a reading of *Angel De Mi Guarda* (*Ángel de Mi Guarda* translates to *My Guardian Angel*), a play he authored and published as a children's book (Moreno, 2007). The play follows José and María Martínez, and their three children—Concepción, Angel, and Esperanza—through the turmoil leading to their departure from the state of Michoacán, México in their journey to the San Joaquín Valley agricultural town of Planada. The 13-scene play critically deals with the Martínez family's social, political, and economic context prior to departure, including hunger and joblessness. This forces José Martínez to draw upon his social and familial capital (Yosso, 2005) by seeking the help of his *compadre* Manuel, who now resides in California, and setting off a chain of events that climaxes when he and his family arrive at the Mexican border.

Angel de Mi Guarda exposes the wide array of social and familial capital that migrant families rely on in order to borrow the $15,000 that "*coyotes*" charge to smuggle each family into the United States. These seldom told perspectives reveal the many dangers that families face as they attempt to cross the U.S.–México border. Once in the U.S., exploitative labor conditions arguably structure a modern-day version of indentured servitude for farmworker families. For José and María Martínez, this arduous transnational journey inculcated in their children the importance of obtaining a formal education (Nava, 2012) in order to escape labor and economic exploitation, attain a higher standard of living, and no longer be subjected to such policies of dehumanization.

The most significant scenes of the play focus on the pressures the Martínez children face in terms of cultural assimilation. At 17-years-old and as the oldest of the three Martínez children, Concepción has grown tired of her family's harsh struggles, drops out of school, and elopes with her boyfriend. As time goes by, Angel, the middle child, deceives his non-English speaking parents into signing a consent form to enlist into the U.S. Army. Ashamed of his cultural background and the poverty he grew up in, Angel views his enlistment in the Army as a way to assimilate into mainstream U.S. society and leave behind his cultural background and heritage. In contrast, the youngest daughter, Esperanza, graduates high school near the top of her class and aspires to leave for a top-ranked four-year university, but struggles to gain her father's approval. While, Mr. Martínez supports his daughter's desire to obtain a higher education, his unfamiliarity with the educational system makes it difficult to give his permission. Ultimately, though, Mr. Martínez acquiesces and allows his daughter to go to college with the condition that her family remain a priority. The culminating scene captures the brutal irony of Angel—now an agent for the Department of Homeland Security and the Border Patrol—shooting and killing his own Godfather as he attempts to cross the U.S.–México border in pursuit of similar opportunities as his *compadre* José and the Martínez family had done only a couple of years before. The play ends with Angel embracing and comforting his dying Godfather—Angel has finally realized that cultural assimilation and his own desire to dutifully serve his new country have been fraught with serious contradictions and consequences.

Following the play, parents were invited to reflect and dialogue on their reactions to it. One of the mothers, María, shared her *testimonio* to address the contradictions of familial pursuit of the American Dream:

> In the play, what was most sad was the young man Angel, who was Mexican. He came from México, he studied here, and then he became an ICE agent. The saddest thing to me was that he was there to repress and kill his own people. And it was sad what happened to his Godfather and that is what happens with us, with our children today. If they came here or were born here, now they become part of the same machine that does not let us pass through.

María spoke to the tragedy inherent in the sociopolitical processes that lead people to migrate across borders. In these scenarios, immigrants face immense dangers, as well as leave much of what they know and love behind. María's commentary can also be understood as the fear that many immigrant families have of U.S. institutions like the military, or that formal education will erode the cultural imprint that parents leave on their children. In his story of becoming a border patrol agent, in many ways Angel symbolizes the failure to cultivate an *educación* (Burciaga & Erbstein, 2012)—or the role a family plays "in inculcating in children a sense of moral, social, and personal responsibility and serves as the foundation for all other learning" (Valenzuela, 1999, p. 23). Not limited to formal education in the form of certificates and degrees, this notion of *educación* refers to "competence in the social world." This competence in the social world would lead Angel to "respect the dignity and individuality" and humanity of border crossers grounded on empathy and learned from the lived experiences of his family and as a fellow migrant.

Another parent shared her *testimonio* highlighting the challenge to traditional gender roles, the evolving role of fathers, and the potential to also transform cultural knowledge and cultural roles in father–son relationships. The mother shared an exchange where her son began demanding a stronger presence in educational matters of her husband:

> "Look dad I need you to understand that I will be graduating from high school soon, and I want to continue to study." And my husband would

tell him, "It's just that studying is not for . . . you can't keep going to school because you don't have papers." And my son would respond, "But you have to help to continue to fight so that I can continue to study. You only seem to worry about providing me with something to eat, to give me money with what I may need, but you don't pay attention to what I may need you beyond those things." And now I understand, it is true that some parents worry more so about providing the necessities, and school and the children get left in last place.

In the beautiful *testimonio* above, a mother shares the unconditional love a son has for his father and explains to him that he can play a much larger role for him beyond being a provider. Despite being undocumented, the son's desire to continue to higher education reformulated for his father the concept of familial capital, or an evolved "caring, coping, and providing" (Burciaga & Erbstein, 2012; Yosso, 2005) that necessitates expanded roles adapted to the new realities facing migrant students and their families in the U.S. Furthermore, Raúl Moreno helped crystalize this session by reminding parents that evolving gender and leadership roles are important in a family. In fact, Moreno then challenged them to take the message to those who could not make it to the retreat.

Activating Resistant Capital

Resistant capital is defined as those "knowledges and skills fostered through oppositional behavior" that are put in motion to challenge political neglect, social inequality, and oppression (Yosso, 2005). While one form of cultural awakening involves understanding oppressive structures, this process also necessitates counteracting them. Formal school spaces where parents are typically invited and expected to participate are often not welcoming to migrant Latina/o parents (Nava, 2012). The leadership retreats facilitated and cultivated the resistant capital of parents through individual and group reflections, in creating spaces for parents to articulate the new knowledge co-created in this space, and in helping them build confidence that they can and do play very significant roles in the educational trajectory of their children.

The final day of the retreats served as an opportunity for participants to collectively reflect on their participation in the retreat and to share their desires of what they wished to engage in with their newfound knowledge. For example, Magdalena, who resided in a community outside of Fresno, shared how the retreat provided her an opportunity to practice some of the challenges parents will face in "real life" once they return to their respective communities. A benefit for her was gaining the motivation to follow through on her commitment toward getting her city to build a stoplight at a dangerous intersection across the street from the elementary school, hoping to save the lives of children who cross that intersection on a daily basis. María, another parent, revealed in her *testimonio* difficulties that her child has endured as a result of their undocumented immigration. When she sees injustices perpetrated against migrants, María asks herself, "Why don't you want us? We only come to work the most difficult jobs. I never see a 'White person' bending down and picking lettuce like me."

Other parents, including Guillermina and Socorro, took it upon themselves to challenge parents to broaden and expand the migrant education network of participants who attend leadership retreats. For example, Guillermina challenged other parents to recruit more and more participants for an upcoming retreat by urging, "We need to fill three or four buses next time. We need to have different parents next time as well." She then stated how she pushes her children in school, "We tell them to always work hard so you don't have to struggle like we do." Socorro, another parent who provided her powerful *testimonio*, reminded the audience that her own community had originally begun their migrant parent meetings with four parents; now, more than 85 parents are often present at their meetings. She asserted, "We need to get and hook those parents that are in the background and reel them in! We can do it." Her successful past strategies included raffles and an assortment of fundraisers to help raise money for scholarships for undocumented students attending college. During moments of reflection, Socorro was often seen knitting beautiful blankets that she then used to raffle off to raise funds for scholarships for college-going students.

The culminating event of the retreat was the creation of Individual Action Plans (IAP) where parents made family, educational, and community action commitments. In their IAPs, parents listed commitments including being more supportive of their children, attending more parent–teacher meetings, paying closer attention to the educational progress of their kids, becoming involved in school-sanctioned activities, sharing the newly acquired information with community members, recruiting more parents (especially fathers) to upcoming events and retreats, and organizing their neighbors for social/educational issues, among others.

The retreats helped shift the consciousness of many parents by providing them opportunities to reflect on how they already provide *apoyo* (Nava, 2012), or support, to further promote the education of their children, and to imagine particular ways—both as individuals and as a collective—that they can assume leadership roles to help advance academic success and the pressing needs of their communities. Perhaps this parent said it best on why the retreats were transformative:

> I've been to many workshops but what I liked about this one is that we worked as a team here, that we all had a place. It was fun, and we went more in depth in many of the things we did. I feel more motivated to return to my district. The information on the service agreement will help me out a lot. And also the event planning information that was given to us.

These *testimonios* depict how migrants in underserved communities can come together, build relationships, identify common problems in their communities, engage in deep critical reflection, while building leadership skills, and begin to exert and enact agency to mobilize for action upon their return to their communities.

Conclusion

This chapter shows that community-based organizations can and do play an important role in bringing parents together to collectively reflect on the educational needs of their community and to devise corresponding action plans and policies. The leadership retreats serve as spaces where broader and deeper engagement and policy development can begin to take place in ways that are rooted in the migrant experience and also build on the community cultural wealth of migrant communities.

The retreats also reveal the powerful role that *testimonios* play as pedagogical tools that serve to affirm and legitimate the presence of migrant parents. This study reveals that when migrant families are engaged in the education of their children in culturally responsive and community responsive approaches, and when their culture and history are seen as assets, transformative learning experiences happen.

This study illuminates how CBOs like the Education Leadership Foundation play an important role in supporting migrant leadership development by authentically drawing from the forms of cultural wealth that migrant families and communities bring to bear in the education of their children. By utilizing *testimonios* as pedagogy that emphasizes critical consciousness (Freire, 2000), educators can center the voices and experiences of families, learn from their struggles, and build upon their strengths in generating forms of educational engagement that are true to migrant families and the broader community. This chapter highlights the specific ways that CBOs can utilize asset based pedagogies and practices to legitimize the cultural wealth among Latino families, particularly in migrant communities. We conclude with our recommendation on how future policy discussions should examine how schools can learn from the framework established by the leadership retreats in order to rethink the goals and purposes of their parent engagement approaches that are deeply rooted in the cultural wealth of non-dominant communities.

Note

1 Portions of this chapter previously appeared in (2016) *Association of Mexican American Educator's Journal* 10 (3): 90–107.

References

Auerbach, S. (2002). "Why do they give the good classes to some and not to others?": Latino parent narratives of struggle in a College Access Program. *Teachers College Record*, 104(7), 1369–1392.

Bogdan, R. C., & Biklen, S. K. (2003). *Qualitative research for education: An introduction to theories and methods* (4th ed.). New York, NY: Pearson Education.

Bourdieu, P. (1986). The forms of capital. In Richardson, J. G. (Ed.), *Handbook of theory and research for the sociology of education* (pp. 241–258). Westport, CT: Greenwood Publishing Group.

Burciaga, R., & Erbstein, N. (2012). Latin@ dropouts: Generating community cultural wealth. *Association of Mexican American Educators Journal*, 6(1), 24–33.

Burgos-Debray, E. (1984). *I, Rigoberta Menchu: An Indian woman in Guatemala* (A. Wright, Trans.). London: Verso.

Ceja, M. (2006). Understanding the role of parents and siblings as information sources in the college choice process of Chicana students. *The Journal of College Student Development*, 47(1), 87–104.

Cruz, C. (2012). Making curriculum from scratch: Testimonio in an urban classroom. *Equity & Excellence in Education*, 45(3), 460–471.

Delgado Bernal, D., Burciaga, R., & Flores Carmona, J. (2012). Chicana/Latina testimonios: Methodologies, pedagogies, and political urgency. *Equity and Excellence in Education*, 45(3), 392–410.

Dixon-Román, E. J. (2014). Deviance as pedagogy: From non-dominant cultural capital to deviantly marked cultural repertoires. *Teachers College Record, 116*(8), 1–30.

Freire, P. (2000). *Pedagogy of the oppressed* (30th Anniversary Edition). New York, NY: The Continuum International Publishing Group Inc.

Giroux, H. A., & Purpel, D. E. (1983). *The hidden curriculum and moral education: Deception or discovery?* Richmond, CA: McCutchan.

González, M. S., Plata, O., García, E., Torres, M., & Urrieta, L., Jr. (2003). Testimonios de inmigrantes: Students educating future teachers. *Journal of Latinos and Education*, 2(4), 233–243.

Henderson, A., & Mapp, K. (2002). *A new wave of evidence: The impact of school, family, and community connections on student achievement*. Paper presented at Annual Synthesis, Southwest Educational Development Lab, Austin, TX.

Johnson, M. (2012). *The 21st century parent: Multicultural parent engagement leadership strategies handbook*. Charlotte, NC: Information Age Publishing Inc.

Lopez, G. (2001). The value of hard work: Lessons on parent involvement from an (im)migrant household. *Harvard Educational Review, 71*(3), 416–438.

Moreno, R. Z. (2007). *Angel de mi guarda*. Fresno, CA: Education Leadership Press.Nava, P. E. (2012). Sin Sacrificio No Hay Recompensa: Apoyo as (Im)migrant Parental Engagement in Farmworking Families of the California Central Valley. (Unpublished doctoral dissertation). University of California, Los Angeles, CA.

Olivos, E. M. (2006). *The power of parents: A critical perspective of bicultural parent involvement in the public school*. New York, NY: Peter Lang.

Pérez Carreon, G., Drake, C., & Calabrese-Barton, A. (2005). The importance of presence: Immigrant parents' school engagement experiences. *American Educational Research Journal*, 42(3), 465–498.

Saldaña, J. (2015). *The coding manual for qualitative researchers* (3rd ed.). Los Angeles, CA: Sage.

Tintiangco-Cubales, A., Kohli, R., Sacramento, J., Henning, N., Agarwal-Rangnath, R., & Sleeter, C. (2015). Toward an ethnic studies pedagogy: Implications for K—12 schools from the research. *The Urban Review*, 47(1), 104–125.

Valenzuela, A. (1999). *Subtractive schooling: U.S. Mexican youth and the politics of caring*. New York, NY: State University of New York Press.

Warren, M. R., Hong, S., Rubin, C. L., & Uy, P. S. (2009). Beyond the bake sale: A community-based relational approach to parent engagement in schools. *Teachers College Record, 111*(9), 2209–2254.

Yin, R. K. (2014). *Case study research: Design and methods.* London: Sage Publications.

Yosso, T. J. (2005). Whose culture has capital? A critical race theory discussion of community cultural wealth. *Race Ethnicity and Education, 8*(1), 69–91.

15 Bilingual and Biliterate Skills as Cross-Cultural Competence Success

Ricardo González-Carriedo
and Alexandra Babino

Historically, the United States has never had purposeful language policies—at least at the federal level. While many would assume that English is the official language of the land, it is not law. Instead, the state-level has rendered de facto language policies, as 32 states have given English an official status—albeit 27 of them made this declaration since the 1980s. The latest state making English official was West Virginia in 2016, signaling a continuation of this trend.

Parallel to this movement, some states have banned in recent decades bilingual education programs from their schools. This was the case in California (1998), Arizona (2000), and Massachusetts (2002). In much of the country, there is a clear concerted effort to impose an ideology based on the hegemony of the English language. The reasons behind this are beyond the scope of this chapter (for a thorough account of the English-Only movement, see Crawford, 2004). For the purposes of this chapter, it suffices to say that two conflicting language ideologies, sometimes acting in the same spaces, are taking place in the United States in present times. One posits the assimilation of those for whom English is not the primary language—an assimilation not only to the English language but also to the White, Anglo, middle-class values. The other affirms that society is better served when cultural pluralism principles are applied, respecting and supporting the cultural and linguistic heritage of the diverse ethnic groups present in American society. It is amidst this ideological push and pull that our students find themselves.

This chapter will argue that bilingual and biliterate skills can lead to cross-cultural competence success among Latino youth. The Seal of Biliteracy is an award given by a school in recognition of students who attain proficiency in two or more languages by high school graduation (Seal of Biliteracy, n.d.), and can play a major role in incentivizing students to become bilingual and biliterate. The study described in this chapter shows how the Seal of Biliteracy initiative, in the context of dual language (DL) programs, can help creating equitable success for Latino students.

The Push for Dual Language Programs

Aligned with the idea of cultural pluralism is the current push for DL programs in schools across the United States. In the city of New York alone, 180 DL programs exist in their public schools, serving students in grades K–12 in languages such as Arabic, Chinese, French, Haitian-Creole, Hebrew, Korean, Polish, Russian, and Spanish. Similar efforts to expand DL programs are being made in states as diverse as Utah, Oregon, Delaware, and North Carolina (Harris, 2015). The reasons education officials offer for the creation and expansion of DL programs are based on the idea that bilingualism and biliteracy are desirable outcomes in society. After all, most of the inhabitants of the world are bilingual or multilingual, and speaking more than one language is a normal state of affairs in most societies.

The influence of the phenomenon known as *globalization*, which has resulted in greater numbers of individuals moving within countries or across borders than at any point in previous history (Hornberger & McKay, 2010), has undoubtedly influenced the push toward DL programs. A substantial number of school districts in the United States are taking active steps in a direction toward second language acquisition, aware of the fact that the competition for jobs today depends on specific skills such as the ability to speak, read, and write in more than one language (Callahan & Gándara, 2014). An illustration of the support of DL programs is the recent federal policy statement from the U.S. Departments of Health and Human Services. The statement aimed to offer more strategic, specific support for early childhood dual language learners by providing a welcoming environment that is linguistically accessible to students and their families in order to expressly foster emerging bilingualism (White House, 2016).

Research studies back up the implementation of DL programs. First, DL programs benefit minority-language and majority-language speakers to the point that both groups of students outperform their peers in transitional bilingual and mainstream monolingual programs in reading and mathematics skills (Marian, Shook, & Schroeder, 2013). Second, DL programs are also effective in the development of cross-cultural competence, a key component of education in today's increasingly interconnected world (Feinauer & Howard, 2014). Finally, the additive nature of DL programs makes them the strongest form of bilingual education (e.g., Baker, 2011; Cummins, 1996; Lindholm-Leary, 2001; Thomas & Collier, 2010).

In DL programs, language and content are taught concurrently (de Jong, 2011) in the context of an enrichment model of instruction where students acquire a second language in a bilingual environment (Warhol & Mayer, 2012). This is in stark contrast with transitional models of bilingual education where the goal is to reach full proficiency only in English (Babino & González-Carriedo, 2015). The bilingual environment of DL programs is accomplished not only by means of the use of two languages for instruction, but also through the classroom demographics. In two-way DL programs, classrooms are divided equally between native English speakers and native Spanish speakers. When the demographics of the school do not permit this, an alternative option may be a one-way DL program. In this case, instruction is still allocated equally between the two languages, but all the students in the classroom are native speakers of one language, usually the minority language.

At the federal level, Title VII of the Elementary Education Act of 1968, later known as the Bilingual Education Act, marked the first legislative effort to develop and implement bilingual education programs. One year later, the Texas legislature passed HB 103, the first bilingual education bill of the state. This bill repealed an English-only statue dating from 1918, which made it a misdemeanor for teachers and administrators to use a language other than English in school. The dropout rate among Latinos at the time of the passage of HB 103 was 80%. The bill did not require schools to offer bilingual education but allowed them to do so after approval from the Texas Education Agency (Latino Education Policy in Texas, n.d.). It would be a later bill, SB 121, passed in 1973, which would direct school districts to institute bilingual education programs when 20 or more English learners in the same grade share the same language classification (Texas Education Agency Bilingual/ESL Unit, 2004).

The next section will describe a more recent attempt at incentivizing bilingualism and biliteracy, the Seal of Biliteracy.

The Seal of Biliteracy

The Seal of Biliteracy initiative was born out of the grassroots efforts of *Californians Together*, a group encompassing parents, teachers, education advocates, and civil rights groups focused on policy and practice related to English learners (Seal of Biliteracy, n.d.). The seal serves as recognition for high school graduates who attain high levels of proficiency in one or more languages in addition to English. It has three main purposes: (a) to encourage students to pursue multilingual competencies; (b) to commend students for their efforts in becoming multilingual; and (c) to serve as evidence of the multilingual skills achieved by the students. All three goals promote a positive view of multilingualism by essentially commodifying second language proficiency.

The first state to adopt the Seal of Biliteracy was California, in 2011. Since then, 23 more states (at the time of this writing) have passed laws instituting the Seal of Biliteracy. Several more are taking steps toward the adoption of this program. The state of Texas endorsed the Seal of Biliteracy through House Bill 5, signed into law by then-Governor Rick Perry on May 10, 2013. This bill focused on changes to the state's curriculum and graduation requirements, but also contained a provision to provide high school graduates with a performance acknowledgement placed on their diploma and transcript on the basis of their achievements in bilingualism and biliteracy (Texas Administrative Code, n.d.). The measure was meant to be a motivational factor for the pursuit of mastery in English plus one or more additional languages.

Given the recent adoption of the Seal of Biliteracy, studies related to this program are still scarce. In fact, only two studies have been conducted, both in California. The first examined the importance of the seal from an employer perspective (Porras, Ee, & Gándara, 2014). In this study, employers overwhelmingly showed favorable views toward hiring bilingual personnel. A large majority also expressed finding a candidate with a Seal of Biliteracy on their diploma as advantageous. The second study explored the implementation of the seal from a district leadership perspective (DeLeon, 2014). The study found that awardees of the seal represented a wide array of languages, including French, German, Mandarin, Japanese, and Korean. Almost half of the recipients were former English learners.

A Multiple Case Study of the Seal of Biliteracy in Texas

Interested in knowing the students' perspective about their participation in the DL program and the Seal of Biliteracy initiative, we conducted a phenomenological, multiple case study. The intention was to capture the lived experiences of three students in regard to their involvement in the DL program and their impressions about the Seal of Biliteracy (Bakker, 2010). The multiple-case study design intended to look for common patterns and explanations of two phenomena: participation in a DL program and attainment of the Seal of Biliteracy. The comparison of the cases allowed for the identification of shared features and characteristics (Bleijenbergh, 2010).

The study took place at a large (over 35,000 students) school district in north Texas. In this school district, almost 80% of the students come from low-income families, and Latinos comprise the majority of the student body (72%). Over one in three students (39%) are classified as an English language learner. Upon obtaining permission from the Institutional Review Board, the school district was contacted to seek authorization to conduct the study. The district provided the researchers with a list of 28 graduating students eligible for the Seal of Biliteracy. In addition to meeting all the requirements for graduation, these students had completed a minimum of eight credits in the DL program, four in the content areas and four in the electives. After attempting to make contact with the 28 students in the list, three agreed to be part of the study, two females and one male, all aged 18 and recent high school graduates. The following sections will describe the findings. All names are pseudonyms.

Sofía

Sofía was born in El Salvador but she moved with her family to the United States at the age of seven. Upon arriving in Texas, her parents enrolled her in a school where the only option available for students who did not know English was a pull-in English as a second language (ESL) program. In this type of program, an ESL teacher goes into the classroom and provides support to the English learner (Wright, 2010). All instruction is in English. However, two years later, Sofía's family moved to a nearby city, and she was enrolled in a school where English learners were placed in a DL program. In her new school, Sofía had two teachers. One taught her certain subjects in English and the other taught other subjects in Spanish. Overall instruction was balanced between the two languages.

This changed when Sofía started middle school. Beginning in 6th grade, only two classes were taught in Spanish, an elective (theater) and a core subject (mathematics). For Sofía, it was important to take mathematics in Spanish because this gave her the ability to understand advanced concepts that would have presented a challenge in English. Although her English oral language skills (listening and speaking) were advanced by the time Sofía started 5th grade, only two years after her arrival, the use of academic language was far more challenging. This was in consonance with findings from several studies that have pointed to a period of between three and five years to develop English oral proficiency and between four and seven years to become proficient in the academic aspect of the language (e.g., Hakuta, 2000). The challenge for students, consequently, is to learn the content areas *at the same time* that they acquire English. However, students in DL programs attain higher academic results than students in ESL programs. This is because English learners in DL programs "master much more of the curriculum, academically and linguistically, than English learners in ESL-programs," including the English language (Thomas & Collier, 2012, p. 1). Taking classes where the medium of instruction was Spanish allowed Sofía not only to keep up with her English-speaking peers in the core subjects but also gave her the foundation to learn English. Research studies have shown that certain language skills related to literacy may transfer across languages, especially if the languages use the same writing system and share a common origin, as is the case with English and Spanish, two Indo-European languages. The transferable skills include decoding and reading strategies, such as scanning, making inferences, and using background knowledge about the text, to cite a few (Baker, 2011).

In high school, Sofía continued taking two classes in the Spanish language, one of them Spanish language arts. Taking the most advanced language classes the school offered, Sofía continued developing her biliterate skills. These classes included Spanish V and Spanish literature. This was accompanied by a constant reinforcement of the Spanish language at home, where this language was commonly used. Language use changed frequently with her two siblings, alternating Spanish and English, a pattern typical in families with bilingual children (Barron-Hauwaert, 2011). However, Spanish was the only language used with her mother, a monolingual Spanish speaker. Periodic trips to El Salvador also contributed to Sofía's language development. All these elements helped her to develop a balanced bilingualism, a term that refers to situations where competencies in two languages are well developed (Baker, 2011). The result of the highly developed skills in both languages was not only that Sofía was able to choose what language to use with her bilingual friends but also that she could read and write with ease in English and Spanish.

Another aspect of Sofía's bilingualism worth noting was her perception that knowing two languages had been a crucial element in her development as a student. She became aware of this when a Spanish-speaking late-enrolling student came to her school, a student with no previous knowledge of English. Sofía's ability to switch back and forth between both languages allowed her to help a new classmate in school. The significance of Sofía's bilingualism also became obvious when she decided to take advanced mathematics courses such as calculus. In her estimation, her understanding of the concepts in this class was made possible by her strong foundation in algebra, a course that she took in Spanish at a time when her English was still developing.

Decidedly important for Sofía was the support that she received from her teachers in the DL program. The school goals for this program were for the students to reach full bilingualism and biliteracy, as well as to develop cross-cultural understandings. Sofía's perception was that her teachers in the DL program were aware of the importance of developing her bilingualism, whereas her teachers not in the DL program were not concerned with the linguistic aspect of her education. However, she also had a positive perception about all teachers' acceptance of the linguistic and cultural diversity of the school. She also mentioned her mother as a decisive factor in her ability to become bilingual. This support complemented the help she received in school and pushed her to continue in the DL program even though this meant at one point giving up sports.

In regard to the importance of bilingualism in her future life, Sofía affirmed that her Spanish language skills will be an important factor, both personally and professionally. Not only will these skills allow her to communicate fluently with Spanish monolingual family members and bilingual friends, but also she thought that being literate in Spanish will allow her to have access to jobs where the bilingual skills will be appreciated. Sofía's feeling was that speaking Spanish will give her access to jobs serving the community. In fact, she expressed a desire to become a bilingual teacher in an elementary school with a DL program. Her perspective was that by doing this, she would be helping others as she was helped in school. Certainly, the high expectations that teachers had of her while in the DL program helped her envision a professional life focused on using her bilingual and biliterate skills to help others.

These high expectations translated in high academic marks for most of the students in the DL program and, very importantly, a desire in the case of Sofía to continue with her education after high school. In fact, her plans were to attend one of the higher education institutions in the area. Finally, it is important to note the highly motivating factor that the Seal of Biliteracy had on Sofía. Although the seal was not stamped in her diploma, she received a letter from the school district congratulating her for her graduation from the DL program and encouraging her to continue viewing her bilingualism as an asset.

Isabella

Unlike Sofía, who was schooled in El Salvador between the ages of five and seven and had very little access to the English language until she moved to Texas, Isabella was born into a Mexican and Salvadoran origin family where the use of two languages was common. Her mother is fluent in both English and Spanish while her father is a Spanish-dominant speaker with some knowledge of English. However, Isabella's primary language when she was enrolled in kindergarten was Spanish. This gave her access to services as an English language learner and to the DL program at her school. She remained in the program until her graduation from high school.

Isabella's memories of her elementary years in the DL program are similar to Sofía's. Each year, two subjects were taught in Spanish and another two subjects in English. The school's model provided for the teaching of language arts (including explicit teaching of listening, speaking, reading, and writing), mathematics, science, and social studies in both languages. This model departs from other models of DL education, where there is a compartmentalization of subjects by language across all grades at the elementary level. Isabella's school also differed from other models that offer an unbalanced distribution of instructional time between the languages in the early grades and progressively reaches a balance in the late elementary years. In Isabella's school, however, the model provided for students to receive 50% of instruction in Spanish and 50% in Spanish. Starting in 6th grade, Isabella received instruction in Spanish in two courses per grade level. Table 15.1 shows the middle and high school DL Spanish course offerings.

This linguistically balanced distribution of instructional time allowed Isabella to be fluent in both languages not long after the start of her schooling, developing literacy skills simultaneously in Spanish and English. During her kindergarten year, like many other students exposed predominantly to Spanish before entering school, she found English challenging. However, this did not last long, and soon she reached a point where she felt equally comfortable with both languages. Although Baker (2011) affirms that balanced bilinguals are scarce, Isabella's bilingualism developed to the point where she could adroitly move from one language to the other. This situation prolonged itself though the middle and high school years to the present day, when Isabella uses Spanish and English with her siblings and friends. Like Sofía, Isabella also is expected to use Spanish with her parents at home and during vacation trips to visit extended family in Mexico and El Salvador.

Table 15.1 Middle and High School Dual Language Spanish Course Offerings

6th grade	7th grade	8th grade	9th grade	10th grade	11th grade
Social Studies-World Cultures	Science 7th 7th GT	Math 8 Algebra I Geometry	History-World Geography	Chemistry PreAP Physics GT	Latin American Studies Juvenile Justice
Spanish 3A	Spanish 3B	Spanish 4AP	Spanish Cultural and Linguistic Topics	Spanish 5 AP	Spanish 5 AP
			Health and Communications	Theater Arts	Theater Arts
			3rd Language (French, Mandarin, Chinese, ASL)	3rd Language (French, Mandarin Chinese, ASL)	3rd Language (French, Mandarin Chinese, ASL)

For Isabella, the announcement in 8th grade that an honorary mention would be included in their diplomas upon graduation from high school was an important motivation to remain in the DL program. She also felt encouraged by her teachers, who stressed the importance of continuing developing her bilingualism and biliteracy by taking core courses in Spanish in addition to advanced courses in Spanish language and literature. The school counselors also provided the necessary guidance, informing the students in the DL program about their options. Although it was not clear to her the shape that the Seal of Biliteracy would take, the knowledge that her bilingualism would be recognized was a significant stimulus that helped her determination to remain in the DL program until her graduation.

The emphasis that the school gave to her linguistic development was also an important factor in regard to her perspective of languages and bilingualism. Isabella feels that being bilingual will give her additional professional opportunities and that the Seal of Biliteracy will allow her to demonstrate her skills in English and Spanish to potential employers. Isabella's plans, like Sofía's, are to become a bilingual teacher in an elementary DL program. She feels happy when she imagines herself using Spanish and English to help children learn. To accomplish this goal, she is set to study at a local community college for two years, after which she plans to transfer to a teacher education program at a nearby university. Her perception about the role that the DL program has had in her elementary and secondary education years is that it helped her have high academic expectations for herself. Courses in the program were rigorous and teachers transmitted the importance of a strong work ethic. Her teachers consistently reminded Isabella and her classmates about the importance of being bilingual and biliterate. During her graduation ceremony, teachers and administrators made a special mention about the group of students graduating from the DL program.

Santiago

The number of immigrant children in the United States grew by 51% in the period between 1995 and 2014 (Camera, 2016). Santiago was born in Mexico, where he spent the first few years of his life. Although Santiago's teachers taught him some English, when he moved to Texas at the age of eight, it was very difficult for him to maintain a conversation in this language. His natural shyness and the fact that most children experience a *silent period* when first exposed to a second language undoubtedly contributed to feelings of isolation and withdrawal (for a comprehensive review of studies related to the silent period, see Ellis, 1994). However, a decisive factor alleviated Santiago's detachment during those first few months in 3rd grade. He was classified as an English language learner (ELL) and placed in a DL program. Students in Texas, like their peers across the country, are identified as ELLs after they are tested for English language knowledge. This test is a consequence of the completion of a survey by the parents at the moment of registration in school. In this survey, parents state the primary language of their child. If the response to the survey is anything else than English, the child is automatically tested. Teachers can also refer students for testing in situations where parents declare English to be the primary language but the teachers have doubts about the students' mastery of this language.

Taught in both English and Spanish, Santiago was able to keep up with his peers in all core subjects. The use of the two languages allowed him to understand the main concepts and participate in activities and assignments at the same pace as the rest of the class. The greater challenge for Santiago during the first few years in Texas was learning English, more so than learning mathematics, science, or social studies. Nevertheless, the constant support of his teachers allowed him to eventually feel more at ease with English, and by the time he reached 5th grade, the language stopped being an obstacle.

In middle school, the amount of instructional time that Santiago received in Spanish decreased drastically, as was the case in high school. Starting in 9th grade, however, Santiago had a number of Spanish-taught classes to choose from, which allowed him some flexibility in the design of his schedule. An element of the DL program that Santiago came to appreciate through the years was the inclusion of cultural components in the instruction. This allowed him to develop a broad cultural awareness. The result was an appreciation for his heritage and an understanding of the cultural diversity present at his school.

As was the case with Sofía and Isabella, Santiago also had the feeling that the DL program maintained high academic expectations for all students. In fact, he attributed his high marks in school to the rigor in the teachers' instructional methods and the depth of analysis of the different components of the curriculum. Santiago interpreted high school only as a step toward a professional career, and to this end he had made plans to attend the local community college, where he would study two years before transferring to an area university to major in psychology.

The first time that Santiago heard about the Seal of Biliteracy was when he was in 11th grade. At that time, students were told that a seal would be imprinted in their graduation diplomas. Knowing about the seal gave him an increased motivation to do well in school and a pride stemming from the value that the school was giving to his bilingualism and biliteracy. Although the seal did not finally appear in his diploma, Santiago received a letter from the school district certifying that he had fulfilled the requirements for a successful completion of the DL program. Overall, Santiago considered himself fortunate to have had the opportunity to be part of the program.

What does this all Mean?

Unlike other countries (e.g., Canada, Mexico, and France), the United States has never had an official language. In fact, the nation has never had a planned and national language policy. Instead, there have been ad hoc language policies to respond to immediate needs or political pressures (Crawford, 2004). Sometimes, these policies have been directly approved by voters through referenda, as was the case with the English-Only education laws passed in Arizona, California, and Massachusetts at the turn of the century. In other occasions, the state legislatures have intervened to regulate the use of language in schools. The latter was the case in Texas, where bilingual education programs were first allowed and then required in certain instances in the late 1960s and early 1970s. In recent times, the federal government and the states have issued declarations and policies incentivizing the acquisition of bilingual skills among the students. Among these policies is the Seal of Biliteracy.

The purpose of the study described in this chapter was to analyze the perspectives of three students about their participation in a DL program. We also intended to explore the perceptions of the students about the Seal of Biliteracy. Specifically, we were interested in knowing whether this policy produced any motivation on the students to graduate from the DL program. Both the DL program and the Seal of Biliteracy were the consequence of legislative actions resulting in policies aimed at helping second language learners. It is important to note that although the majority of students in DL programs are classified by the state of Texas as English learners, two-way DL programs serve native-English speakers as well.

The amount of evidence in favor of DL programs has been growing steadily in the last two decades (e.g., Alanís & Rodríguez, 2008; Collier & Thomas, 2004; Gómez, Freeman, & Freeman, 2005). DL programs allow students to perform well in school while learning an additional language. The students in this study were clear in their satisfaction about the program. Sofía, who started school in Texas in 2nd grade, and Santiago, who was enrolled in 3rd grade, affirmed that having the option of using Spanish was an essential component of their education during their first two years in Texas schools. Having their primary language as the medium of instruction for half of the day allowed them to keep up with peers who started in the DL program in kindergarten and who by the age of seven or eight had reached proficiency in English. All three students interviewed stated that teachers in the DL program had held high expectations. The students also had the perception that they had to work harder in school because they were part of the DL program and they were expected to do so. This feeling was attached to a sense that students in the DL program excelled academically. The three students had plans for their future that involved attending institutions of higher education. Interestingly, the three intended to use their bilingual skills in the future, Sofía and Isabella as bilingual teachers and Santiago as a psychologist. They assigned a high value to their knowledge of Spanish and, in the case of Sofía and Isabella, had a desire to pass on their experiences in the DL program to other students.

The interviews yielded vague responses in relation to the Seal of Biliteracy. The students were aware of its existence and its significance, since

212 Ricardo González-Carriedo and Alexandra Babino

the seal had been mentioned several times in school. However, the students assumed that the seal would be imprinted in the graduation diplomas and they were confused when, after receiving the diplomas, they saw that the seal was not there. However, the students did receive a letter from the school district stating that they had met the requirements of the DL program. This letter emphasized the commitment of the school district to bilingualism and biliteracy and stressed the importance of these skills. The students were appreciative of the letter, which reinforced their perceptions about their linguistic skills.

In summary, students perceived the DL program they attended as very valuable, particularly in their early elementary years, when Spanish was their dominant language. As they progressed in school, the program varied in regard to the time allocated to both languages, with English becoming the principal language of instruction and Spanish being limited to two classes every day. Ideally, the balanced allocation of time between languages should have continued through middle and high school. The lack of sufficient bilingual teachers at the secondary level may explain why most DL programs do not extend in their true form beyond elementary school. However, in spite of this, students reported a high level of satisfaction with their DL program until their graduation, primarily because of the high academic expectations that were an inherent part of the program. Feelings about the Seal of Biliteracy, on the other hand, were more ambiguous, possibly on account of the conflicting information they received throughout the years. The program was conceived as a tangible reward for attaining fluency in English and another language. The requisites of the DL program fulfilled the requirements expressed in the policy approving the Seal of Biliteracy. However, the seal did not appear in the diploma. As few school districts in Texas are fully implementing the Seal of Biliteracy at the time of this writing, future research needs to consider the school and district administrators' views about the seal and the perceived obstacles for a full implementation.

The Seal of Biliteracy, in the context of DL programs, has the potential to serve as a strong motivating element for students developing their bilingualism. Fostering bilingualism and biliteracy are key steps toward building a more equitable society able to fulfill the demands of this increasingly globalized 21st Century. Enacting policies such as the Seal of Biliteracy initiative, which foster the development of the rich cultural and linguistic assets of this country, is a step in the right direction. Students will feel supported and their bilingualism validated. This policy represents a key landmark in the journey toward a more equitable, dynamic Latino student success.

References

Alanís, I., & Rodríguez, M. A. (2008). Sustaining a dual language immersion program: Features of success. *Journal of Latinos and Education*, 7(4), 305–319.

Babino, A., & González-Carriedo, R. (2015). Advocating for dual-language programs: Implementation of a public policymaking model. *Journal of Bilingual Education Research & Instruction, 17*(1), 12–27.

Baker, C. (2011). *Foundations of bilingual education and bilingualism.* Bristol, UK: Multilingual Matters.

Bakker, J. I. (2010). Phenomenology. In Mills, A. J., Durepos, G., & Wiebe, E. (Eds.), *Encyclopedia of case study research* (pp. 673–677). Los Angeles, CA: Sage Publications.

Barron-Hauwaert, S. (2011). *Bilingual siblings: Language use in families.* Bristol, UK: Multilingual Matters.

Bleijenbergh, I. (2010). Case selection. In Mills, A. J., Durepos, G., & Wiebe, E. (Eds.), *Encyclopedia of case study research* (pp. 61–63). Thousand Oaks, CA: Sage Publications.

Callahan, R. M., & Gándara, P. C. (Eds.). (2014). *The bilingual advantage: Language, literacy and the US labor market* (Vol. 99). Bristol, UK: Multilingual Matters.

Camera, L. (2016, January 5). The increase of immigrant students tests tolerance. *U.S. News.* Retrieved from www.usnews.com/news/blogs/data-mine/articles/2016-01-05/number-of-immigrant-students-is-growing

Collier, V. P., & Thomas, W. P. (2004). The astounding effectiveness of dual language education for all. *NABE Journal of Research and Practice, 2,* 1–20.

Crawford, J. (2004). *Educating English learners: Language diversity in the classroom.* Los Angeles, CA: Bilingual Education Services.

Cummins, J. (1996). *Negotiating identities: Education for empowerment in a diverse society.* Ontario, CA: California Association of Bilingual Education.

de Jong, E. (2011). *Foundations for multilingualism in education: From principles to practice.* Philadelphia, PA: Caslon.

Deleon, T. M. (2014). *The new ecology of biliteracy in California: An exploratory study of the early implementation of state seal of biliteracy.* (Unpublished doctoral dissertation). Loyola Marymount University, Los Angeles, CA.

Ellis, R. (1994). *The study of second language acquisition.* Oxford: Oxford University Press.

Feinauer, E., & Howard, E. R. (2014). Attending to the third goal: Cross-cultural competence and identity development in two-way immersion programs. *Journal of Immersion and Content-Based Language Education, 2*(2), 257–272.

Gómez, L., Freeman, D., & Freeman, Y. (2005). Dual language education: A promising 50–50 model. *Bilingual Research Journal, 29,* 145–164.

Hakuta, K. (2000). How long does it take English learners to attain oroficiency. University of California Linguistic Minority Research Institute. UC Berkeley: University of California Linguistic Minority Research Institute. Retrieved from: https://escholarship.org/uc/item/13w7m06g

Harris, E. (2015, October 8). DL Programs are on the rise, even for native English speakers. *The New York Times.* Retrieved from www.nytimes.com/2015/10/09/nyregion/DL-programs-are-on-the-rise-even-for-native-english-speakers.html?_r=0

Hornberger, N., & McKay, S. (2010). Introduction. In Hornberger, N., & McKay, S. (Eds.), *Sociolinguistics and language education* (xv–xx). Bristol, UK: Multilingual Matters.

Latino Education Policy in Texas. (n.d.). *Major historical antecedents to Texas Bilingual Legislation.* Retrieved from www.edb.utexas.edu/latino/bilingual_edu_page.html.

Lindholm-Leary, K. (2001). *Dual language education.* Clevedon, UK: Multilingual Matters. As cited in Baker, C. (2011). *Foundations of bilingual education and bilingualism.* Clevedon, UK: Multilingual Matters.

Marian, V., Shook, A., & Schroeder, S. R. (2013). Bilingual two-way immersion programs benefit academic achievement. *Bilingual Research Journal, 36*(2), 167–186.

Porras, D., Ee, J., & Gándara, P. (2014). Employer preferences: Do bilingual applicants and employees experience an advantage? In Callahan, R., & Gándara, P. (Eds.), *The bilingual advantage: Labor, literacy, and the U.S. labor market* (234–259). Bristol, UK: Multilingual Matters.

Seal of Biliteracy (n.d.). *What is the seal?* Retrieved from http://sealofbiliteracy.org/

Texas Administrative Code (n.d.). *Chapter 74: Curriculum requirements: Subchapter B: Graduation requirements.* Retrieved from http://ritter.tea.state.tx.us/rules/tac/chapter074/ch074b.html

Texas Education Agency Bilingual/ESL Unit. (2004). *Chronology of federal and state law & policy impacting language minority status.* Retrieved from http://www2.sfasu.edu/enlace/modules/Chronology%20of%20Federal%20Law%20Guiding%20ELL%20Policy%20and%20Practice%20from%20TEA.pdf

Thomas, W. P., & Collier, V. P. (2010). *Educating English language learners for a transformed world.* Albuquerque, NM: Fuente Press.

Thomas, W. P., & Collier, V. P. (2012). *Dual language education for a transformed world.* Albuquerque, NM: Dual Language Education of New Mexico/Fuente Press.

Warhol, L., & Mayer, A. (2012). Misinterpreting school reform: The dissolution of a dual-immersion bilingual program in an urban New England elementary school. *Bilingual Research Journal, 35*(2), 145–163. doi:10.1080/15235882.2012.703636

White House. (2016). *Fact sheet: Supporting dual language learners in early learning settings.* Retrieved from www.whitehouse.gov/the-press-office/2016/06/02/fact-sheet-supporting-DL-learners-early-learning-settings

Wright, W. E. (2010). *Foundations for teaching English language learners. Research, theory, policy, and practice.* Philadelphia, PA: Caslon.

16 Diversity-Driven Charters and the Construction of Urban School Success

Priscilla Wohlstetter, Amy K. Wang, and Matthew M. Gonzales

Charter schools are a unique breed—part of the public education system, open to all students tuition-free, and yet unburdened from many of the rules and regulations that govern and sometimes constrain district-run public schools. Each charter school operates within the detailed framework of its own performance contract or "charter," agreed upon between the charter authorizer and the school. Collectively, charter schools were intended to diversify the providers of public education; to encourage and incubate innovations with regard to education programs, school governance, staffing, and budgeting; and to improve student achievement. In addition, charter schools were expected to broaden public school choice and to serve as models for improving teaching and learning in district-run public schools.

In the United States, the 1980s was a time of considerable experimentation with individual education reforms. The charter movement was the latest in a series of reforms that were ultimately bundled into a package that became charter schools. School districts across the country experimented with school-based management, an idea borrowed from the private sector on the assumption that when decision-making was decentralized to school sites, school communities would make smart decisions tailored to the needs of their unique communities, thus strengthening the commitment to the reform agenda. Under school-based management, school communities were empowered to make the same kinds of decisions over the school's education program, budget, and staff.

Other experiments in the 1980s explored deregulation—loosening state education codes and the rules and regulations governing schools—so that individual schools would have more discretion in making decisions. Research (Elmore & Fuhrman, 2004) in this area assessed the value of blanket waivers as compared to waivers that were awarded piecemeal, provision by provision. The common conclusion is that blanket waivers were far more liberating to schools and also resulted in school improvement efforts far more rapidly.

Finally, there were reforms that emphasized school choice. While school choice in the modern era of public schooling had been linked to magnet schools for desegregation purposes, the new wave of choice reforms pioneered in Minnesota created the first legislated charter school. This ground-breaking Minnesota law allowed the formation of eight results-oriented, student-centered public schools: the first, City Academy in St. Paul, opened its doors in 1992. Minnesota adopted its charter school law as an incremental change from existing education policy. Minnesota enacted the Post-Secondary Education Options (PSEO) Act in 1985, which allowed junior and senior high school students to enroll in postsecondary education institutions, earning credits simultaneously toward high school and college graduations. State and district tuition dollars followed the student to the school of his or her choice, adding competition to local educational systems with clear winners and losers.

At the same time states were experimenting with these reforms, the Reagan administration's National Commission on Excellence in Education released its report titled "A Nation at Risk," concluding that U.S. schools were failing. This report touched off a wave of efforts to restructure education. The national discussion about restructuring eventually brought together the ideas of Ray Budde, an educator and administrator in Massachusetts, with those of Albert Shanker, president of the American Federation of Teachers. Ray Budde had a strong interest in "the way things are organized" and "how things work or don't work in organizations." His paper, entitled "Education by Charter," written back in the mid-1970s, offered ideas for the reorganization of school districts. Subsequently, Budde had his paper published by the Northeast Regional Lab in 1988, and it was disseminated widely. It eventually got into the hands of Al Shanker, who had a weekly column in *The New York Times*. In one of his columns during July 1988, Shanker discussed a speech he had recently given at the National Press Club supporting the idea of teachers setting up autonomous schools within schools. Shanker mentioned that Ray Budde had the best name for these schools: charter schools. Shanker also expanded on Budde's idea by proposing that teachers ought to be able to start new schools outside an existing school building. In sum, the key principles of the charter movement—school-site autonomy, deregulation, choice, competition, and accountability—were proposed as elements of a new school model designed to empower teachers, desegregate schools, and cultivate innovative educational practices (Kahlenberg & Potter, 2014). Figure 16.1, below, sets forth the theory of change underlying charter schools.

With the first generation of charter schools beginning in the early 1990s, and continuing through most of the decade, attention was focused on the states—the pace at which charter laws were being adopted, the difference in content across laws, and whether or not charters were a passing fad to be replaced by the next reform de jour. During this decade, the number of states enacting charter laws grew exponentially, from one in 1991 to the opening of nearly 2,000 charter schools in 2000–2001 across the United States, which enrolled nearly half a million students. Figure 16.2 illustrates this growth both in the number of students enrolled and the number of charter schools from 1990–2014.

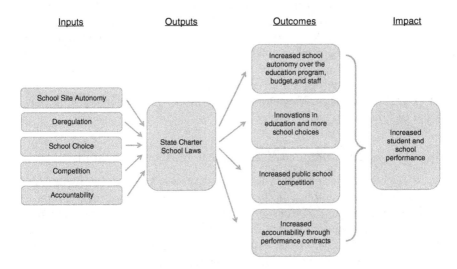

Figure 16.1 From Here to There: The Charter School Theory of Change

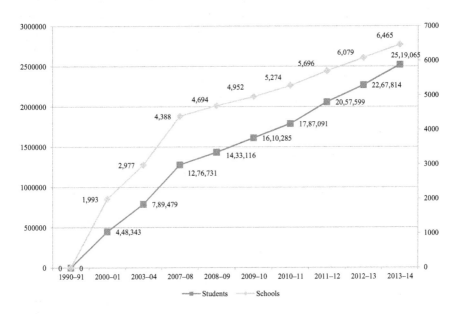

Figure 16.2 Growth of Charter Schools 1991–2014

From 2000 to 2008, nearly half a million more students enrolled in charter schools (1.2 million in total), which led to the opening of 4,388 schools. Since 2008, there has been a consistent increase of between 100,000 and 200,000 students enrolling in charter schools each year. Currently, over 2.5 million students attend charter schools, and close to 6,500 public charter schools have opened. According to the National Center for Educational Statistics, "From school years 2003–04 to 2013–14, the percentage of all public schools that were public charter schools increased from 3.1 to 6.6 percent, and the total number of public charter schools increased from 3,000 to 6,500." Today, 44 states and the District of Columbia have charter school laws, leaving just six states (Montana, Nebraska, North and South Dakota, Vermont, and West Virginia) without charter laws (U.S. Department of Education, 2016).

Backfires and Unintended Consequences of Charter Schools

In reviewing research on charter schools, we identified three major challenges to implementation. First is the notion that proponents of charter schools anticipated that school-by-school change would ultimately produce system change. But this did not happen until the philanthropic community invested heavily in networks of charter schools to speed up system change. The second implementation challenge related to charter schools as engines of innovation. As we discuss below, charter schools have not experimented much with innovation, and as a result, traditional models of education prevail. Finally, contrary to Shanker's vision of charter schools attracting diverse groups of students, many charter school populations are homogeneous in terms of race, socioeconomic status, and parents' educational attainment. In this section, we discuss these three challenges, which ultimately laid the foundation for new policy demands in response to the backfires and unintended consequences during early implementation of the charter school movement.

The slow pace of system change. The original champions of charter schools envisioned that individual charter schools acting on their own would be able to change entire school systems. Over the years, the one-by-one approach to charter schools was joined by the growth of networks of charter schools in order to spur the speed of systemic reform. The network approach also grew in direct response to the operational and financial challenges faced by many stand-alone charter schools. Network configurations, whose home offices offer financial management, facility acquisition, human resources, legal compliance, and grants acquisition assistance, help combat the pervasive resource scarcity experienced by stand-alone charters by taking advantage of economies of scale as service providers.

The growth of CMOs has been attributed to the infusion of foundation funding. NewSchools Venture Fund (NSVF), created in 1998, was the first to identify and support multi-site charter management organizations, which launch and operate integrated networks of public charter schools. From 2006–2015, NSVF concentrated its investments in key cities, including Boston, Washington D.C., Oakland, Newark, New York City, Chicago, Los Angeles, and New Orleans. In each city, NSVF worked to build a portfolio of successful, scalable, and sustainable entrepreneurial organizations, mostly

CMOs, that provide high-quality educational opportunities for underserved children (Russo, 2013; Scott & Quinn, 2014; Scott, 2005).

Later on in 2006, the Charter School Growth Fund (CSGF), another venture philanthropy, was created as a national non-profit to make multi-year, philanthropic investments in talented education entrepreneurs to build networks of great charter schools, and to provide them with support as they grew. According to the CSGF Website (charterschoolgrowthfund.org), they funded the expansion of charter networks across 23 states in a wide range of communities, from Los Angeles and Phoenix to the Rio Grande and the Mississippi River Delta.

As the CMO landscape blossomed, the federal government emerged with a new grant in 2010 under its existing Charter School Program to provide federal dollars to CMOs to spur the replication and expansion of high-quality charter schools with demonstrated records of success, including success in increasing student academic achievement. The purposes of these federal grants were to: "1) expand the enrollment of one or more existing charter schools; and 2) open one or more new charter schools that are based on the charter school model for which the eligible applicant has presented evidence of success" (U.S. Department of Education, 2011). This federal grant program, moreover, stipulated that the money would support CMOs with a minimum of 60% minority students, once again tilting funding toward majority-minority charter schools. New venture philanthropies, buoyed by this federal assistance, launched a new route to expansion—scaling up charter schools of proven success. In thinking about the charters that were able to take advantage of scaling up, many were majority-minority, no-excuses charter schools focused on students "at-risk" of dropping out of school—Achievement First (CT and NY), Inner City Education Foundation (Los Angeles), Knowledge is Power Program (national), Success Academies (NY), and YES Prep (TX), to name a few.

Lack of program innovation/experimentation. A key driver of the charter movement was the desire to free up public schools from constraints that were thought to impede their ability to design innovative education programs. Indeed, Wohlstetter, Smith, and Farrell noted that 90% of state charter laws included as one of the purposes behind the law to encourage school communities to use their autonomy in the classroom to experiment, innovate, and create new educational options for students (2013, p. 16).

As noted earlier, charter school proponents stressed the need for deregulating schools—pushing for waivers from state and local regulations—and for shifting decision-making responsibilities closer to school communities. These principles of deregulation and school-site autonomy, at least in theory, would allow the education programs at charter schools to be tailored explicitly to the needs of particular student populations.

The research, based on implementation of school curriculum, pedagogy, and governance and management, concluded that school innovations in charters tended to target a specific subset of students—students who had already dropped out of school or whose circumstances placed them at-risk of doing so; this approach, moreover, was more common in charter schools than non-charter schools (Zimmer & Buddin, 2009).

Lubienski, drawing on 56 reports of innovation in charter schools, found that "although some organizational innovations are evident, classroom strategies tend toward the familiar" (Lubienski, 2003, p. 395). Organizational, administrative, and structural changes were prominent, such as experimenting with parent contracts, merit pay for teachers, and smaller class size. While Lubienski did take note of some innovative classroom practices (e.g., the use of technology as a way to individualize instruction), he concluded that if the role of charter schools is to provide "laboratories for R&D" for new instructional practices, they are not, in fact, meeting this goal.

Others also claimed that classroom innovation in charter schools was limited. Ausbrooks et al., in their 2005 review of promotional information from Texas charter schools, found that, "20 percent of the schools list no unique teaching method." Similarly, Yatsko, Gross, and Christensen (2009), concluded, "Even among the highest performers, few charter schools have deviated much from the traditional American notion of high schooling." Smith, Wohlstetter, and Brewer (2007) concluded that while charter schools have produced pockets of innovation in teacher empowerment, community partnerships, and governing board operations, "the movement as a whole employs fairly traditional models." Most recently, Renzulli, Barr, and Paino (2015) demonstrate growing national diversity among "specialist" charter schools that target distinct curricular or thematic approaches to schooling or aim to serve a specified target population. However, they find an overall increase in the percentage of charter schools that are presenting themselves as the kind of "generalist" schools often found among traditional public schools, like those focusing on college preparation.

Re-segregation. While early critics of charter schools feared the schools would target White middle-class students, research has found that charter schools actually served disproportionate numbers of low-income and minority students (Armor & Duck, 2010; Bifulco, Ladd, & Ross, 2009; Diem, 2012; Frankenberg, Siegel-Hawley, & Wang, 2010; Henig & Mac-Donald, 2002; Orfield & Frankenberg, 2012; Reardon & Owens, 2014; Roda & Wells, 2013; Scott, 2005; Wohlstetter, Smith, & Farrell, 2013). Evidently, charter schools operating in a market-based system opted to pursue students who had *not* been well served by the traditional K–12 system (Wohlstetter, Smith, & Farrell, 2013). Often this meant student populations whose circumstances placed them at-risk of dropping out and economically disadvantaged minority students in urban areas.

As a result, a large segment of the charter school population concentrated in urban areas and educated minority students in majority-minority schools (National Alliance for Public Charter Schools, 2015). The federal Charter School Program, with its funding priority on majority-minority schools, also probably influenced this outcome. Black and Latino students make up nearly two-thirds of the entire charter school student population, and while the White student population continues to decline, evidence cited above suggests that the White students that do attend charter schools are increasingly isolated among other White students (Renzulli & Evans, 2005; Garcia, 2007).

Frankenberg et al. (2010) reported that in a number of jurisdictions, Minneapolis, New Jersey, California, and Texas, charter schools were associated with increasing racial and economic segregation for low-income Black and Latino students. Conversely, researchers uncovered patterns of White isolation in Minneapolis and Arizona, suggesting that charter schools "may act as havens for 'White flight' " (p. 10), noting that the average White student in an Arizona charter school "is exposed to 74% other White students. . . ." (p. 809) (Renzulli & Evans, 2005; Garcia, 2007). In addition to ethno-racial isolation, NCES notes, "In school year 2012–13, the percentage of students attending high-poverty schools—schools in which more than 75 percent of students qualify for free or reduced-price lunch (FRPL) under the National School Lunch Program—was higher for charter school students (36 percent) than for traditional public school students (24 percent)" (U.S. Department of Education, 2016).

As Kahlenberg (2011) has suggested, many charter designs help facilitate segregation. "Minnesota . . . has thirty charters that cater mostly to a particular ethnic or immigrant group, such as Somali, Ethiopian, or Hmong students" (p. 3). Hebrew language charter schools in New York and Florida have emerged to instill Jewish identity, and across the nation, over 200 Afrocentric charter schools have opened their doors since 1996.

The expansion of CMOs, combined with the fact that most charter schools were located in urban areas, gave support to the complaint that charter schools were effectively re-segregating the public school system. The 2011 National Study of Charter Management Organization Effectiveness confirmed that CMOs, by comparison to their host districts, served a "disproportionately large number of Black, Hispanic, and low-income students. . . ." (p. 23). At one of the fastest growing CMOs, the Knowledge is Power Program (KIPP), 88% of the students qualify for free and reduced-price lunch, and 90% are African-American or Latino (KIPP, 2015). Bolstered by a $50 million federal grant, KIPP's student population grew dramatically from 27,000 to 68,000 over the span of five years (Layton, 2015).

Demands for New Laws, Local School-Based Policies, and Socioeconomic Diversity

In 2007, the U.S. Supreme Court's decision in *Parents Involved in Community Schools vs. Seattle School District No. 1* (*PICS*, 2007) ruled that integration policies which relied on a student's individual race in selecting students were unconstitutional when race-neutral alternatives may be able to produce racial diversity. In his concurring opinion, Chief Justice Roberts stated: "The districts have . . . failed to show that they considered methods other than explicit racial classifications to achieve their stated goals. Narrow tailoring requires 'serious, good faith consideration of workable race-neutral alternatives'" (*PICS*, p. 34). A natural alliance formed between those who advocated socioeconomic diversity and those who advocated racial diversity, and groups began to endorse socioeconomic integration. Since *PICS*, a record number of school districts across the country have relied on income-based categories as part of their school assignment procedures (Frankenberg et al., 2015). In 2016, The Century Foundation identified a total of 91 school districts and charter schools across the nation that consider socioeconomic status as a factor in school assignment (Potter, Quick, & Davies, 2016).

From the demands initially brought to the courts by a group of parents, there emerged a wave of reform simultaneously across public school districts and charter organizations that emphasized the benefits of diversity. With the effort to desegregate public schools using race effectively thwarted by the Supreme Court and the rapid expansion of CMOs contributing to re-segregation, integration advocates turned their focus to socioeconomic integration. There are several other key reasons for the growing interest in socioeconomic integration.

First, the limitations placed on race-based integration plans by the *PICS Supreme Court* case and subsequent federal guidance placed limitations on race-based integration plans. Arguments raised by the Poverty & Race Research Council (PRRAC)[1] and others in their "Amicus Brief of Housing Scholars and Research and Advocacy Organizations" questioned the government's role in creating and sustaining residential segregation and the relationship between housing and school segregation. Arguments in the brief were cited in the concurring and dissenting opinions of the fragile 5–4 *PICS* decision of the Court.

The following year after *PICS*, the Bush administration sent a letter to school districts interpreting this decision even more narrowly, suggesting that only fully race-neutral integration plans were legal (Tefera, Siegel-Hawley, & Frankenberg, 2010). This interpretation and guidance by the Bush administration encouraged schools to develop enrollment plans that used race-neutral indicators. While many saw this guidance as a limitation to racial integration, advocates and school leaders focused their attention on socioeconomic diversity. In a time, when many CMOs educated high-poverty Black and Latino student populations, the recruitment, location, and enrollment strategies of diverse charter schools were designed to attract socioeconomically diverse student populations. The earliest of these included Capital City Charter School, which opened in the year 2000 in Washington, D.C.

In 2009, PRRAC helped to form the National Coalition for School Diversity (NCSD) to demand federal policies to promote school diversity and reduce racial isolation in K–12 public schools. NCSD is a network (whose membership overlaps considerably with PRRAC) of national civil rights organizations, university-based research centers, and state and local education and advocacy groups. One of NCSD's first victories was to persuade the U.S. Attorney General and Secretary of Education to jointly issue a statement affirming the importance of both socioeconomic and racial integration as appropriate strategies for achieving greater diversity in K–12 education (U.S. Department of Education and Office of Civil Rights, 2011). NCSD also advocated SES diverse schools as a turnaround strategy.

At the same time as the advocacy coalitions were stepping up their demands for diversity, the U.S. Supreme Court issued a series of decisions ruling on the constitutionality of various desegregation solutions proposed by local school districts. These rulings, in concert with the media attention they attracted, helped to launch a new reform movement: charter schools that by design intentionally diversify their student populations.

Below in Table 16.1 are the diversity-centered missions that a sample of these charter schools developed.[2]

Researchers have lauded SES integration programs as one of the most effective methods for increasing the academic achievement of low-income and minority students. Recent work by Wells, Fox, and Cordova-Cobo (2016) has confirmed this, highlighting the many benefits of integrated schools for White middle class students, as well as low-income and minority students. They specifically note that diverse schools are associated with decreased dropout rates, increased graduation rates and learning outcomes, positive intergroup relationships, and the promotion of "creativity, motivation, deeper-learning, critical thinking, and problem-solving skills" (p. 14), many of which are skills desired by employers (Hart Research Associates, 2013). The research has been used by key influencers like PRRAC and NCSD to justify their demands to the federal government.

By 2014, a small group of 14 intentionally diverse charter schools had sprung up across eight states, and together they formed another coalition, the National Coalition on Charter School Diversity (NCCSD), which was composed primarily of school members and outside advisers, including education practitioners and researchers. While NCSD and PRRAC have considerable expertise on the legal/policy/advocacy side, NCCSD, according to one of its co-founders, had a strong sense of the practice of building, sustaining, and improving diverse schools (B. Beabout, personal communication, July, 2016). According to the most recent data available, NCCSD has grown to over 100 diverse charter schools, serving about 25,000 students in grades K–12 across 12 different states.

In origins, the diverse charter movement appears to be primarily locally based, with federal policies enabling their creation and expansion. The role of the states has been less active with a few exceptions. As a result of NCSD's lobbying of the federal government to include diverse charter schools as a turnaround strategy, one state—New York—took advantage of this window of opportunity. Departing from the tradition of diverse

Table 16.1 Mission Statements at Each Charter School Organization

Charter Organization	School Missions	School Policy/Practice
Blackstone Valley Prep[1]	Blackstone Valley Prep (BVP) Mayoral Academy is an intentionally diverse network of tuition-free public schools chartered by the Rhode Island Department of Education.	BVP intentionally accepts students from four unique sending districts, two from traditionally higher-income suburban communities and two from the predominantly lower-income communities.
Bricolage Academy[2]	Bricolage Academy advances educational equity by preparing students of diverse backgrounds to be innovators who change the world.	Our school is still very new and very small—80 kids, 4 sections. We try to make sure that the classrooms are reasonably balanced by ethnicity, SES, gender, and by academic level (Founder, Personal communication, June 3, 2015).
Capital City Charter[3]	Capital City Public Charter School enables a diverse group of students to meet high expectations, develop creativity, critical thinking, and problem-solving skills, achieve a deep understanding of complex subjects, acquire a love of learning, along with a strong sense of community and character.	Our school is diverse in so many ways: we have a large number of gay families, families from different countries, lots of ELL, and students with disabilities. Our mission is that all kids can be successful at Capital City (Founder, Personal communication, June 16, 2015).
Community Roots[4]	By offering students the opportunity to learn and grow side by side with peers from varied backgrounds, we believe that graduates will leave our school with a sense of community, which transcends the traditional borders of race, culture, and socioeconomic status, as well as an ability to challenge the misconceptions around gender and sexuality.	It's part of the culture of the school to make sure we have mixed groups. We rely heavily on theory and think about which theory makes sense for us in practice (Personal communication, Director of Community Engagement, October 27, 2015).

Summit[5]	Regardless of race, neighborhood, or prior academic experience, we believe every student is capable of high levels of academic and social achievement. Students benefit from a diverse school environment that mirrors our complex world, and deepens both academic and social learning.	We have one track at our school, and that is the college track. There is a college prep curriculum, and you are supported every step of the way. I'd say we have about 99% who are accepted into a 4-year college. That in and of itself means our kids are fully integrated together—they're not in a remedial or an accelerated track (Executive Leader, September 13, 2015).
Citizens of the World[6]	Citizens of the World Charter Schools (CWC Schools) is a national network of academically rigorous, free public schools where students of diverse backgrounds learn to high levels and grow into caring and responsible citizens of the world.	We want these schools to succeed so we're keeping tabs on what's going on in the schools with various indicators. For example, what are the diversity breakdowns, how are they doing in terms of achievement-wise, are there gaps in those groups, and are those groups closing? What are they doing to close those gaps? (Founder, Personal Communication, June 19, 2015).

Source: 1: http://blackstonevalleyprep.org/about/; 2: www.bricolagenola.org/about-us/mission-vision; 3: www.ccpcs.org/about/mission-and-history/; 4: www.communityroots.org/; 5: http://summitps.org/whoweare/mission; 6: www.citizensoftheworld.org/our-mission

charters emanating organically from school founders, the New York State Department of Education mandated that failing schools applying for School Improvement Grants prioritize SES diversity in their missions and school improvement plans. Early feedback from this pilot program suggests that turnaround schools resisted having school missions and goals foisted upon them. Schools focused on education programming—Montessori and project-based learning—while SES integration was an after-thought.

The other state-initiated diverse charter school plan emerged from Rhode Island, where the state law created Mayoral Academies. By statute, Mayoral Academies (charter schools in Rhode Island) must draw their students from "both urban and non-urban communities" (Rhode Island Board of Education, 2009). In contrast to New York's school turnaround strategy, the Rhode Island law vested authority with the local level—charter school founders—as to whether they would adopt student integration as a school focus.

Diverse Charters and the Structuring of School Success

School success can often look very different depending on numerous factors and contextual elements. Through a combination of top-down and bottom-up reforms, diverse charters are growing to be more reflective of what Al Shanker and others envisioned, by embodying elements of teacher empowerment, innovative practices, and deregulation. Research has emphasized the importance of micro-level and bottom-up aspects of implementation, with *street-level bureaucrats* positioned at the center of inquiry (Wohlstetter, Houston, & Buck, 2014).

While education falls under state responsibility—all powers not mentioned in the constitution are reserved for the states—the federal government has played an important role as an enabler. The federal government has opened up windows of opportunity through constitutional rulings and other policies, giving rise to a new educational innovation—diverse charter schools. From the top-down, we have witnessed help from federal policies, such as the Supreme Court's 2007 decision in *PICS* (U.S. Office of Civil Rights, 2011), as well as the most recent update of the Charter School Program to allow high-poverty charter schools to preferentially admit educationally disadvantaged students (U.S. Department of Education, 2014). Furthermore, the allowance of the creation of set-asides in school lotteries based on parent's income or educational attainment further enabled local actors to push socioeconomic integration.

From the bottom up, reforms are locally tailored to the needs of the specific school populations. Importantly, they are determined at the local school level, by those closest to the students, such as school founders, teachers, and principals. These street-level bureaucrats often approach policy through the lens of their occupational demands, which scholars have argued is the key to implementation success (Lipsky, 1971). Wohlstetter et al. (2014) also claim that greater implementation fidelity can be achieved when relevant local institutions assist in capacity building within the street-level bureaucrats. Together, this two-pronged support structure allows charter schools to have site-based autonomy, which positions them for success.

Once schools have successfully attracted and admitted a diverse student population, school success is then dependent on internal school-based practices. Within schools, we see the use of diversity, both as a means to an end, and also as a strategy to turn around failing or low-performing schools. One study of a failing school in Lansing, Michigan revealed promising results after the school was converted into a magnet school that integrated students by socioeconomic status. In Cambridge, Massachusetts, a struggling, predominantly low-income school reopened as a Montessori school that was economically balanced, which attracted five times the number of applicants as the year before (Kahlenberg, 2009).

Among a group of intentionally integrated charter schools, founders cited the benefits of integration for all students as one of the primary reasons they founded the school in the first place. In establishing the school, they ensured that diversity was a cornerstone of the school mission. Thus, diversity-driven practices naturally emerged in all decision-making, whether by means of targeted student and teacher recruitment, or deliberate community-building strategies.

Though still in its preliminary stages, a landmark study (Wohlstetter, Gonzales, & Wang, 2016) that examined the internal policies within such integrated schools has witnessed improved achievement scores, as well as more positive school cultures. Findings show diverse charter schools that have been around longer, particularly elementary schools, are among the top performers when compared to traditional public schools in both ELA and mathematics. The older CMOs serving high school students earned bragging rights too: high levels of proficiency in reading and mathematics on state tests, high percentages of graduating seniors accepted into a four-year college or university, and one diverse high school ranked in the top 20% of all state public high schools and #3 in the state serving students with disabilities.

Is Choice the Answer?

As our analysis suggests, charter schools—as schools of choice—can employ some of the mechanics of choice that have in the past been drivers of segregation, to reverse those trends in favor of socioeconomic integration. However, it is important to note that simply allowing uncontrolled choice will not achieve these goals. As we have shown, choice-based systems can only ensure effective integration when there are specific controls in place. The allowance of set-asides and weighted lotteries are tools that can and should be used to develop diverse charter schools.

Further, when considering district-wide enrollment policies, there is good evidence that controlled choice policies can facilitate integrated, choice-based systems that empower parents to choose better schools. There have been a number of successful efforts, in Cambridge (MA), White Plains (NY), and Berkeley (CA). But the power of choice is not sufficient. Families also need access to information about the range of choices and access to free transportation to schools of choice.

Notes

1 PRRAC is a civil rights policy organization convened in 1989–1990 by major civil rights, civil liberties, and anti-poverty groups.
2 These charter school organizations constitute the sample from new research on intentionally diverse charter schools in six states across 21 schools (Wohlstetter, Gonzales, & Wang, 2016).

References

Armor, D., & Duck O'Neill, S. (2010). After Seattle: Social science research and narrowly tailored school desegregation plans. *Teachers College Record, 112*(6), 1705–1728.

Ausbrooks, C., Barrett, E. J., & Daniel, T. (2005, March 21). Texas charter school legislation and the evolution of open-enrollment charter schools. *Education Policy Analysis Archives, 13*(21). Retrieved July 10, from http://epaa.asu.edu/epaa/v13n21/

Bifulco, R., Ladd, H. F., & Ross, S. L. (2009). Public school choice and integration evidence from Durham, North Carolina. *Social Science Research, 38*(1), 71–85.

Diem, S. (2012). The relationship between policy design, context, and implementation in integration plans. *Education Policy Analysis Archives, 20*(23), 2–39.

Elmore, R., & Fuhrman, S. (Eds.). (2004). *Redesigning accountability*. New York: Teachers College Press.

Frankenberg, E., Siegel-Hawley, G., & Wang, J. (2010). Choice without equity: Charter school segregation and the need for civil rights standards. Civil Rights Project/ Proyecto Derechos Civiles. Retrieved from https://www.civilrightsproject.ucla.edu/research/k-12-education/integration-and-diversity/choice-without-equity-2009-report

Frankenberg, E., McDermott, K., DeBray, E., & Blankenship, A. (2015). The new politics of diversity: Lessons from a federal technical assistance grant. *American Educational Research Journal, 52*: 440–474.

Garcia, D. (2007). The impact of school choice on racial segregation in charter schools. *Educational Policy, 22*(6), 805–829.

Hart Research Associates. (2013). "It takes more than a major: Employer priorities for college learning and student success". *An online survey among employers conducted on behalf of the Association of American Colleges and Universities.* Retrieved from https://www.aacu.org/sites/default/files/files/LEAP/2015employer studentsurvey.pdf

Henig, J. R., & MacDonald, J. A. (2002). Locational decisions of charter schools: Probing the market metaphor. *Social Science Quarterly, 83*(4), 962–980.

Kahlenberg, R. (2009). *Turnaround Schools that work: Moving beyond separate but equal*. New York: Century Foundation.

Kahlenberg, R. (2011). *Popular, bipartisan, and mediocre*. New York: New Republic.

Kahlenberg, R., & Potter, H. (2014). *A smarter charter: Finding what works for charter schools and public education.* New York: Teachers College Press.

KIPP. (2015). *How we measure success.* Retrieved from www.kipp.org/results/national-results

Layton, L. (2015). KIPP's explosive growth came with slight dip in performance study, study says. *Washington Post.* Retrieved from https://www.washington-post.com/local/education/kipps-explosive-growth-came-with-slight-dip-in-perfor-mance-study-says/2015/09/16/c065cee0-5ca5-11e5-8e9e-dce8a2a2a679_story.html?utm_term=.e8258b02ab4f

Lipsky, M. (1971). Street-level bureaucracy and the analysis of urban reform. *Urban Affairs Review,* 6, 391–409.

Lubienski, C. (2003). Innovation in education markets: Theory and evidence on the impact of competition and choice in charter schools. *American Educational Research Journal,* 40(2), 395–443.

National Alliance for Public Charter Schools. (2015). *The public charter schools dash-board.* Retrieved June 17, 2015, from www.publiccharters.org/dashboard/home

Orfield, G., & Frankenberg, E. (2012). *Educational delusions: Why choice can deepen inequality and how to make schools fair.* Berkeley, CA: University of California Press.

Parents Involved in Community Schools v. Seattle School Dist. No. 1, 551 U.S. 701 (2007).

Potter, H., Quick, K., & Davies, E. (2016). *A new wave of school integration.* Washington D.C.: The Century Foundation. Retrieved March 08, 2016, from http://apps.tcf.org/a-new-wave-of-school-integration

Reardon, S. F., & Owens, A. (2014). 60 years after Brown: Trends and consequences of school segregation. *Annual Review of Sociology,* 40, 199–218.

Renzulli, L. A., Barr, A. B., & Paino, M. (2015). Innovative education? A test of special-ist mimicry or generalist assimilation in trends in charter school specialization over time. *Sociology of Education,* 88(1), 83–102. doi: 10.1177/0038040714561866

Renzulli, L. A., & Evans, L. (2005). School choice, charter schools, and white flight. *Social Problems,* 52(3), 398–418.

Rhode Island Board of Education. (2009). *Mayoral Academies: Title 16 Education,* Chapter 16–77.4. Rhode Island: Rhode Island Board of Education.

Roda, A., & Wells, A. S. (2013). School choice policies and racial segregation: Where White parents' good intentions, anxiety, and privilege collide. *American Journal of Education,* 119(2), 261–293.

Russo, A. (2013). Diverse charter schools: Popular, controversial and a challenge to run successfully. *Education Next,* 13(1), 28–34.

Scott, J. T. (Ed.). (2005). *School choice and diversity: What the evidence says.* New York: Teachers College Press.

Scott, J., & Quinn, R. (2014). The politics of education in the post-Brown era race, markets, and the struggle for equitable schooling. *Educational Administration Quarterly,* 50(5), 749–763.

Smith, J., Wohlstetter, P., & Brewer, D. (2007). Under new management: Are charter schools making the most of new governance options? In Lake, R. (Ed.), *Hopes, fears, & reality: A balanced look at American charter schools in 2007* (pp. 17–27). Seattle, WA: Center On Reinventing Public Education.

Tefera, A., Siegel-Hawley, G., & Frankenberg. E. (2010). *School integration efforts three years after parents involved.* Los Angeles, CA: UCLA Civil Rights

Project/Proyecto Derechos Civiles. Retrieved from https://www.civilrightsproject. ucla.edu/legal-developments/court-decisions/school-integration-efforts-three-years-after-parents-involved

U.S. Department of Education, National Center for Education Statistics. (2015). *The condition of education 2015* (NCES 2015–144). Retrieved from https://nces. ed.gov/pubsearch/pubsinfo.asp?pubid=2015144

U.S. Department of Education, National Center for Education Statistics. (2016) Common Core of Data (CCD), "Public Elementary/Secondary School Universe Survey," 1990-91 through 2014-15. Retrieved from https://nces.ed.gov/programs/ digest/d16/tables/dt16_216.20.asp

U.S. Department of Education, National Center for Education Statistics. (2016) Common Core of Data (CCD), "Public Elementary/Secondary School Universe Survey," 2014–15. See *Digest of Education Statistics 2016*, table 216.30. Retrieved from https://nces.ed.gov/programs/digest/d16/tables/dt16_216.30.asp

U.S. Department of Education. (2014), Charter School Program, Title V, Part B of the ESEA Nonregulatory Guidance.

U.S. Department of Education, Charter School Program Application (2011, March). *Application for Grants under the Charter Schools Program Grants for States Educational Agencies.* p. 20. Office of Innovation and Improvement.

U.S. Departments of Education and Justice, (2011). *Non-Regulatory guidance on the voluntary use of race to achieve diversity and avoid racial isolation in elementary and secondary schools.* Office of Civil Rights.

Wells, A., Fox, L., & Cordova-Cobo, D. (2016). *How racially diverse classrooms can benefit all students.* New York, NY: The Century Foundation.

Wohlstetter, P., Gonzales, M., & Wang, A. (2016). What diverse charter schools do differently. *Education Week.* Retrieved from www.edweek.org/ew/articles/2016/ 06/24/what-diverse- charter-schools

Wohlstetter, P., Houston, D. M., & Buck, B. (2014). Networks in New York City: Implementing the common core. *Educational Policy, 29*(1), 85–110. doi: 10.1177/ 0895904814556753

Wohlstetter, P., Smith, J., & Farrell, C. C. (2013). *Choices and challenges: Charter school performance in perspective.* Cambridge, MA: Harvard Education Press.

Yatsko, Sarah; Gross, Betheny; & Christensen, Jon. (2009, November). *Charter high schools: Alternative paths to graduation.* White Paper Series, No. 3. NCSRP, Center on Reinventing Public Education. Retrieved from http://www.crpe.org/sites/ default/files/whp_ics_altpaths_nov09_0.pdf

Zimmer, R., & Buddin, R. (2009). Is charter school competition in California improving the performance of traditional public schools? *Public Administration Review, 69*(5), 831–845. Retrieved from http://dx.doi.org/10.1111/j.1540-6210. 2009.02033.x

17 Reflecting on the Institutional Processes for College Success Among Chicanos in the Context of Crisis[1]

Louie F. Rodríguez, Eduardo Mosqueda, Pedro E. Nava, and Gilberto Q. Conchas

The education crisis facing the Latino community in the U.S. has received considerable attention. Recognizing the demographic growth, low educational attainment levels, high dropout rates, and low college-going rates among Latinos, research suggests that Latino males specifically are struggling. In recognition of the various factors that shape the disparity in Latino male outcomes, this essay aims to focus on the experiences of four low-income Chicanos within the U.S. context. Our counternarratives demonstrate that beyond *"ganas"*—motivation to succeed—key institutional processes, practices, and policies shaped our experiences, providing a complex analysis of Latino student mobility from kindergarten to college and career.

The education crisis facing the Latino community in the U.S. has received considerable attention. In April 2011, the U.S. Department of Education and the White House Initiatives for Hispanic Excellence in Education released *Winning the Future: Improving Education for the Latino Community* (2011). Recognizing the demographic growth, low educational attainment levels, high dropout rates, and low college-going rates among Latinos, the report served as a "call to action" for the country to address the crisis. Within this crisis, a burgeoning area of research has addressed the "vanishing" Latino male in higher education (Rios, 2006; Saenz & Ponjuan, 2008; The College Board, 2010).

In the United States' current climate, where the American paradox of inequality and opportunity looms, research suggests that Latino males specifically are struggling (Castellenos, Gloria, & Kamimura, 2006). While recognizing the various factors that can account for the disparity in Latino male outcomes, such as culture, peers, and labor market demands (Saenz & Ponjuan, 2008), this chapter aims to focus on the experiences and narratives of four low-income Chicanos within the context of the American dilemma. Although we are four professional Latino males now—as adolescents—we experienced social inequality firsthand as witnesses and recipients of the counterproductive policy initiatives of the Reagan era (Miron, 1996), yet we managed to navigate the complex system of higher education. Rather than falling into a narrative about our motivation to succeed or "*ganas*" as the sole explanation of our college mobility, we believe the explanation deserves much more complexity and nuance. In fact, extant research on the success and failure of Chicano/Latino students from the kindergarten through higher education pipeline shows that Chicanos who persevere tend to receive meaningful mentorship, have supportive families, and capitalize on funding, research, and internship opportunities afforded to them from institutions such as colleges and universities, often through initiatives supported by the federal government (Conchas, 2006; Gándara, 1995).

The purpose of this chapter is to tell our stories—four narratives that capture formative moments within our college experiences as Chicanos that contributed to our mobility through the U.S. education system. While our histories are individually unique, they are also expectedly overlapping. Our stories epitomize the true American dilemma—originating from a culture and history in the U.S. of struggle, injustice, and contradiction as well as hope, possibility, and opportunity. As children we faced many challenges—concentrated poverty, race and class segregation, parents with little to no formal schooling, and limited formal role models with the knowledge required for mainstream success (i.e., social capital). However, we also came from communities with a significant amount of optimism and hope. Our parents' long hours in the fields, in factories, or pushing brooms instilled within us a sense of obligation, responsibility, and will. As high school students, academic tracking, in both positive and negative ways, helped raise our individual consciousness about the structure of opportunity and inequality that only became clearer as we each found our ways through college, graduate school, and as scholars in the field of education.

This chapter first describes how we met, how our pathways intersected, and how we came to assemble a narrative from our individual experiences. We then briefly describe our individual stories using the structure-culture-agency framework as a guiding conceptual lens. Finally, we provide reflection and recommendations to institutions that serve Latina/o students who fit our profile for the purposes of equity and excellence. It is our intent, using reflective narratives of our experiences, to shed light on best practices, processes, and policies that work as means to inform pathways leading to college and career success. As a collective group of Chicano scholars, we also believe it is our responsibility to share our stories as researchers, educators, and advocates, so that emerging students can learn and connect, institutional agents can recognize and advocate, and so that policymakers can realize the power of their decisions on the lives of real people.

Intersecting Pathways

The methodology employed in this chapter was rather unconventional. Our history extends over a decade and was born at the Harvard Graduate School of Education. Upon becoming colleagues, we immediately developed a friendship and network of support, and it was through coffee shop conversations, classroom experiences, and hours of processing, theorizing, and sharing that we united to share our story in an academic paper. As we shared some of our most formative undergraduate experiences as Chicanos, we recognized the unavoidable and expected overlap in our experiences. As we each wrote and shared our individual stories, we recognized the common themes and identified a common conceptual framework that captures key institutional policies and processes that shaped our experiences. Thus we developed this reflection organically and at the same time through our personal, political, and intellectual/theoretical strengths and experiences that define who we are as Chicano scholars.

Our Formative Narratives in Theoretical Perspective

Understanding our college experiences is rooted in our pathways prior to that. Our individual family histories, our experiences in the K–12 system, and the effects of federal and international policy were all significant forces that shaped our individual and collective success. The stories prior to college are beyond the scope of this essay, but require some attention. Louie, for instance, came from a third-generation working class Chicano family. His father instilled a strong sense of Chicano pride at a very early age and emphasized the importance of education. As his father shuffled around from job to job as the Reagan trickle-down economics theory failed miserably in low-income and mostly communities of color in southern California in the 1980's, Louie learned the benefits and sacrifices of hard physical labor while in elementary school. He witnessed his father's sore feet and blistered hands, yet he pressed forward to provide for his family. This foundation is what drives Louie's determination for success.

Eddie, the son of Mexican-origin immigrants with little formal schooling, managed to move from high school to a four-year college despite substandard schools, an apartheid-like high school, and a violent community. His high school experiences were particularly foundational as they demonstrated the true nature of inequity in America—vast opportunities for White and middle-class students and limited opportunities for Chicano/Latino and other minority students. These experiences eventually led Eddie to study the effects of segregation on the educational opportunities of immigrant and non-immigrant youth in U.S. schools.

Like Eddie, Pedro is the son of Mexican immigrant parents. At the age of 14, Pedro worked alongside his father picking peppers in the Central Valley. Instilling the values of hard work, Pedro's parents wanted him to know what awaited him if he didn't do well in school. While earning a paltry $4.35 an hour for an entire day's work bent over picking vegetables, he had to endure the daily insults the rancher hurled at workers for not working fast enough under temperatures in excess of 100 degrees. It is from these experiences that Pedro entered college.

Finally, Gil hails from the pleasant beach community but low-income "Avenue" of Ventura, California. His father ventured into unknown territory during the early 1960s as part of the *Bracero* Program; an unjust and exploit-ative labor policy that brought in low-skilled, low-paid agricultural workers to the U.S. His father's life was a life of sweat, toil, and outright discrimi-nation. His mother then followed with his two older brothers as undocu-mented and unwanted sojourners. However, when Gil was born in the winter of 1969, immigration policy allowed his family to become legal residents yet permanently brown and uneducated foreigners in a raced, classed, and gendered society. When Gil was five, both his father and mother secured employment in the local plant harvesting mushrooms in substandard work-ing conditions. Like his father, Gil's mother worked long hours, but was burdened with the second shift of maintaining the home and five children. He notes that his mother and father never complained and it was in their sacrifice that Gil entered college.

While we believe that sharing our stories is spiritually renewing, we also find it equally significant to tell stories that are complex, critical, and poten-tially useful for practitioners, scholars, and policymakers responsible for serving and retaining Latino students in higher education. We invite the readers, practitioners, researchers, professors, and policymakers to analyze our experiences through interdisciplinary lenses around structure-culture-agency relational contexts. This framework revolves around the interplay between institutional structure and cultures that intersect with individual agency to predict and understand social and individual outcomes and pro-cesses (Brown & Rodriguez, 2008). In their work on understanding the pro-cess of Latino dropouts, authors found that institutional policy (structure), school level expectations (culture), and individual drive and determination (agency) helped provided a much more informative framework for under-standing why Latino students drop out or are pushed out of school.

We challenge readers to examine how the structure-culture-agency par-adigm assists in complicating the theoretical framework and empirical research that attempts to explain Latino academic success and failure. For instance, how did the opportunity structures within our individual experi-ences (i.e., federal and state programs) help construct a localized culture of accountability (i.e., high expectations, influential peer groups), that in turn shaped our agency (i.e., actions and identities) to become thriving, progres-sive, and professionally minded scholars? In an attempt to move beyond variable-driven research inquiry, we tell our perspectives using critical race counterstories (Solórzano & Yosso, 2002; Yosso, 2006). We paint rich por-traits of our day-to-day experiences that capture our struggles and hopes as Chicanos finding our way through college, and on a quest to serve our *gente*.

Our Four Narratives

Making it to the Other Side: Louie's Experience

As a third-generation Chicano and first-generation college student, I was forced into the community college system after high school because

I learned during the middle of my senior year that I was in the wrong classes all through high school. Upon entering San Bernardino Valley College, it seemed like high school all over again, but this time there weren't any adults telling you to go to class. Growing frustrated with my lack of direction, I went to see a counselor, Laura Gomez. We set a two-year pathway and I transferred to the California State University, San Bernardino. With sparse social capital, I sought out opportunities to maximize my college experience and was on a mission to succeed. I was proactive, not because I was special or born with a proactive gene per se, but because I was determined to make my family proud and pave the way for those that would be following in my footsteps.

As a rookie transfer student, I spent a lot of time watching others. With no friends who transferred with me, I, to a certain degree, trained myself as an ethnographer who was on a truth-seeking mission and I wanted answers. Who was doing college right? Who was successful? How could I be successful? In many ways, I felt like a college outsider, and through my observations, I started to see things from critical perspectives. The students who seemed to be succeeding didn't necessarily look like me, and there seemed to be few Chicanas/os present on my college campus. The students who were interacting with faculty, assuming leadership roles on campus, and those who seemed to be enjoying the college experience didn't look like me. I constantly wondered, how can you just talk to a professor and who am I to go to a professor's office hours and waste their time?

Then one day I ran into Sergio. He was an advanced undergraduate Chicano student in my department and always seemed to know where he was going and what he was doing. Before this, I never initiated a conversation with Sergio but we seemed to acknowledge each other's existence when passing through our department's hallways. On this day, he said, "you should come to this McNair information meeting. It's about graduate school." Poking his head out of his office was my future mentor, Dr. David Chavez, a Chicano professor in psychology who studied cross-cultural issues, education, and psychology. Dr. Chavez too gave me a nudge of encouragement to attend the McNair meeting. I later found out that Dr. Chavez served as Sergio's McNair mentor and helps explain, in part, why Sergio seemed so focused.

The McNair Scholar's Program was a federally funded, affirmative action program aimed at promoting graduate school for underrepresented minorities. After attending the McNair information meeting and learning about research, mentorship, and a degree called a Ph.D., I was sold and qualified with my modest 3.3 grade point average. I thought to myself, "I can actually do this. I belong here. This is something especially for me."

Now I was on the other side. With the designation of McNair Scholar, I was connected to Dr. Chavez as my summer research mentor. We shared a working-class background and I was impressed by his credentials and down-to-earth disposition. Pamela Christian, the McNair Director at CSUSB, thought that Dr. Chavez would be a good fit for me. Pamela, as a university administrator and cheerleader for underrepresented students, made it her priority to make me feel like I had a direction. She and I checked in on a monthly basis, only making me feel more confident and focused. I would always walk out of her office feeling empowered, driven, and goal-oriented. McNair provided opportunities to present research at national conferences, visit Research I universities, receive mentorship, and interact with graduate students and professors who were in our shoes at one time, and apply for off-campus research opportunities. These opportunities led me to buy a neck-tie for the first time in my life, get on a plane for the first time in my life, present my research in Wisconsin, and dream of opportunities beyond the space I called home for 20 years. I immediately became connected to a network of other undergraduates who were smart, driven, and passionate about their respective discipline. During our on-campus research experience, we engaged in deep philosophical debates about the role of Chicana/o ethnic studies on university campuses, nature vs. nurture debates, and the duality between individual will versus structures of opportunity. These opportunities made me feel privileged, special, and included in one of the most, what seemed to me, important groups on campus. We received recognition from the university's highest administrators, and I became connected with yet another source of social capital (one university administrator ended up writing a letter of recommendation for me for graduate school).

In many ways, my experiences with McNair began to forge a shift in my identity from regular college student to graduate school-bound scholar. Because of McNair and the mentorship I received, I felt entitled to approach professors during office hours. I walked across campus with my head held high. I was Sergio. I was focused, determined, and always looking for that next opportunity to get me to graduate school. As I progressed into my senior year, I became the go-to person in my department. I began to mentor younger McNair and non-McNair students. I felt that every opportunity was wide open for me. As a junior, I applied for the departmental honors cohort, a highly competitive and elite group experience that promoted graduate school, mentorship, and research. This experience only reinforced my McNair experience. Only in the honors program, I was the only person of color, and this is when I became acutely aware of the racial disparities of opportunity and only imaged what it would have been like for me without the McNair experience. At this point in my college trajectory, I began to develop a more critical sense of consciousness about my own success and those that weren't as lucky as I was, particularly from the Chicano community. My sense of social responsibility was emboldened and I always wondered about those who were looking at me wondering what it was like to be part of the McNair Scholar's Program.

The mentorship I received from Pamela and Dr. Chavez gave me the confidence to apply to a summer research consortium in the Northeast. One school on the list of participating institutions included Harvard University. Not even sure of Harvard's exact location, I was plugged into a network of resources and opportunities that eventually led me to complete two Master's degrees and a doctorate from Harvard. Now my role is to help get others from the outside looking in, to the inside looking out at a world of opportunity and hope.

Tracking Success (and Failure): Eddie's Experience

For the majority of my high school peers, college was not an option. I attended a high school that had (and probably still has) the dubious distinction of having one of the highest dropout rates in the Los Angeles Unified School District. The school was large and overcrowded. And like many other schools that serve low-income students of color, the number of courses offered to students diminished at the higher-grade levels. Thus the school was structured to accommodate the students that dropped out of school each year. Opportunities for school success were limited to a small number of students that were placed in the college preparatory track. Placement in the college preparatory track since middle school and throughout high school was one of the primary reasons why I was able to attend college. The college track provided me access to what Jeannie Oakes (1985) termed "high-status knowledge," that is, the knowledge that is a prerequisite for college attendance. I also had access to social capital through UC Irvine's (UCI) Equal Opportunity Program's high school outreach component. The outreach representatives provided us with information and guidance about the college application process—a service that was crucial since it was difficult for a single college counselor to meet the needs of over 3,000 students.

In spite of the many barriers I faced in high school, I managed to attend UCI after graduation. As an undergraduate student at UCI, I was determined make the most out of my opportunity to attain a college education. Although it initially wasn't clear to me what my career goal would be postgraduation, my interests began to converge toward the end of my undergraduate years. I had worked every summer as a mentor and tutor with programs designed to prepare students of color for undergraduate majors in mathematics and science. Working in this capacity with undergraduate students helped me realize how much I enjoyed teaching.

At Irvine, I had a hard time fitting into the larger structure. I joined an undergraduate student organization, *el Movimiento Estudiantil Chicano de Aztlan* (MEChA), that focused on understanding and ameliorating adverse conditions faced by low-income Chicano/Latino communities through organizing and advocacy. In MEChA I was able to become integrated into an organization that provided me with social and academic support. MEChA provided the space to discuss issues of inequality that impacted Latinos on the UCI campus and in the local community. I also was able to form study groups with other MEChA members that allowed us to provide each other with help on our academic assignments. It was through MEChA that I was able to think deeply about issues of social and structural inequities that impacted Chicanos and Latinos in the U.S. This experience helped me to further develop critical consciousness around issues of inequality and the agency and commitment to work to redress them.

At UC Irvine, I also benefited from institutional structures that exposed me to the possibility of graduate school. Toward the end of my undergraduate experience, I participated in an undergraduate research program that for the first time in my life prompted me to consider higher education. Following my junior year at UCI, I was involved in the Summer Academic Enrichment Program (SAEP), an intense research program sponsored by the Associate Dean of the School of Social Sciences, Dr. Caesar Sereseres, designed to prepare students for graduate school and graduate-level research. My experience in this program had a transformative influence on what my future would be. For the first time in my undergraduate experience, I was exposed to quantitative and qualitative research methods coupled with information about graduate schools that included workshops on the application process. Beyond learning research methods through SAEP, I was able to apply them to inequalities in education that impacted low-income Latino communities such as the one where I was raised, and helped explain why so few of my high school peers went on to college.

The research project I worked on during SAEP allowed me reflect on my high school experience and I began to make sense of the struggles I had to overcome in order to continue my education. I began to question why it was that in my former high school, only a small number of Chicanos were placed in the college track in spite of the fact that the student body was composed of nearly 85% Chicano students. In fact, it was the small number of White and Asian students at my high school that primarily made up the college preparatory track. I was fortunate to have succeeded having attended a school system that reproduced the enduring social patterns of academic failure and success that persistently reflect White and Asian students outperforming Latinos and African-Americans.

In preparation for graduate school, SAEP Director, Dr. Caesar Sereseres, provided mentorship. His guidance and support was instrumental in helping me actualize the transition from UC Irvine to graduate school. I attended the Harvard Graduate School of Educations Master's program. Following my Master's degree, I taught mathematics and science in a middle school in Santa Ana, CA. As a teacher, I witnessed how Latino English Learners (ELs) were concentrated in low-level mathematics courses. After three years of teaching, I was promoted to the role of mathematics curriculum specialist to help develop and disseminate strategies for teaching mathematics to ELs throughout the district. In this capacity, I noticed the practice of consigning Latino ELs to low track classes was district wide. It was then that I decided to apply to graduate school to pursue a doctorate in education with an emphasis on how to improve the opportunities for Latino ELs to learn and perform in mathematics at high levels. Following my doctoral work,

I accepted a job as an assistant professor of Education at the University of California, at Santa Cruz.

From the Fields to the Classroom: Pedro's Experience

Chicano/Latino Studies courses at California State University, Fresno were for me the first time that I had the opportunity to learn about the historical and cultural contributions of Mexicans, and specifically of farmworkers in the United States. Prior to that critical juncture in my life, I had been conditioned with a "sense of always looking at one's self through the eyes of others," a double consciousness (Du Bois, 1903). At the time, I subscribed to dominant achievement ideology and had internalized the limited educational success of those around me largely as a result of not working hard enough. In my Chicano Studies classes, I began to systematically explore and question many of the "common sense" assumptions I held. For example, in one class we incorporated the methodology of "*El Teatro Campesino*" into the class curriculum and performed key historical moments from the perspectives of *Mexicanos*. Moments like the Spanish invasion of Mexico, the Mexican-American War, and the United Farmworkers Union (UFW) movement in the 1960s. Through *Teatro*, we developed agency in enacting our own histories and our own theories, our point of departure was no longer a deficit, but a strength! We became empowered to ask, why? Why was history traditionally taught that way, and how could we change it? Why were the farmworking communities we came from poor? Why were the schools we attended highly segregated and underfunded? Why did my high school not have a single AP course? Why did more of us not graduate from high school and go to college? What if we worked hard but it wasn't enough? Why did the hard labor of our parents go unappreciated? In what other profession would the boss intimidate their employees daily with insults of their worthlessness and disposability? As I progressed through my undergraduate years, I often reflected on my work in the fields picking and packing peppers and tomatoes in the summers in 100+ degree heat while being denigrated for doing something that 99% of the American population would be unwilling to do. I found the racialized nature of farmwork highly problematic, where 100% of the workers I saw around me were of Mexican origin and the growers White.

Before Chicano studies, I accepted the structural realities I was exposed to as normal, as the way things were supposed to be. I continued to take more Chicano and Ethnic Studies course and came across the work of Brazilian educational philosopher Paulo Freire, among other social theorists, and became armed with the theoretical armature to challenge many of the assumptions that I had previously accepted as reality. These new optics gave me a sense of agency and nurtured my spirit, as those courses were often the only spaces in which we were allowed to question the hidden curriculum of the academy. I began to develop an academic language to "name" the forms of oppression I experienced (Freire, 2000) and at the same time became cognizant of the relative privileges I acquired as a university student. By naming the problem, I could work to transform the structural inequities that have denied other students similar to me the opportunities to succeed.

I took this new sense of agency and continued to excel in my undergraduate studies. Under the mentorship of Chicano Studies professor Manuel Bersamin, I applied, and was accepted into, the McNair Scholars program, a federally funded program designed to promote graduate school for low-income and first generation students. My acceptance into the McNair program provided an avenue to conduct research and receive much needed mentorship and guidance. A key benefit I derived from my participation in the McNair program was my attendance at a Harvard Graduate School of Education recruitment conference at CSU San Bernardino. There I met Louie Rodriguez (a doctoral student at the time) and Gilberto Conchas (an Assistant Professor) who encouraged me to apply. Through the guidance and support of my faculty mentors in Fresno and Louie Rodriguez, I applied and was accepted to Harvard University for a Master's degree. As I reflect on my educational trajectory, I see the critical importance that having attended that recruitment conference held for me. The impact of meeting these two working class Chicanos who were at Harvard concretized the possibilities that someone like me could be there too.

The value for an education cultivated in me by my parents, as well as my experiences working the fields and food packing houses of the California Central Valley, served to color my perspective. The mentorship, guidance, and intellectual stimulation that emerged from Chicano and Ethnic Studies courses have profoundly shaped my career goals and plans of becoming a critical educator. As a Ph.D. student at UCLA, I have worked as a research mentor for undergraduate McNair Scholars on campus. My motivation toward becoming a university professor stems from the critical mentorship that I have received; my hope now is to do for students what I was fortunate to have others do unto me.

"Para la Raza": Gil's Experience

Unlike many of my peers, my parents did not fully understand my chosen profession. For many years my parents would inquire in Spanish about my schooling endeavors and, in particular, my doctoral work at the University of Michigan. "When will you be done?" "And, what is it that you are doing?" "Psychology?" "No," I would reply. "I am studying S-O-C-I-O-L-O-G-Y." Keep in mind that in Spanish, sociology sounds like psychology. "*Hijo, y que es eso?*" (Son, and what is that?), my father would ask. "*Es el estudio de la sociedad y como instituciones afectan a la gente,*" (It is the study of society and how institutions affect people,) I would explain. "*Bueno, nomas con que seas para la raza!*" (Well, as long as you are for our people!), my father explained. "*Sí papa,*" (Yes father,) I responded.

Although my father did not live to hear about my academic work as a sociologist and especially live to see his son as a Harvard Professor, tenured professor in the University of California, and as a senior officer at the Bill & Melinda Gates Foundation, my teaching and my research represent my parents' commitment and perseverance for equity and equality. My parents opened the door for me, and my undergraduate experience provided the social scaffolds to acquire and activate the necessary social capital to further expand upon the limited opportunities afforded upon the son of poor immigrant laborers.

All of this would not have been possible without the support and guidance I experienced as an undergraduate at the University of California, Berkeley. I was fortunate to have been part of three significant institutional processes that laid the foundation to my eventual matriculation at the University of Michigan's prestigious graduate program in sociology. The first came from living in the Chicano/Latino theme house, Casa Joaquin Murrieta, on the Berkeley campus. At Casa, I was fortunate to have received the structural and cultural aspects of the undergraduate experience that privileged classes all too often take for granted. I was exposed to caring and supportive adults, peer mentoring, cultural activities, and, above all, a safe and high-achieving atmosphere. I clearly recall that as a freshman at Cal, I spent countless hours in the computer lab working on my "developmental" English class assignments. I did not pass my English essay exam and therefore had to enroll in a catch-up intensive writing course. I was such a horrible writer and struggled with my essays. In one semester, I had to undue the five-paragraph rule that I had wrongly learned in high school English classes. I was fortunate to have been exposed to peers who had a great high school education and who took the time to tutor me and guide me through the processes of articulating my thoughts on paper. "Gil, don't be lazy and go back down and re-write this piece," my peer would constantly state. What a challenge, but what an experience! Had it not been for the access to computers in the first place and to being exposed to high-achieving and supportive peers, I might not have made it past Subject A English at Cal. It was this high-achieving and supportive climate that exposed me to my second and perhaps strongest influence.

Through contacts gleaned from living at Casa, I was introduced to sociologist Professor Denise Segura at the University of California, Santa Barbara after my sophomore year. Professor Segura was a good friend with the director of Casa who secured for me an internship at UCSB. The summer program, Summer Academic Research Institute, forever changed my identity. Under the tutelage of Professor Segura, I embraced graduate school and wholeheartedly embraced an identity as a sociologist. I remember working long hours in the computer lab learning to crunch numbers with the other students and the graduate student. Professor Segura (an eminent feminist and labor sociologist) was working on a research project on the job satisfaction among Chicanas. I carved out a small research project on the job satisfaction among immigrant and U.S.-born Mexican American women. I was interested in how their educational level mediated their job satisfaction. I was so engaged in this project and was fortunate to have worked with Professor Segura and her doctoral student who equally showed enthusiasm in my project. I conducted the analysis, wrote the paper (yes, I became a better writer), and presented the results at the conclusion of the internship to my peers and other faculty advisors at UCSB. Again, this was an important event in my undergraduate experience that shaped my intellectual interests in research related to social equity. In addition, I believe that I impressed Professor Segura, for one sunny day on the UCSB campus, Professor Segura suggested that I apply for the American Sociological Association's Minority Opportunity Summer Training (MOST). I was consequently chosen to participate in MOST on the Berkeley campus the following summer.

MOST represents the third scaffold during my undergraduate experience. MOST sought to recruit, prepare, and help admit the next generation of graduate students of color into top doctoral programs in sociology. I had the honor to not only work with renowned sociologists like Robert Blauner and Mike Hout, but to be exposed to equally impressive peers. This was an opportunity that began to mold my identity as a budding sociologist. While I did not write a formal thesis for this internship, I took several courses with other MOST peers and had the honor to dialogue with Professors Blauner and Hout on a daily basis. We also attended seminars and cultural events throughout the Bay Area. MOST introduced us and prepared us for graduate school life and initiated important professional networks in academia. You have to keep in mind the majority of MOST participants were first-generation college students. Through MOST, it was not enough to emphasize enrollment in graduate school, but completion and eventual acquisition of the Ph.D.

To date, Professors Segura, Blauner, and Hout remain my strongest advocates. Moreover, many fellow MOST peers are close colleagues throughout academia. Most of us successfully secured tenure as associate professors. Unfortunately, Casa Joaquin Murrieta, SARI, and MOST no longer exist. This is truly unfortunate, for these programs provided the opportunity for first generation students to pursue successful careers in the ivory tower.

America is wrought with both inequality and opportunity. I represent that complicated dilemma. My individual determination was not enough to complete college, obtain a Ph.D., and acquire tenure. I benefited from institutional processes that mediated my engagement and success. It all began with my parents' hard work and the institutional agents along the way that paved the path for me. Now, I try to mentor the next wave of scholars who embrace equity and social justice. I am very proud of Louie Rodríguez, Eddie Mosqueda, Pedro Nava, and the many more that these three fine scholars will mentor along their academic trajectories. I still have much mentoring to do as well. I believe that we must remember those that came before us, those that opened the door for us, and those that will come after us. Let us all make our parents proud and always be "*para la raza.*"

Future Directions for Institutions of Higher Education

From our experiences, we believe that many of the K–12 and institutions of higher education have the resources to proactively and effectively serve Latino students. However, in recognizing the framework of structure-culture-agency, structures alone do not automatically transform institutional practices (Elmore, 1995). That is, the resources, programs, and policies alone will not ensure that drastically more underserved and underrepresented students will be served by what is perceived to be available. Like we found in our experiences, there must be a set of institutional commitments that aim to transform the culture of those institutions so that the agency of individuals (i.e., administrators, program staff, faculty, and higher level policymakers) is supported, stimulated, and ultimately held accountable. Everyone needs to feel the urgency, and it is largely up to the leadership to prioritize the success of students, such as Latinas/os, so that the entire institution and the surrounding community know that the mission to serve these groups is a priority. Below are three socially and culturally driven recommendations that can help institutions recognize and respond to the opportunities that are often facing them daily.

Conduct Dialogues Involving Latino Students and University Practitioners

It is striking to find that most institutions of higher education, like most high schools, fail to understand and capture the voices and experiences of the very students they serve. While the opportunities that exist, such as sports, academic clubs, and interest-based campus organizations, serve a segment of the university population well, there is an entirely different segment of the student population that does not engage in those activities. Many Latina/o students work, are responsible for their family's financial well-being, and juggle many other responsibilities that most middle-class students do not have to consider. These are the students that typically struggle to engage with the university community, academic life, and overlook or are overlooked by the many opportunities that do exist. Spaces need to be created to engage these students, listen to their voices and experiences, and use these perspectives as practical and policymaking tools to reach and propel these students onto pathways of success.

Enlist a Relationship-Building Campaign across the Campus

Research on the significance of student-teacher relationships as a mediating factor between student success and failure has been a significant theme in progressive education research over the last 15 years (Valenzuela, 1999). At the university level, the significant adults, or institutional agents (Stanton-Salazar, 2001), are vital to the development, well-being, and success of students, particularly those that have been historically marginalized by these very institutions. A relationship-building campaign can take the form of a mentor/mentee effort, but the effort does not need to be so formal. Professors, for instance, need to step back and recognize their roles as buffers between students and the vast opportunities that exist within and beyond education. However, the nature of the relationship-building is not just to deliver information. The institutional agents need to recognize the political nature of their roles as member of the university community. Acting and not acting *with* students can be the determining factor that launches a student to graduate school or to leave college without attaining a diploma. Critics often state that forging such relationships with all students is impossible, and it is. However, it is also important to state that not all students require the degree of relationships that we are suggesting.

Cultivate a Pro-Research Environment

For all of us, exposure to research opportunities as undergraduates was instrumental in facilitating opportunities to dialogue about our experiences, explore opportunities on and off campus, and foster those significant relationships and connections with institutional agents. Learning from programs like the McNair Scholars Program is key to developing an academic culture that establishes a pro-research environment, particularly for students who rarely have access to such opportunities. For us, engaging with research opportunities was largely responsible for positioning us onto a trajectory where research, and all its accompanying skills that are acquired, are the norm.

Conclusion

In this chapter, we both narrate some of our critical and most formative college experiences that explain pathways of success while weaving in some important theoretical observations that help explain our perseverance. While we all attended college at different times and places, our experiences demonstrate the importance of one critical fact—institutional culture played a critical role in our success as first generation college students. It is clear that culture matters. The literature suggests that relationships, student engagement, trust, and issues of belongingness and connectivity to the institution all have a significance impact on students. Often missing are the voices and experiences of students who actually attend these institutions. Our common experiences demonstrate that leveraging social capital through key institutional agents contributed to our college success. While all four of us were afforded federal- or state-funded opportunities, our social networks allowed us to capitalize upon these important mechanisms. Despite humble beginnings and adversity due to counterproductive policies over the course of our childhood experiences, the institutional culture that prioritized mentoring, support, and opportunity created environments that expected hard work and determination. To this day, we continue to work hard and are determined to push for equity and excellence in education. It is our responsibility as institutional agents to continue the legacy and mentor those in the higher education pipeline—from Westwood to Ann Arbor and Cambridge and back into communities like Planada, San Bernardino, Ventura, and Wilmington. Our aim is to build upon the toils of previous generations and keep the doors of opportunity open to all *raza*—this ought to be at the heart of equity minded educational policy.

Note

1 The authors would like to acknowledge the original version of this chapter which was published as follows: Rodríguez, L., Mosqueda, E., Nava, P., and Conchas, G.Q. (2013). Reflecting on the Institutional Processes for College Success: The Experiences of Four Chicanos in the Context of Crisis. *Latino Studies Journal, 11* (3), 411–427.

References

Brown, T. M., & Rodríguez, L. F. (2008). School and the co-construction of school dropout. *International Journal of Qualitative Studies in Education,* 22(2), 221–242.

Castellenos, J., Gloria, A. M., & Kamimura, M. (2006). *The Latina/o pathway to the Ph.D.: Abriendo Caminos.* Sterling, VA: Stylus.

College Board. (2010). *The educational crisis facing young men of color.* New York: The College Board Advocacy and Policy Center.

Conchas, G. Q. (2006). *The color of success: Race and high-achieving urban youth.* New York: Teachers College Press.

Du Bois, W. E. B. (1903). *The souls of Black folk.* New York: W.W. Norton.

Elmore, R. F. (1995). Structural reform in educational practice. *Educational Researcher, 24,* 23–26.

Freire, P. (2000). *Pedagogy of the oppressed.* New York: Continuum.

Gandara, P. C. (1995). *Over the ivy walls: The educational im\mobility of low-income Chicanos.* New York: SUNY Press.

Miron, L. (1996). *The social construction of urban schooling: Situating the crisis.* New York, NY: Hampton Press.

Oakes, J. (1985). *Keeping track: How schools structure inequality* (2nd ed.). New Haven, CT: Yale University Press.

Rios, V. (2006). The hyper-criminalization of Black and Latino male youth in the era of mass incarceration. *Souls, 8*(2), 40–54.

Saenz, V., & Ponjuan, L. (2008). The vanishing Latino male in higher education. *Journal of Hispanic Higher Education, 8*(1), 54–89.

Solórzano, D., & Yosso, T. (2002). Critical race methodology: Counterstorytelling as an analytical framework for education research. *Qualitative Inquiry, 8,* 23–44.

Stanton-Salazar, R. D. (2001). *Manufacturing hope and despair: The school and kin support networks of U.S.-Mexican Youth.* New York, NY: Teachers College Press.

U.S. Department of Education and White House Initiatives for Hispanic Excellence in Education. (2011). *Winning the future: Improving education for the Latino community*. Washington, DC. Retrieved from https://www2.ed.gov/about/inits/list/hispanic-initiative/winning-the-future-improving-education-latino-community.pdf

Valenzuela, A. (1999). *Subtractive schooling: U.S.-Mexican youth and the politics of caring*. New York: State University of New York Press.

Yosso, T. (2006). *Critical race counterstories along the Chicana/Chicano educational pipeline*. New York, NY: Routledge.

18 Reframing the Problematic Achievement Gap Narrative to Structure Educational Success

Robert K. Ream, Sarah Ryan, and Tina Yang

Among the wide-ranging educational challenges facing American society, perhaps no issue is more important to the nation's civic and economic well-being than inequities in educational opportunities and outcomes among diverse socioeconomic, racial/ethnic, and language-learning student groups. James Coleman was a sociologist at Johns Hopkins University when his controversial 1966 report to the U.S. Congress, *Equality of Educational Opportunity*, became the first national study to offer a systematic description of racial/ethnic differences in academic performance among children of various ages. Since then, analyses of nationally representative survey data have documented a persistent history of achievement differences, according to which Whites and especially east Asians enjoy relatively high average socioeconomic standing and student performance in comparison with African-Americans and some Hispanic subgroups (Jencks & Phillips, 1998; Reardon & Galindo, 2009, Zhou & Kim, 2006).

The stakes continue to rise as the population base of U.S. voters and workers becomes increasingly diverse and divided by widening social class inequality (Russell Sage Foundation, 2015). In response to the coincidence of changing U.S. demographics and new information about performance gaps accompanying the standards and accountability movement, federal and state education reform policies have increased pressure almost entirely on K–12 schools to close the so-called "achievement gap"—a problematic misnomer insofar as its emphasis on standardized test score outcomes work to deemphasize the "achievement debt" exacerbated by a long history of discriminatory gaps in educational inputs (Ladson-Billings, 2006; Patel, 2015; Ream, Ryan, & Espinoza, 2012).[1] Yet even though education reform policies of the past 40 years coincided with increased achievement for the overall student population, that same siloed approach to holding schools accountable has failed to substantially narrow racial, social class, and linguistic disparities in education opportunity and outcomes (Duncan & Murnane, 2011).

To shed light on the unrealistic expectation that schools alone should be capable of remedying widely structured and deeply rooted inequity, we divide this chapter into four parts. In the initial three sections, we summarize the nature, sources, and consequences of the gaps in opportunity and achievement. The first section describes the incidence of the gaps over time, highlighting the sizable gap-narrowing that occurred between the early 1970s and the late 1980s. The next part draws on ecological systems theory (Bronfenbrenner, 1979) to identify the multiple and overlapping potential causes behind these gaps, shifting focus away from a blame-oriented deficit view of individuals and minoritized communities and toward how unequal family, school, and neighborhood conditions affect educational and life outcomes (Heckman & Mosso, 2014). The third part illustrates the consequences of, and society's interest in eliminating, pernicious gaps in opportunity and achievement.

In the final section, we shift our attention toward how to close the gaps in educational opportunity, drawing on new research that upends two questionable assumptions about how educational processes function beyond the formal K–12 setting. The first assumption contends that the beneficial effects of early childhood interventions inevitably fade by the 3rd grade, while the latter asserts that few educational benefits derive from affordable housing reforms designed to improve the neighborhoods of marginalized families. Both assumptions rely on a selective reading of research and have long limited the imaginable policy moves that might be used to reduce the achievement debt by advancing educational and social equality.

The language of achievement gaps, however imperfect, has played a significant role in drawing widespread public attention to disparities in standardized test scores across groups. And longstanding, systematic group-level disparities in test scores signal something important and observable—again, however imperfect—about the historical, economic, sociopolitical, and moral inequities woven through societal structure. Yet, it is possible, we believe, to extricate ourselves from entrenched patterns of idiomatic language, thought, and policy practices that have worked, ironically, to perpetuate the inequality they were meant to redress. As we ultimately conclude below, new research offers the potential to reframe the problematic achievement gap paradigm, and, importantly, the policy agenda.

Incidence and Pliability of the Gaps

Perhaps the most widely used evidence on achievement gaps comes from the National Assessment of Educational Progress (NAEP). Although the history of the problematic achievement gap phrase dates back at least to the early 1960s (Kirkland, 2010), common media reference to NAEP, with its emphasis on disparities in test score outcomes, has helped to perpetuate the achievement gap idiom by deemphasizing the legacy of inequitable policies and practices and discriminatory gaps in funding educational inputs.

Yet NAEP also provides empirical data that help puncture holes in both the public's and policymakers' overly rigid expectations about what is feasible when it comes to options toward eliminating persistent gaps in opportunity and achievement (Ream et al., 2012). Illustratively, Black-White and Hispanic-White gaps in NAEP mathematics and reading narrowed substantially between 1971 and 1988 (Berends & Peñaloza, 2008). In reading, for example, a 52-point Black-White gap for 17-year-olds in 1971 was reduced to a 21-point gap in 1988. Trends toward test score convergence reversed, however, in the late 1980s. Some gaps stabilized and others actually widened throughout the 1990s (Barton & Coley, 2009), per Figure 18.1.

The first decade of this century saw a slight narrowing of Black-White and Latino-White performance gaps at the elementary school level, perhaps especially among Latino immigrants not yet deemed proficient in English (Reardon & Galindo, 2009). In mathematics, for example, a 26-point Latino-White gap for 9-year-olds in 2000 was reduced to a 19-point difference in 2013, per Figure 18.2.[2]

Yet despite the recent narrowing among 9-year-olds, the standards and accountability reforms of the past several decades (touted as key to closing achievement gaps) have failed to match the dramatic gap-narrowing that occurred during the decades of the 1970s and 1980s, when for some age-cohorts the gaps were cut by as much as half or more.

Today, 4th graders eligible for the federally assisted National School Lunch Program (NSLP) score .40 standard deviations below the national math test score average (.50 SD approximates one year of academic growth). The differences are even more pronounced for the one in five students in U.S. public schools who speak a language other than English at home. For age-9 English Language Learners (ELLs), it would require approximately 1.5 years (.77 SD) of academic growth to match the average math scores of their English-fluent counterparts, per Figure 18.3.

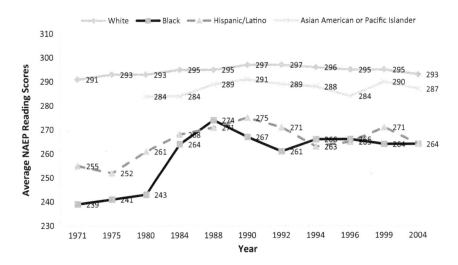

Figure 18.1 Age 17 Trends in NAEP Reading Scores by Race/Ethnicity (1971–2004)

Source: Rampey, B. D., Dion, G. S., and Donahue, P. L. (2009). NAEP 2008 Trends in Academic Progress (NCES 2009–479). National Center for Education Statistics, Institute of Education Sciences, U.S. Department of Education, Washington, D.C. Retrieved from https://nces.ed.gov/nationsreportcard/pdf/main2008/2009479.pdf

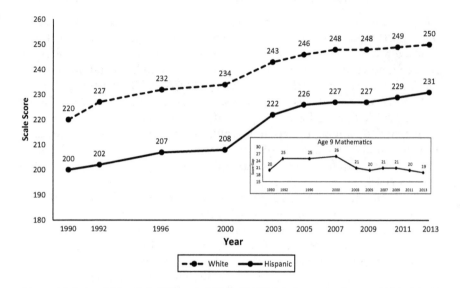

Figure 18.2 Age 9 Trends in Hispanic/White NAEP Mathematics Scores (1990–2013)

Source: U.S. Department of Education, National Center for Education Statistics (2013). *The National Assessment of Educational Progress (NAEP)* [Data file]. Retrieved from http://nces. ed.gov/nationsreportcard/naepdata/

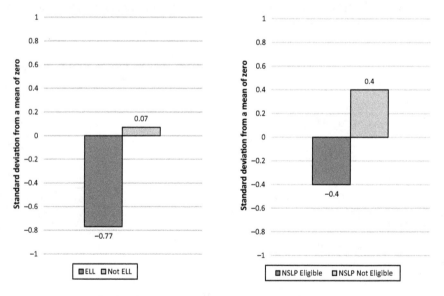

Figure 18.3 Standardized NAEP Mathematics Scores by Family Income Level (NLSP) and English Learner (ELL) Status, 9-year-olds (2013)

Source: U.S. Department of Education, National Center for Education Statistics (2013). *The National Assessment of Educational Progress (NAEP)* [Data file]. Retrieved from http://nces. ed.gov/nationsreportcard/naepdata/

Our present path offers school-centered formulations of the problems and possible solutions, most often without weighing how other social institutions influence educational results. To continue on this path with an almost singular focus on standardized test scores is to remain complicit in the perpetuation of the very student group achievement gaps that decades of reforms have been framed as being designed to eliminate.

The Ecology of Educational Opportunity and Achievement

Both ecological systems theory (Bronfenbrenner, 1979) and the economics of human development (Heckman & Mosso, 2014) hold that the interconnectedness of several environmental systems—including families, peers, schools, neighborhoods, and the broader policy environment—plays a major role in the dynamics of unequal skill formation and educational and social outcomes. One challenge, then, is to determine the extent to which the attributes of formal education policies and school practices have a unique impact on the magnitude of systemic differences in educational inputs, opportunities, and outcomes, apart from family and community influences, per Figure 18.4.

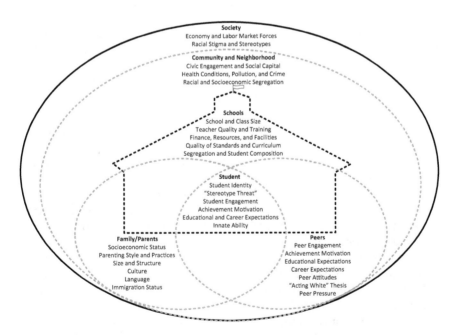

Figure 18.4 The Ecology of Educational Opportunity and Achievement

Source: Robert K. Ream et al., "The Opportunity/Achievement Gap," in *Psychology of Classroom Learning: An Encyclopedia*, 1E, eds. Eric M. Anderman and Lynley H. Anderman (Gale, a part of Cengage Learning, inc., 2009): 657–664.

For decades we have known that most of the group-level variation in average student achievement outcomes can be attributed to structural and institutional factors outside of K–12 schools, such as disparities in family resources, the health status of learners, and neighborhood contexts (Berliner, 2013; Ream, Cohen, & Lloro-Bidart, 2015). Yet schools also play a crucial role in mitigating inequality, which tends to narrow within the formal school setting, but widen over the summer and as children move through developmental and educational transitions (Benson & Borman, 2010; Downey, von Hippel, & Broh, 2004). What is it about the out-of-school context that can account for summer advantage for some children and a summer slide for others?

Family Resources

As has been acknowledged throughout this volume, intersecting historical, economic, sociopolitical, and moral debt categories have accumulated in an achievement debt. Arguably, these same debt categories have precipitated largely intractable inequities in family socioeconomic status (SES) and wealth according to race, social class, and power dynamics that carry social implications (Coates, 2014; Oliver & Shapiro, 2006). Myriad studies confirm that family socioeconomic status as a measure of parental education, employment, and income is among the most powerful predictors of student achievement (Putnam, 2016; Sirin, 2005). Many prominent social scientists have shown that the correlation between SES and race is inevitably linked to diminished access to quality education, healthcare, and even technology for underrepresented minorities, and thus, to patterned racial inequality in educational outcomes (Duncan & Murnane, 2011; Rothstein, 2004). Approximately one-third of US Latino children and nearly 40% of Black children are now living in poverty. One in ten White and Asian-American children are impoverished, per Figure 18.5.

Related to SES, health also matters. Although all children are affected by physical and mental health issues impacting learning, marginalized children living in poverty and racial and linguistic minorities bear a substantially heavier burden. Health economist Janet Currie (2005) estimates that racial differences in health conditions linked to poverty—including vision problems, persistent asthma, and obesity—may account for as much as one quarter of the racialized gaps in cognitive abilities. Also linked to family SES is the digital divide in access to communication technologies. Almost half of the most marginalized and disadvantaged households do not own a computer (Lee & Barron, 2015).[3]

In short, cumulative disadvantages in family SES, health, and access to technology are a triple whammy disproportionately affecting the performance of students from low-income and linguistic minority backgrounds which helps perpetuate unequal educational outcomes. And these interlaced challenges map onto an uneven geography of opportunity. Residential segregation often traps minoritized children in high-poverty, segregated

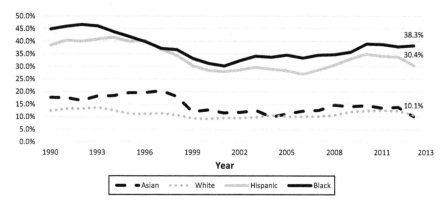

Figure 18.5 U.S. Poverty Rate of Children by Race/Ethnicity, 1990–2013 (percent)

Source: DeNavas-Walt, Carmen, and Bernadette D. Proctor (2014). "Income and Poverty in the United States: 2013 Current Population Reports." *Washington, DC: U.S. Department of Commerce, U.S. Census Bureau.*

communities and schools while families with substantial wealth increasingly live in much more advantaged enclaves (Solari & Mare, 2012).

Residential and School Segregation

Above and beyond immediate family circumstances, neighborhoods have a large impact on educational performance, health trajectories, and over-all well-being (Sampson, 2008), making it especially disturbing that neighborhoods in the 100 largest U.S. cities became steadily more isolated by income between 1990 and 2010 (Owens, Reardon, & Jencks, 2016). And residential and school segregation, both of which have been systematically structured by a century's worth of federal, state, and local policies, go hand in hand (Rothstein, 2017). Indeed, the re-segregation of American schools along lines of race/ethnicity has accelerated since the early 1990s and continues to grow in all parts of the country, most conspicuously among African-Americans and Hispanics (Orfield & Lee, 2005). Not since President Lyndon Johnson signed the Civil Rights Act have schools been as segregated as they are today. Importantly, the segregation of students is accompanied by the uneven distribution of the nation's best-prepared educators across schools.

Teachers and Instruction

Perhaps most important among the malleable within-school factors affecting differential educational outcomes is the quality of teachers and of instruction. An extensive body of research demonstrates that teacher skills and dispositions can boost student achievement over the long term, sometimes dramatically (Ferguson, 1991; Rockoff, 2004). Yet far fewer of the best-prepared teachers are teaching in schools where the vast majority of students are Black or Latino (Barton & Coley, 2009). These disparities in access to high-quality teachers—including more experienced teachers who are especially capable of bolstering academic achievement among historically disenfranchised students (Lankford, Loeb, & Wyckoff, 2002; Lewis et al., 2012)—are large and may be growing worse (Darling-Hammond, 2007; Timar & Maxwell-Jolly, 2012).

Why Differential Achievement Matters

The civic imperative to eliminate disparities in educational opportunity and achievement is strong, but at a simply utilitarian level, better-educated students earn higher incomes, live healthier lives, and are less likely to be involved in crime. Columbia University's Henry Levin has investigated costs to society should we fail to succeed in aiding greater numbers of students to complete at least a high school education. His reports focus on a group of approximately 700,000 20-year-olds who were not high school graduates in 2005. The costs to society, as measured across the hypothetical lifetime of a single one of these students, runs to over $200,000, factoring revenue lost to society in federal, state, and local taxes and costs paid out in the public healthcare and criminal justice systems, per Figure 18.6. On aggregate, the fiscal consequences to society for this single cohort of students without high school diplomas—which we would argue might be more appropriately characterized as an achievement debt *owed* these students and their communities—is projected at $148 billion.

Can the Achievement Debt be Resolved?

After accounting for the effects of families and K–12 schools, still approximately one-third of the variance in achievement between groups remains unaccounted for (Barton & Coley, 2009). Thus, most researchers agree that even eliminating vast resource differences between schools and among families would not entirely close the gaps (Berends & Peñaloza, 2008; Jencks & Phillips, 1998).[4] What other factors merit attention and how might these factors be addressed so that contemporary policies are designed to simultaneously bolster excellence and equity in our education system?

Early Childhood Education

For decades we have known that gaps in reading and math outcomes between minoritized or economically marginalized students and other more enfranchised students are already at roughly a year by the time children enter kindergarten (Fryer & Levitt, 2006; Hart & Risley, 1995; Lee & Burkam, 2002). These differences at the group level remain fairly constant

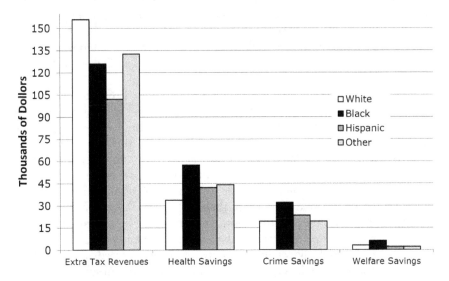

Figure 18.6 Fiscal Consequences for each Student without a High School Diploma (2005)

Source: Henry Levin (2009). The economic payoff to investing in educational justice. *Educational Researcher*, 38(1), 5–20.

between the 1st and 12th grades, indicating that K–12 schools themselves do not create or even necessarily foster inequity (Alexander, Entwisle, & Olson, 2007; Ream et al., 2012).

Many researchers have noted that the positive picture of dramatically narrowing gaps starting in the early 1970s corresponded to a rapid increase in early childhood program enrollment accompanying the Great Society's War on Poverty programs, including Head Start preschools. Between the late 1960s and the early 1990s, preschool enrollment for low-income four- and five-year-olds increased more than threefold, from 16% to 52% (Grissmer, Flanagan, & Williamson, 1998). Today, despite a range of opinion regarding which pre-K programs work best, there is broad consensus that the preschool years provide a critical period during which it is possible to substantially influence the long-term success and well-being of economically marginalized children (Heckman, 2006; Karoly, Kilburn, & Cannon, 2006; Lee & Burkham, 2002).

The consensus builds largely upon a series of longitudinal studies of model pre-K programs, including the Abecedarian Project, the Chicago Child Parent Center program, and the High-Scope Perry Preschool program. Research on each of these programs and others shows that children in the most underprivileged sectors who receive targeted early childhood development have much better education, social, health, and employment outcomes as adults (Campbell et al., 2012; Palfrey et al., 2005; Reynolds et al., 2011). What can we learn from the broad and lasting success of model preschool programs about how to structure cost-effective early childhood interventions that facilitate more equitable educational and social outcomes, in part by addressing not only test scores but also the systems and structural conditions that perpetuate the gaps?

Evidence from the Perry Preschool which, from 1962 through 1967 provided one or two years of high-quality, part-day educational services to three- and four-year-old African-American children living in poverty in Ypsilanti, Michigan, is particularly instructive on this question, largely because founder David Weikart had the foresight to commission randomized experiments that could tell us about both the short- and long-term effectiveness of Perry. The early evidence proved encouraging; by the time Perry children entered kindergarten, their test scores had jumped to nearly one standard deviation over the cognitive gains made by similar children in the comparison group. Yet by the 3rd grade, the Perry advantage had faded.

Although the early boost in test scores had disappeared in elementary school, as middle schoolers Perry participants demonstrated school-oriented behaviors that proved conducive to their success later on. They had significantly more optimistic views toward school, were more able to manage distractions and stay focused, and were less likely to be held back a grade than the no-program group. They continued on to secure better grades and complete more schooling. By age 40, they enjoyed higher earnings, greater home ownership, increased marriage stability, and less reliance on social services than the control group (Schweinhart et al., 2005).

The Perry design produced an early jolt in cognition and also helped children develop lasting social-emotional competencies not captured by standardized tests but no less potent in fostering important economic and health-related outcomes (Nagaoka et al., 2015). The economic return to society (in 2000 dollars) from education savings and increased taxes was nearly $250,000 per Perry participant (Schweinhart et al., 2005). Nobel Economist James Heckman estimates the aggregate Perry cost-benefit ratio over the life of the participants at over eight to one (Heckman, Seong, Pinto, Savelyev, & Yavitz, 2010).

Despite growing consensus about the long-term positive effects of small-scale high quality preschool, the predictability of test score "fadeout" in the early grades continues to spark debate about whether small model programs can be effectively taken to scale (Lipsey, Farran, & Hofer, 2015). Can much larger programs implemented by education bureaucrats with constrained budgets approximate similarly lasting effects? In the direct line of questioning has been the nation's major early childhood program, Head Start (Puma et al., 2012; Wong, Cook, Barnett, & Jung, 2008).

As early as the 1960s, Head Start was already being criticized for not sustaining a raise in participants' test scores through elementary school. Most recently, a number of high profile studies have reignited concerns about test score fadeout (Lipsey et al., 2015; Puma et al., 2012), leading

The Brookings Institution's Grover Whitehurst to caution against pre-school becoming "a creed in which adherents place faith based on selective consideration of evidence and without weighing the costs against the benefits" (Whitehurst, 2013).

The evidence about Head Start is typically limited to elementary grade test scores, while the program's long-term impacts are rarely the focus of research. In one exception, however, Harvard's David Deming used data from the National Longitudinal Survey of Youth (NLSY) to compare siblings who differed in their participation in Head Start (Deming, 2009). The early test score fadeout surfaced in Deming's analyses as well, and were most pronounced among the most disenfranchised youth. But by taking the long view, Deming also uncovered long-term gains in high school graduation, work ethic, and improved health—gains which were largest among the very children who experienced the most precipitous cognitive fadeout early on.

As we discuss next, the tendency to evaluate reforms implemented beyond the formal K–12 setting based primarily on whether or not they produce better standardized test scores in school is not limited to early childhood research.

Assisted Housing Opportunities

For decades, government-sponsored housing voucher programs designed to lift families out of marginalized communities by relocating them to more advantaged neighborhoods, including the Gautreaux housing voucher program in Chicago and its sister program, the Moving to Opportunity (MTO) experiment, have both been roundly criticized for failing to boost children's test scores (Orr et al., 2003; Sanbonmatsu, Kling, Duncan, & Brooks-Gunn, 2006).[5] New analyses, however, under a new set of design assumptions, push back against longstanding skepticism about the adequacy of these programs (Chetty & Hendren, 2015; Chetty, Hendren, & Katz, 2016).

In their groundbreaking 2016 study published in *The American Economic Review*, Harvard economists Raj Chetty, Nathaniel Hendren, and Lawrence Katz re-analyzed data from 4,600 families who entered the MTO experiment in the mid-to-late 1990s. MTO lottery winners were offered a voucher that enabled them to move to low-poverty communities; some of the lottery winners experienced a substantial improvement by moving to a much better neighborhood; others moved to less selective neighborhoods.

In the process of re-examining MTO, Chetty and colleagues implemented two new design assumptions that had been largely overlooked in prior housing voucher studies:

> Assumption 1: *Timing matters.* Prior MTO studies typically grouped children who moved to neighborhoods as infants with children who moved in their late teens.

Assumption 2. *Neighborhood quality matters.* Prior MTO studies typically grouped children whose families moved to high-resourced suburban neighborhoods with those who moved to neighborhoods that were only marginally better.

The authors' re-analyses overturned decades of studies claiming that assisted housing opportunities and accompanying gains in neighborhood and school quality are mostly ineffective. Instead, they find that well-timed housing vouchers that enable families to move when their children are young can be tremendously beneficial. The children who moved when they were younger than 13 were more likely to attend college and enjoyed much greater economic success than similarly aged children who had not won the lottery.[6] MTO children who experienced the move as adolescents saw no gains, however—probably due to fewer years experienced in better neighborhoods combined with the disruption entailed in uprooting during adolescence.

The most striking results emerged when Chetty and his colleagues accounted both for how much time a child experienced in a more advantaged neighborhood and for how much more advantaged that neighborhood happened to be. The younger children who moved to less advantaged neighborhoods saw gains in subsequent incomes only half as large as the children who moved to more privileged neighborhoods. When low-income minoritized youth are given an early opportunity to live in more enfranchised middle-class neighborhoods and partake of the privileges that accompany schools serving more well-off students, they make gains that reduce test score gaps (Schwartz, 2010).

"It is rare," commented labor economist Justin Wolfers (2015, p. 2) in a summary analysis of this new work, "to see social science overturn old beliefs so dramatically." And beliefs have powerful implications. Taken-for-granted social, and research design, assumptions about the causes and consequences of opportunity gaps, including about how neighborhoods or pre-K experiences matter, ultimately shape the evidence base that is used to develop and defend policy reforms.

Promoting Educational Success Going Forward

We began this chapter by depicting those periods during the 1970s and 1980s in which test score gaps narrowed significantly as encouraging, insofar as they provided evidence that persistent disparities in educational and social opportunities and outcomes can be remedied. Indeed, if this progress had continued apace, discriminatory gaps in educational outcomes might well have entirely closed by now (O'Day & Smith, 2010). Lamentably, the positive picture of dramatically narrowing gaps has since been replaced by relatively small up-and-down changes along with periods of stagnation. Even as most contemporary efforts in educational reform consistently ignore the structured underpinnings of inequality to focus almost entirely on school-centered efforts to eliminate the gaps, the central finding of the Coleman Report bears repeating: no more than 40% of group-level variation in educational outcomes can be attributed to K–12 schools themselves in isolation from other non-school factors. Because the diverse causes of opportunity and achievement gaps—or what Gloria Ladson-Billings (2006) more appropriately characterizes as an educational debt—overlap and are inextricably linked, we need an equally nuanced and integrative approach to solving these inequities.

The combined perspectives of ecological systems theory and the economics of human development enable us to properly recognize the nature and causes of social inequities, both within and beyond schools, as layered and overlapping (see Figure 18.4). Both perspectives redirect our attention toward the role that "out-of-school" programs and policies, when designed to target the social and institutional factors that extend beyond the schoolhouse, can play in narrowing group-level educational and social inequities. Many such programs—including early childhood education and housing vouchers—were initiated decades ago during the War on Poverty and, almost since that time, have faced scrutiny, which only intensified amidst the more recent preoccupation with educational efficiency and the politics of education productivity (Cibulka, 2001). Yet new research takes another look at long-held assumptions about how and by what measures we should expect these programs to matter.

Against the backdrop of this new research, the significance of decisions about what we decide to measure, and, clearly, when we decide to measure it, cannot be overstated. In contrast to much of the research on early childhood programs over the last 50 years, David Weikart insisted on a longitudinal approach to evaluating Perry program effectiveness, along with the evaluation of multiple outcomes. Despite test score fadeout, Perry children ultimately did much better in life. Something important and lasting, yet not detectable on a standardized test, had happened for them during preschool.

And, of course, early childhood and neighborhood reforms are intertwined to the extent that investments in early childhood are most productive when coupled with investments in the sustaining environments, including neighborhoods, in which children develop (Bailey, Duncan, Odgers, & Yu, 2017). Thus, perhaps it should come as no surprise that new research on housing vouchers (Chetty & Hendren, 2015; Chetty et al., 2016) suggests long-term benefits from a well-timed move to a better neighborhood similar to those of high-quality early childhood programs. James Heckman underscores the broader point in reference to preschool:

> The success of an early childhood program ultimately comes down to what is being evaluated, and too many evaluate the wrong things.
> (Heckman, 2015, p. 1)

Where research and policy intersect, a powerful dynamic can be at play. Crucial choices about which outcomes matter most help to shape which problems are feasible to study and which programs are ultimately worthy of investment. The language we use to characterize policy problems in turn shapes these choices.

As advances in theory and research provide better information about how policy might address the conditions that create and perpetuate the longstanding achievement debt, there is also the potential to reframe the problematic achievement gap paradigm. Given the power of language to anticipate and structure thought and, ultimately, action, a first step should be to discontinue our use of misleading phrases such as "no excuses schools" and "the achievement gap." These stock terms, widespread in both academic and public parlance, uncritically locate blame with schools and students while giving the rest of us a free pass. Without reframing the achievement gap narrative as one of educational debt, policymakers will likely remain unwilling to refocus their attention on the array of social institutions and practices that condition formal schooling and influence its effectiveness.

Notes

1 Our sensitivity toward narrowly construed discourse about achievement gaps derives from the understanding that language is powerful because it actually anticipates thought (Whorf, 1956; Gumperz & Levinson, 1996). The pervasiveness of the achievement gap rhetoric may limit the scope of data collection and analysis researchers imagine undertaking, diverting attention from the historical, economic, sociopolitical, and moral inequities that condition formal schooling and influence its effectiveness.
2 If U.S. Hispanics/Latinos are asked to choose between these pan-ethnic terms, Hispanic is preferred to Latino by a three to one margin. Thus, we employ the term Hispanic and Latino interchangeably, although neither label adequately acknowledges the diverse ethnic and cultural heritage in the populations they describe (National Research Council, 2006).
3 A digital divide may place marginalized and impoverished students at a particular disadvantage with respect to the Common Core State Standards testing mode shift from paper/pencil to computerized tests (Judge, Puckett, & Bell, 2006).
4 Coleman and colleagues (1966) found that (1) although schools certainly influence student achievement and (2) although school quality varies widely in the United States, nevertheless, the large documented differences in the quality of schools attended by minoritized and White children failed to explain most of the differences in their average levels of achievement.
5 For a comprehensive descriptive of Gautreaux and the Moving to Opportunity (MTO) housing voucher experiments, see Duncan and Zuberi (2006).
6 For those who moved at age 8, the net present value of the extra earnings s/he will eventually accrue is $99,000, which would generate approximately $11,000 in new taxes.

References

Alexander, K. L., Entwisle, D. R., & Olson, L. S. (2007). Lasting consequences of the summer learning gap. *American Sociological Review, 72*(2), 167–180.
Bailey, D., Duncan, G. J., Odgers, C. L., & Yu, W. (2017). Persistence and fadeout in the impacts of child and adolescent interventions. *Journal of Research on Educational Effectiveness, 10*(1), 7–39.

Baker, M. (2011). Innis lecture: Universal early childhood interventions: What is the evidence base? *Canadian Journal of Economics/Revue canadienne d'économique*, 44(4), 1069–1105.

Barton, P. E., & Coley, R. J. (2009). *Parsing the achievement gap II: Policy information report*. Princeton, NJ: Educational Testing Service.

Benson, J., & Borman, G. D. (2010). Family, neighborhood, and school settings across seasons: When do socioeconomic context and racial composition matter for the reading achievement growth of young children? *Teachers College Record*, 112(5), 1338–1390.

Berends, M., & Peñaloza, R. V. (2008). Changes in families, schools, and the test score gap. In K. Magnuson & J. Waldfogel (Eds.), *Steady gains and stalled progress: Inequality and the Black-White test score gap*. New York, NY: Russell Sage Foundation.

Berliner, D. (2013). Effects of inequality and poverty vs. teachers and schooling on America's youth. *Teachers College Record*, 115(12), 1–26.

Bronfenbrenner, U. (1979). Contexts of child rearing: Problems and prospects. *American Psychologist*, 34(10), 844.

Campbell, F. A., Pungello, E., Burchinal, M., Kainz, K., Pan, Y., Wasik, B., et al. (2012). Adult outcomes as a function of an early childhood educational program: An Abecedarian Project follow-up. *Developmental Psychology*, 48(4), 1033–1043.

Chetty, R., & Hendren, N. (2015). *The impacts of neighborhoods on intergenerational mobility: Childhood exposure effects and county-level estimates*. Working paper. Harvard University and NBER.

Chetty, R., Hendren, N., & Katz, L. F. (2016). The effects of exposure to better neighborhoods on children: New evidence from the moving to opportunity experiment. *The American Economic Review*, 106(4), 855–902.

Cibulka, J. G. (2001). The changing role of interest groups in education. *Educational Policy*, 15(1), 12–40.

Coates, T. (2014, June). The case for reparations. *The Atlantic*.

Coleman, J., Campbell, E., Hobson, C., McPartland, J., Mood, A., Weinfeld, F., & York, R. (1966). *Equality of educational opportunity*. Washington, DC: National Center for Educational Statistics.

Currie, J. (2005). Health disparities and gaps in school readiness. *The Future of Children*, 15(1), 117–138.

Darling-Hammond, L. (2007). The flat earth and education: How America's commitment to equity will determine our future. *Educational Researcher*, 36(6), 318.

Deming, D. (2009). Early childhood intervention and life-cycle skill development: Evidence from Head Start. *American Economic Journal: Applied Economics*, 1(3), 111–134.

DeNavas-Walt, C., & Proctor, B. D. (2014). *Income and poverty in the United States: 2013 current population reports*. Washington, DC: US Department of Commerce, US Census Bureau.

Downey, D. B., Von Hippel, P. T., & Broh, B. A. (2004). Are schools the great equalizer? Cognitive inequality during the summer months and the school year. *American Sociological Review*, 69(5), 613–635.

Duncan, G. J., & Murnane, R. J. (2011). *Whither opportunity: Rising inequality, schools, and children's life chances*. New York, NY: Russell Sage Foundation.

Duncan, G. J., & Zuberi, A. (2006). Mobility lessons from Gautreaux and moving to opportunity. *Northwestern Journal of Law & Social Policy*, 1(1), 110–126.

Ferguson, R. F. (1991). Paying for public education: New evidence on how and why money matters. *Harvard Journal on Legislation, 28*, 465–498.

Fryer, R. G., & Levitt, S. D. (2006). The Black-White test score gap through third grade. *American Law and Economics Review, 8*(2), 249–281.

Grissmer, D., Flanagan, A., & Williamson, S. (1998). Why did the Black-White score gap narrow in the 1970s and 1980s? In C. Jencks & M. Phillips (Eds.), *The Black-White test score gap* (pp. 182–228). Washington, DC: Brookings Institution Press.

Gumperz, J., & Levinson, S. (Eds.) (1996). *Rethinking linguistic relativity: Studies in the social and cultural foundations of language.* Cambridge: Cambridge University Press.

Hamre, B. K., & Pianta, R. C. (2007). Learning opportunities in preschool and early elementary classrooms. In R. C. Pianta, M. J. Cox, & K. L. Snow (Eds.), *School readiness and the transition to kindergarten in the era of accountability* (pp. 49–83). Baltimore, MD: Paul H. Brookes Publishing.

Hart, B., & Risley, T. R. (1995). *Meaningful differences in the everyday experience of young American children.* Baltimore, MD: Brookes Publishing.

Heckman, J. (2006). Skill formation and the economics of investing in disadvantaged children. *Science, 312*, 1900–1902.

Heckman, J. (2015, October). Pre-K researchers can't get past the third grade. *The Hechinger Report.* Retrieved from http://hechingerreport.org/pre-k-researchers-cant-get-past-the-third-grade/

Heckman, J. J., & Mosso, S. (2014). *The economics of human development and social mobility.* (No. w19925). Cambridge, MA: National Bureau of Economic Research.

Heckman, J. J., Seong, H. M., Pinto, R., Savelyev, P. A., & Yavitz, A. (2010). The rate of return to the HighScope Perry Preschool Program. *Journal of Public Economics, 94*(1–2), 114–128.

Huang, F. L., Invernizzi, M. A., & Drake, E. A. (2012). The differential effects of preschool: Evidence from Virginia. *Early Childhood Research Quarterly, 27*(1), 33–45.

Jencks, C., & Phillips, M. (Eds.). (1998). *The Black-White test score gap.* Washington, DC: Brookings Institution Press.

Judge, S., Puckett, K., & Bell, S. (2006) Closing the digital divide: Update from the Early Childhood Longitudinal Study. *The Journal of Educational Research, 100*(1), 52–60.

Karoly, L. A., Kilburn, M. R., & Cannon, J. S. (2006). *Early childhood interventions: Proven results, future promise.* Santa Monica, CA: RAND.

Kirkland, D. (2010). "Black skin, white masks": Normalizing whiteness and the trouble with the achievement gap. *Teachers College Record.*

Ladson-Billings, G. J. (2006). From the achievement gap to the education debt: Understanding achievement in U.S. schools. *Educational Researcher, 35*, 3–12.

Lankford, H., Loeb, S., & Wyckoff, J. (2002). Teacher sorting and the plight of urban schools: A descriptive analysis. *Educational Evaluation and Policy Analysis, 24*(1), 37–62.

Lee, J., & Barron, B. (2015). *Aprendiendo en casa: Media as a learning tool among Hispanic-Latino families.* New York, NY: The Joan Ganz Cooney Center at Sesame Workshop.

Lee, V. E., & Burkam, D. T. (2002). *Inequality at the starting gate: Social background differences in achievement as children begin school.* Washington, DC: Economic Policy Institute.

Levin, H. M. (2009). The economic payoff to investing in educational justice. *Educational Researcher, 38*(1), 5–20.

Lewis, J., Ream, R. K., Bocian, K. M., Cardullo, R. A., Hammond, K. A., & Fast, L. A. (2012). Con cariño: Teacher caring, math self-efficacy, and math achievement among Hispanic English learners. *Teachers College Record, 114*(7), 1–42.

Lipsey, M., Farran, D., & Hofer, K. (2015). *A randomized control trial of a statewide voluntary prekindergarten program on children's skills and behaviors through Third Grade: Research report*. Peabody Research Institute.

Magnuson, K., Ruhm, C., & Waldfogel, J. (2007). "Does prekindergarten improve school preparation and performance?" *Economics of Education Review, 26*(1), 33–51.

Nagaoka, J., Farrington, C. A., Ehrlich, S. B., Heath, R. D., Johnson, D. W., Dickson, S., et al. (2015). *Foundations for young adult success: A developmental framework*. Chicago, IL: Consortium on Chicago School Research, The University of Chicago.

National Research Council. (2006). *Multiple origins, uncertain destinies: Hispanics and the American future*. Washington, DC: The National Academies Press.

O'Day, J. A., & Smith, M. S. (2010). Quality and equality in American education: Systemic problems, systemic solutions. In I. Kirsch & H. Braun (Eds.), *The dynamics of opportunity in America* (pp. 297–358). Princeton, NJ: Educational Testing Service.

Oliver, M. L., & Shapiro, T. (2006). *Black wealth, White wealth: A new perspective on racial inequality*. London: Taylor & Francis.

Orfield, G., & Lee, C. (2005). *Why segregation matters: Poverty and educational inequality*. Los Angeles, CA: Civil Rights Project/Proyecto Derechos Civiles at UCLA.

Orr, L., Feins, J. D., Jacob, R., Beecroft, E., Sanbonmatsu, L., & Katz, L. F. (2003). *Moving to opportunity for fair housing demonstration: Interim impacts evaluation*. Washington, DC: U.S. Department of Housing and Urban Development, Office of Policy Development and Research.

Owens, A., Reardon, S. F., & Jencks, C. (2016). *Income segregation between schools and districts, 1990 to 2010*. Stanford, CA: Center for Education Policy Analysis.

Palfrey, J. S., Hauser-Cram, P., Bronson, B. M., Warfield, M. E., Sirin, W., & Chan, E. (2005). The Brookline Early Educational Project: A 25-year follow-up study of a family-centered early health and development intervention. *Pediatrics, 116*(1), 144–152.

Patel, L. (2015). *Decolonizing educational research: From ownership to answerability*. London: Routledge.

Puma, M., Bell, S., Cook, R., Heid, C., Broene, P., Jenkins, F., Mashburn, A., & Downer, J. (2012). *Third grade follow-up to the Head Start impact study: Final report*. [OPRE Rpt. No. 2012–45]. Washington, DC: Office of Planning, Research and Evaluation, Administration for Children and Families, U.S. Department of Health and Human Services.

Putnam, R. D. (2016). *Our kids: The American dream in crisis*. New York, NY: Simon and Schuster.

Rampey, B. D., Dion, G. S., & Donahue, P. L. (2009). *NAEP 2008 trends in academic progress* (NCES 2009–479). Washington, DC: National Center for Education Statistics, Institute of Education Sciences, U.S. Department of Education.

Ream, R. K., Cohen, A. K., & Lloro-Bidart, T. (2015). Whither collaboration? Integrating professional services to close reciprocal gaps in health and education. In

D. E. Mitchell & R. K. Ream (Eds.), *Professional responsibility* (pp. 287–307). New York, NY: Springer.

Ream, R., Espinoza, J., & Ryan, S. (2009). The opportunity/achievement gap. In E. M. Anderman & L. H. Anderman (Eds.), *Psychology of classroom learning: An encyclopedia* (pp. 657–664). Detroit, MI: Macmillan Reference.

Ream, R., Ryan, S., & Espinoza, J. (2012). Reframing the ecology of opportunity and achievement gaps: Why "no excuses" reforms have failed to narrow student group differences in educational outcomes. In T. Timar & J. Maxwell-Jolly (Eds.), *Narrowing the achievement gap: Perspectives and strategies for challenging times* (pp. 35–56). Cambridge, MA: Harvard Education Press.

Reardon, S. F. (2016). School segregation and racial academic achievement gaps. *The Russell Sage Foundation Journal of the Social Sciences*, 2(5), 34–57.

Reardon, S. F., & Bischoff, K. (2011). Income inequality and income segregation1. *American Journal of Sociology*, 116(4), 1092–1153.

Reardon, S., & Galindo, C. (2009). The Hispanic-White achievement gap in math and reading in the elementary grades. *American Educational Research Journal*, 46(3), 853–891.

Reynolds, A. J., Temple, J. A., White, B. A. B., Ou, S., & Robertson, D. L. (2011). Age 26 cost-benefit analysis of the Child-Parent Center Early Education Program. *Child Development*, 82(1), 379–404.

Rockoff, J. E. (2004). The impact of individual teachers on student achievement: Evidence from panel data. *The American Economic Review*, 94(2), 247–252.

Rothstein, R. (2004). *Class and schools.* New York, NY: Teachers College, Columbia University; Economic Policy Institute.

Rothstein, R. (2017). *The color of law: A forgotten history of how our government segregated America.* New York: Liveright.

Russell Sage Foundation. (2015). *Chartbook of social inequality: Income and earnings.* Retrieved from www.russellsage.org/sites/all/files/chartbook/Income%20 and%20Earnings.pdf

Sampson, R. J. (2008). Moving to inequality: Neighborhood effects and experiments meet structure. *American Journal of Sociology*, 114(11), 189.

Sanbonmatsu, L., Kling, J. R., Duncan, G. J., & Brooks-Gunn, J. (2006). Neighborhoods and academic achievement: Results from the moving to opportunity experiment. *Journal of Human Resources*, 41(4), 649–691.

Schwartz, H. (2010). *Housing policy is school policy.* New York, NY: The Century Foundation.

Schweinhart, L. J., Montie, J., Xiang, Z., Barnett, W. S., Belfield, C. R., & Nores, M. (2005). *Lifetime effects: The High/Scope Perry Preschool study through age 40.* Ypsilanti, MI: High/Scope Press.

Sirin, S. R. (2005). Socioeconomic status and academic achievement: A meta-analytic review of research. *Review of Educational Research*, 75(3), 417–453.

Solari, C. D., & Mare, R. D. (2012). Housing crowding effects on children's well-being. *Social Science Research*, 41(2), 464–476.

Timar, T., & Maxwell-Jolly, J. (Eds.). (2012). *Narrowing the achievement gap: Perspectives and strategies for challenging times.* Cambridge, MA: Harvard Education Press.

U.S. Department of Education, National Center for Education Statistics. (2013). *The National Assessment of Educational Progress (NAEP).* Retrieved from http:// nces.ed.gov/nationsreportcard/naepdata/

Whitehurst, G. J. (2013). *Can we be hard-headed about preschool? A look at universal and targeted pre-k*. Washington, DC: Brookings Institution. Retrieved from https://www.brookings.edu/research/can-we-be-hard-headed-about-preschool-a-look-at-universal-and-targeted-pre-k/

Whorf, B. (1956). Language, thought and reality. In J. B. Caroll (Ed.), *Language, thought, and reality: Selected writings of Benjamin Lee Whorf* (pp. 207–219). Cambridge: MIT Press.

Wolfers, J. (2015, May). Why the new research on mobility matters: An economist's view. *The New York Times*. Retrieved from www.nytimes.com/2015/05/05/upshot/why-the-new-research-on-mobility-matters-an-economists-view.html?_r=0

Wong, V. C., Cook, T. D., Barnett, W. S., & Jung, K. (2008). An effectiveness-based evaluation of five state pre-kindergarten programs. *Journal of Policy Analysis and Management*, 27(1), 122–154.

Zhou, M., & Kim, S. (2006). Community forces, social capital, and educational achievement: The case of supplementary education in the Chinese and Korean immigrant communities. *Harvard Educational Review*, 76(1), 1–29.

Contributor Bios

Miguel N. Abad is a community-based educator from San Francisco, California. Currently, he is a doctoral student in the School of Education at the University of California, Irvine concentrating on educational policy and social context.

Vanessa Anthony-Stevens is an Assistant Professor of Social and Cultural Studies in the Department of Curriculum and Instruction, University of Idaho. Her areas of specialization include Indigenous education and anthropology of education. Her recent teaching and research focus on preparing teachers for rural diversity, and negotiations of Indigenous educational sovereignty in the United States and Mexico.

Alexandra (Ale) Babino is an Assistant Professor at Texas A & M University - Commerce. Her research explores the identities, investments, and biliteracy trajectories of emergent bilinguals in dual language programs.

Brian Boggs serves as the Director of Program Development in the Office of K-12 Outreach and Adjunct Professor of Educational Administration in the College of Education at Michigan State University. His area of expertise is policy development and analysis in the areas of school reform and he holds a dual major Ph.D. in Educational Policy and Administration from MSU. In addition, Brian holds a special certification in urban education from MSU and has taught college rhetoric, critical writing, and policy courses at the University of Michigan – Flint. Brian has held local public office for 14 years where he focuses on community engagement and governmental finance.

Cassie J. Brownell is a doctoral candidate and a Marianne Amarel Teaching and Learning Fellow in the Department of Teacher Education in the College of Education at Michigan State University. Her research reimagines literacies in the English Language Arts (ELA) classroom by interrogating how writing with a variety of communicative resources (e.g., visuals, audio, material items) facilitates new spaces for human diversities.

Shannon M. Calderone is an Assistant Professor in the Department of Educational Leadership at Washington State University. Her research interests include issues related to college affordability, financial literacy, and financial stress.

Gilberto Q. Conchas is Professor of Educational Policy and Social Context at the University of California, Irvine. Conchas' research focuses on inequality with an emphasis on urban communities and schools. He is the author of six books, including *The Color of Success: Race and High-Achieving Urban Youth*, *Small Schools and Urban Youth: Using the Power of School Culture to Engage Youth*, *StreetSmart SchoolSmart: Urban Poverty and the Education of Boys of Color*, and *Cracks in the Schoolyard—Confronting Latino Educational Inequality*.

Amanda Datnow is Associate Dean of the Division of Social Sciences and a Professor in the Department of Education Studies at the University of California, San Diego. Her research focuses on educational reform, particularly with regard to issues of equity and the professional lives of educators.

Mark E. Deschaine is an Assistant Professor in the Department of Educational Leadership at Central Michigan University, Mount Pleasant, Michigan. He received his doctorate from Western Michigan University in the Department of Educational Leadership, Research and Technology with an emphasis in K–12 Leadership. Dr. Deschaine's research agenda examines how theory, policy, and processes support effective differentiated instruction.

Graham Downes is Associate Professor and Programme Leader for Education Studies at Bath Spa University, UK. His teaching and research interests focus on the sociology of education. His doctoral thesis explores the introduction of Free Schools in England and their implications for a state system of education.

Frank Fernandez is Assistant Professor in the Department of Education Leadership and Policy Studies at University of Houston. He earned a Ph.D. at The Pennsylvania State University. He researches educational policy issues, including topics related to adult skills, access and equity for underserved students, and doctoral education.

Michael R. Ford is an Assistant Professor of Public Administration at the University of Wisconsin–Oshkosh. His research interests include public and non-profit board governance, accountability, and school choice. Prior to joining academia, Michael worked for many years on education policy in Wisconsin.

Corinna Geppert is a post-doctoral researcher at the Department of Education at the University of Vienna, Austria. Her research focuses on educational policymaking, educational transitions in selective schooling systems, as well as on conditions of successful educational trajectories.

Mathew M. Gonzales is Director of the School Diversity Project for a non-profit social justice center called New York Appleseed. He works in New York City to promote integrated schools. Prior to working with Appleseed, he was a graduate student in education policy at Teachers College, Columbia University. He is a former special education middle school teacher and has worked in education for over 10 years.

Ricardo González-Carriedo, Ph.D., is an Assistant Professor at the University of North Texas. His research focuses on bilingual teacher training, the effects of international experiences on preservice and inservice teachers, literacy development among second language learners, and the representation of bilingual and immigrant students in the media.

Michael A. Gottfried is an Associate Professor in the Gevirtz Graduate School of Education at the University of California Santa Barbara. He holds a Ph.D. and M.A. in Applied Economics from the University of Pennsylvania and a B.A. in Economics from Stanford University. Professor Gottfried's work focuses on the economics of education and on educational policy. His work spans areas including students with disabilities, early education, attendance and truancy, and STEM.

Briana M. Hinga is an Assistant Professor of Clinical Education at the Rossier School of Education at the University of Southern California. She completed her Ph.D. in education at the University of California, Irvine. Her research illuminates how history, social structure, schooling practices, policies, perceptions, and actions interact to shape educational opportunity. She focuses on partnerships with communities, students, and schools to design and evaluate learning environments that foster possibility and social justice.

Lea Hubbard is Chair and Professor of the Department of Leadership Studies in the School of Leadership and Education Sciences at the University of San Diego. Working nationally and internationally, her work focuses on educational reform and educational inequities as they exist across ethnicity, class, and gender.

Adrian H. Huerta is a Postdoctoral Scholar at the Higher Education Research Institute at the University of California, Los Angeles. His research areas focus on college access and equity, school discipline polices, and marginalized student populations in the K–16 educational pipeline with an emphasis on Latino male youth. He is a 2015–2016 American Educational Research Association Minority Dissertation Fellowship recipient.

Lauren Jervis is a Ph.D. candidate in the Faculty of Education at York University in Toronto, Canada. She researches the interplay between ideas of childhood and agendas of the political sphere through studying public conflicts over educational policies involving parents, governments, and other education advocates.

Jacob Kirksey is a Ph.D. student and researcher at UC Santa Barbara with research interests in the economics of education and education policy. Professionally, Jacob has worked for two non-profit organizations, taught K–12 theater in schools, and designed his own after school programs. Currently, Jacob is working on research projects related to peer effects, absenteeism, and special education via a policy perspective.

Argelia Lara is an Assistant Professor in the School of Education at Mills College. She received her Ph.D. from UCLA's Graduate School of Education and Information Systems, in the division of Social Science and Comparative Education, specializing in race and ethnic studies. Argelia's research interests examine immigrant education, undocumented students along the K–PHD pipeline, college choice, and access and equity in higher education for students of color and first generation college students.

Karla I. Loya is an Assistant Professor of Educational Leadership at the University of Hartford, CT. Her research and teaching interest include instruction, learning, and assessment, equity, and diversity issues in higher education, and research methods.

Patricia M. McDonough is Professor of Education at the University of California at Los Angeles.

Eduardo Mosqueda is an Associate Professor of Education at the University of California at Santa Cruz. His research primarily examines the relationship between the English proficiency of language minority students, their access to rigorous courses, and their performance on standardized mathematics assessments.

Pedro E. Nava is an Assistant Professor of Education in the Educational Leadership Program at Mills College in Oakland, California. Pedro completed his Ph.D. from UCLA's Graduate School of Education in the Urban Schooling division. The focus of his research and teaching are in urban and rural schooling inequality, critical pedagogy and critical race theory, immigration and education, family-school engagement, and participatory action research.

Leticia Oseguera is an Associate Professor of Education Policy Studies at The Pennsylvania State University. Her research focuses on underserved youths' transitions to postsecondary education.

Hugh Potter is a fifth-year Education Policy doctoral candidate at Michigan State University. With a focus on Urban Education, Hugh endeavors to gain greater clarity on the systemic issues of discipline for students of color related to school discipline. Current research centers upon disproportionate discipline and culturally responsive approaches to behavioral interventions.

Catherine A. Simon is an Associate Professor and programme leader for Education Studies at Bath Spa University, UK. She has a specialist interest in English education policy and her research interests encompass schools as organizations, leadership, and management. She is currently researching multi academy trusts and school sponsorship.

Robert K. Ream is an Associate Professor of Education Policy Analysis in the Graduate School of Education at the University of California, Riverside. His research interests include the social dynamics of racial, social class, and linguistic inequality in K-12 and higher education settings.

Louie F. Rodríguez is an Associate Professor in the Graduate School of Education at the University of California Riverside. He is a scholar of urban education and focuses on students' voices and experiences in the school and community context, critical ways to understand and use institutional culture to boost student engagement, and engaging the Latinx community for excellence.

Sarah Ryan is a Senior Researcher at Education Development Center (EDC) where her research focuses on understanding the sources and consequences of group-level disparities in educational processes and outcomes, particularly at the secondary and post-secondary levels.

Aaron Saiger is Professor of Law at Fordham University in New York City. He studies and writes about education and regulatory law. He has a Ph.D. from the Woodrow Wilson School of Public and International Affairs, Princeton University, and a J.D. from the Columbia University School of Law.

William Vélez is Professor Emeritus of Sociology at the University of Wisconsin-Milwaukee. His scholarship is broadly focused on educational and housing issues with specialized research interests in Latino urban populations.

Amy K. Wang is an analyst at Bank Street Education Center, a non-profit organization within Bank Street College of Education. She earned her M.A. in Education Policy from the Department of Education Policy & Social Analysis, Teachers College, Columbia University.

Sue Winton is an Associate Professor in the Faculty of Education at York University in Toronto, Ontario, Canada, and co-director of the World Educational Research Association's International Research Network on Families, Educators, and Communities as Educational Advocates. Her research examines policy advocacy, influences, and enactment.

Priscilla Wohlstetter is Distinguished Research Professor at Teachers College, Columbia University. Her research focuses on the politics of policymaking and K–12 education reform, including charters and school choice, the Common Core, and inter-organizational networks.

Tina Yang is a second-year doctoral student in Educational Psychology at the University of California, Riverside. Her research interests include ethnic and racial disparities in education and educational assessment and measurement.

Index

CPSIA information can be obtained
at www.ICGtesting.com
Printed in the USA
LVHW021410270421
685708LV00012B/435